SHONEN JUMP GRAPHIC NOVEL

Vol. 10

DB: 26 of 42

STORY AND ART BY
AKIRA TORIYAMA

THE MAIN CHARACTERS

Bulma

Goku's oldest friend, Bulma is a scientific genius. She met Goku while on a quest for the seven magical Dragon Balls which, when gathered together, can grant any wish.

Son Goku

The greatest martial artist on Earth, he owes his strength to the training of Kame-Sen'nin and Kaiô-sama, and the fact that he's an alien Saiyan. To get even stronger, he has trained under 100 times Earth's gravity.

Kaiô-sama

The "Lord of Worlds," he is Kami-sama's superior in the heavenly bureaucracy. He lives in the Other World, where he occasionally trains dead heroes.

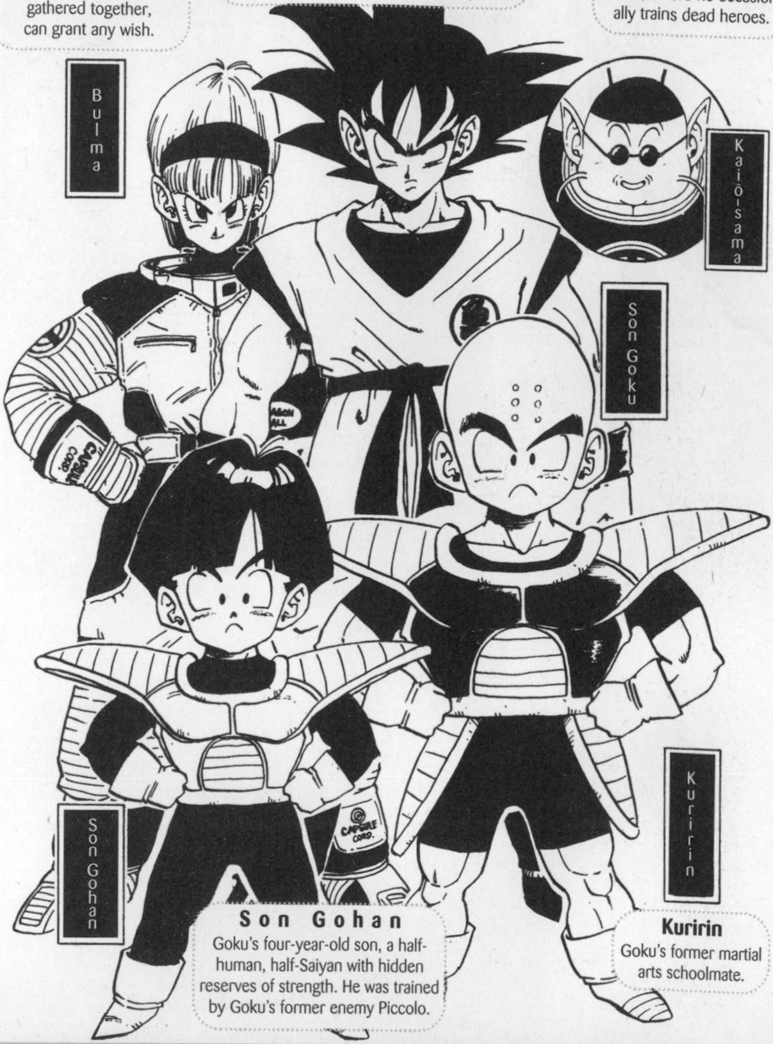
Bulma
Kaiôsama
Son Goku
Kuririn
Son Gohan

Son Gohan

Goku's four-year-old son, a half-human, half-Saiyan with hidden reserves of strength. He was trained by Goku's former enemy Piccolo.

Kuririn

Goku's former martial arts schoolmate.

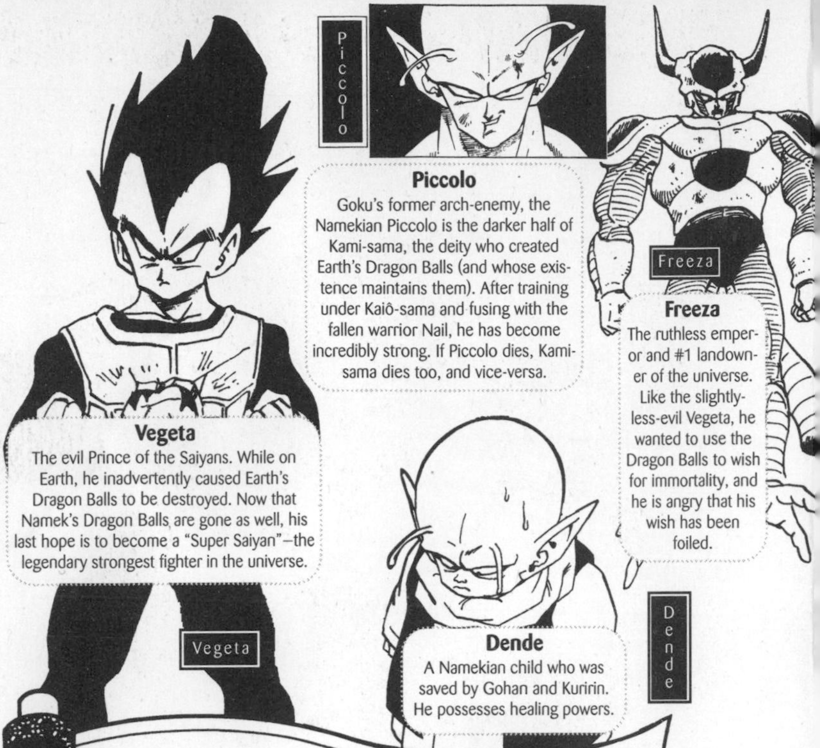
Piccolo
Freeza
Vegeta
Dende

Piccolo

Goku's former arch-enemy, the Namekian Piccolo is the darker half of Kami-sama, the deity who created Earth's Dragon Balls (and whose existence maintains them). After training under Kaiô-sama and fusing with the fallen warrior Nail, he has become incredibly strong. If Piccolo dies, Kami-sama dies too, and vice-versa.

Freeza

The ruthless emperor and #1 landowner of the universe. Like the slightly-less-evil Vegeta, he wanted to use the Dragon Balls to wish for immortality, and he is angry that his wish has been foiled.

Vegeta

The evil Prince of the Saiyans. While on Earth, he inadvertently caused Earth's Dragon Balls to be destroyed. Now that Namek's Dragon Balls are gone as well, his last hope is to become a "Super Saiyan"—the legendary strongest fighter in the universe.

Dende

A Namekian child who was saved by Gohan and Kuririn. He possesses healing powers.

Son Goku was Earth's greatest hero, and the Dragon Balls—which can grant any wish—were Earth's greatest treasure. When Vegeta attacked Earth to steal them, Goku and his friends managed to fend him off, but many lives were lost in the process. In search of a way to wish their friends back to life, our heroes went to planet Namek, where the Dragon Balls were originally made—only to find the planet under attack by both Vegeta and Freeza! Gohan and Kuririn were forced to team up with Vegeta against their common enemy, while keeping the Dragon Balls out of his hands. Meanwhile, Goku was injured and now recuperates in a healing tank. But now, the Dragon Balls of Namek are no more, and Gohan, Kuririn, Vegeta and Piccolo must survive Freeza's rage at losing his wish...

DRAGON BALL Z 10

26 DRAGON BALL

CONTENTS

DRAGON BALL

DBZ:107 • Freeza vs. Piccolo, Part 2

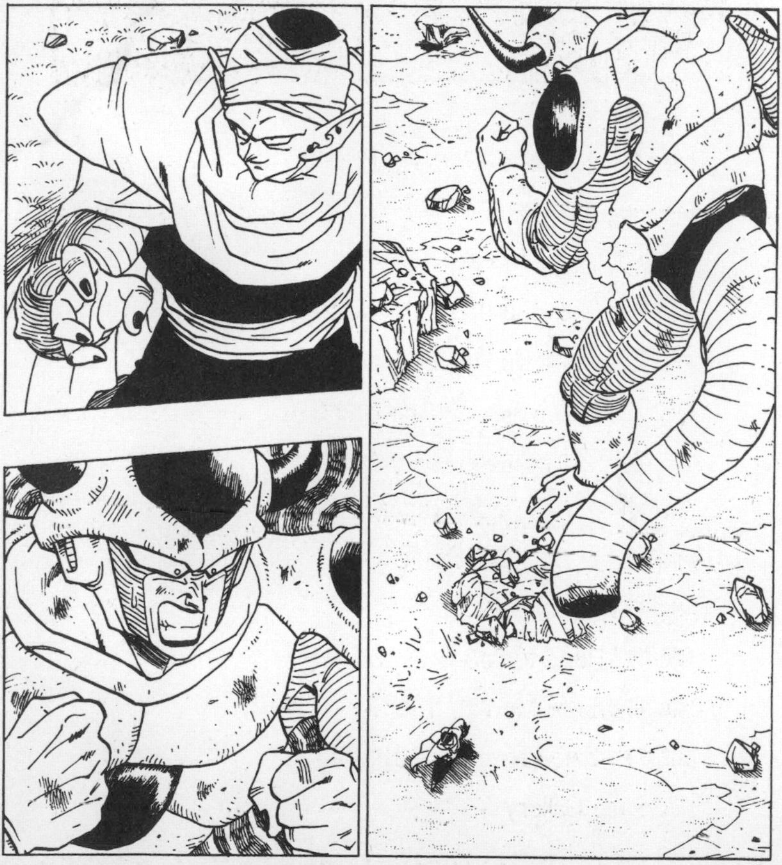

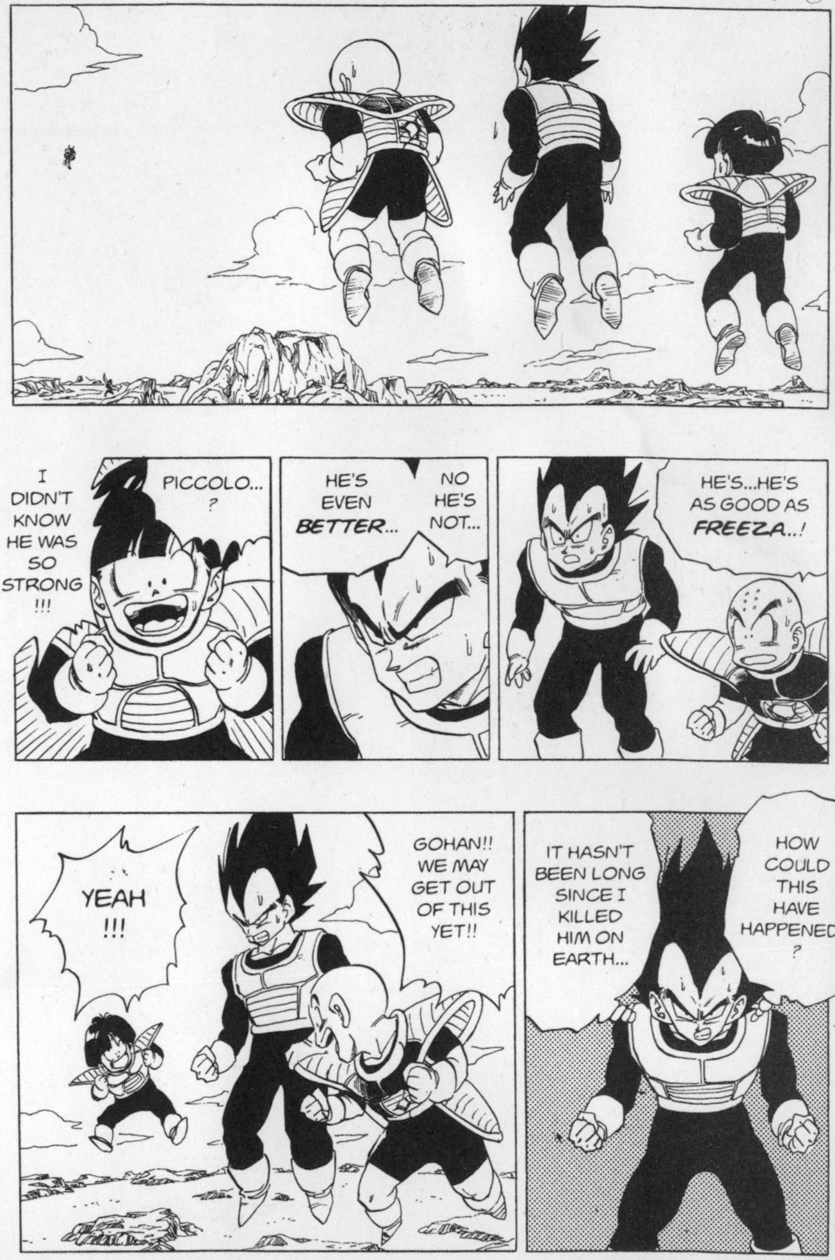
HE'S...HE'S AS GOOD AS FREEZA...!
NO HE'S NOT...
HE'S EVEN BETTER...
PICCOLO...?
I DIDN'T KNOW HE WAS SO STRONG!!!
HOW COULD THIS HAVE HAPPENED..?
IT HASN'T BEEN LONG SINCE I KILLED HIM ON EARTH...
GOHAN!! WE MAY GET OUT OF THIS YET!!
YEAH!!!

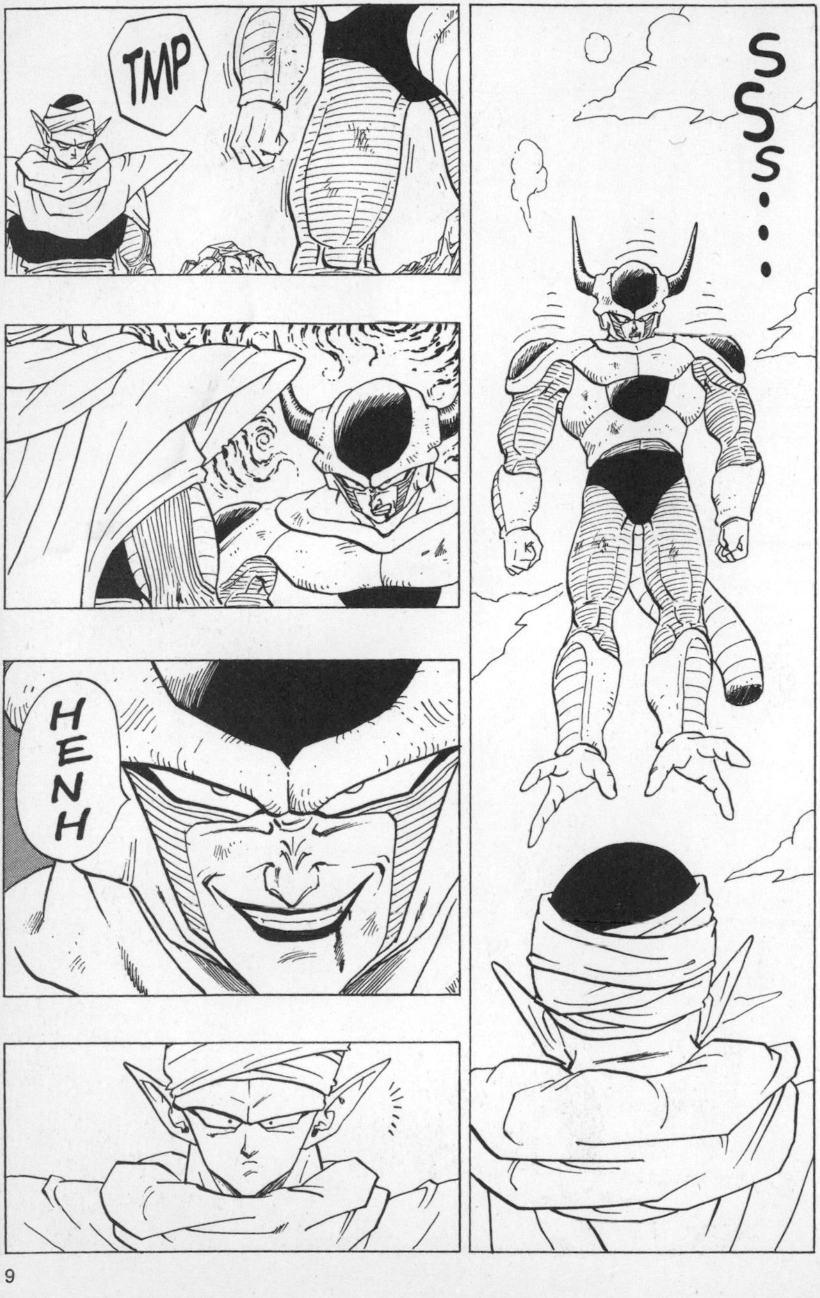
SSs...
TMP
HENH

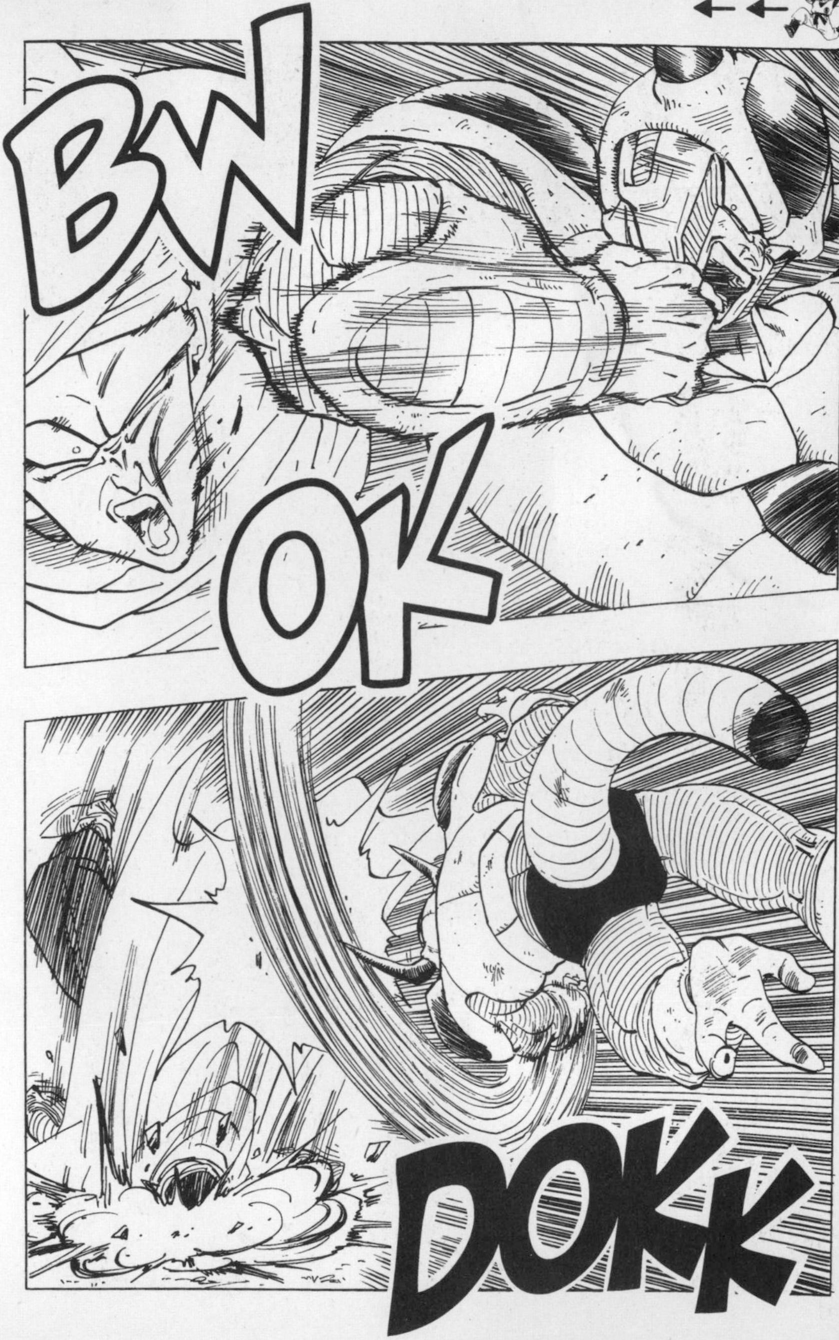
BWOK
DOKK

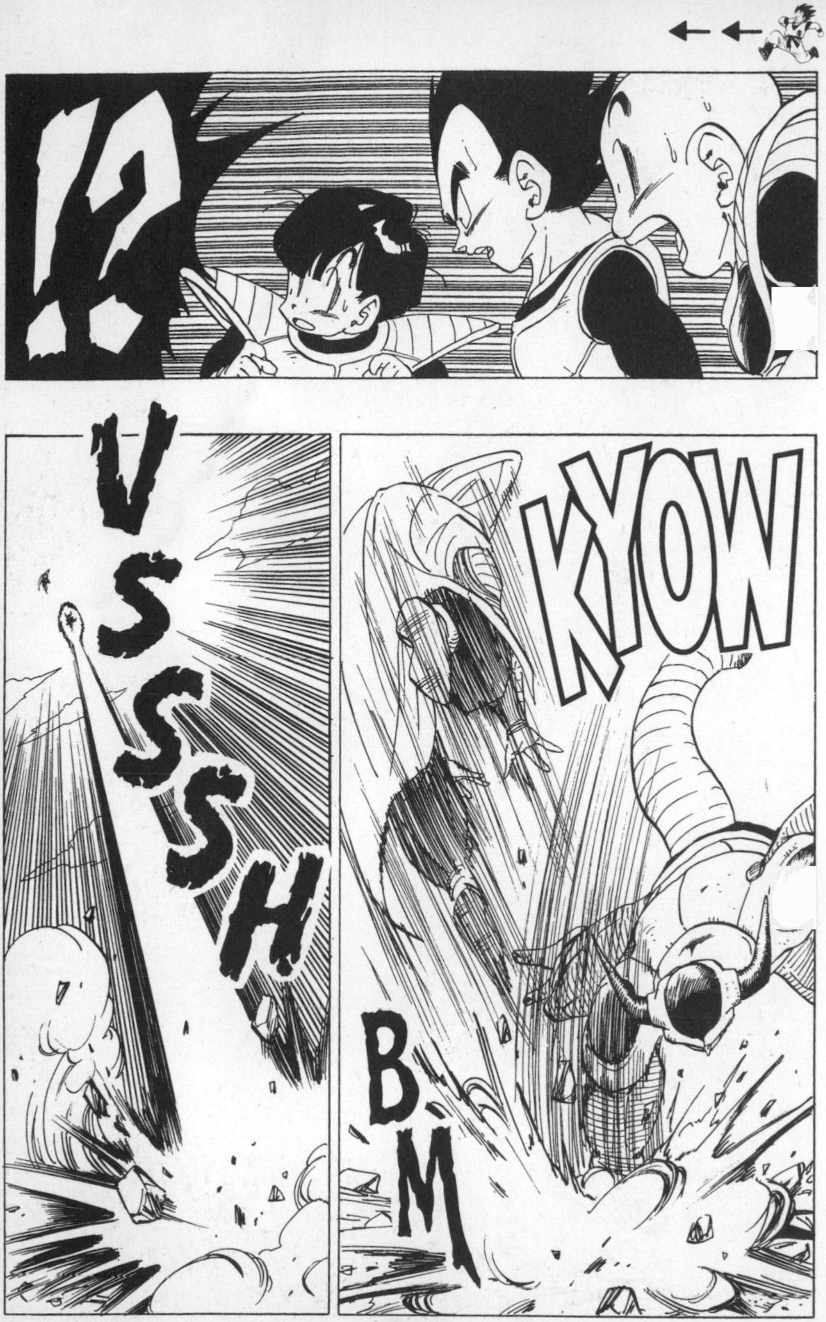
!?
KYOW
B
M
VSSSH

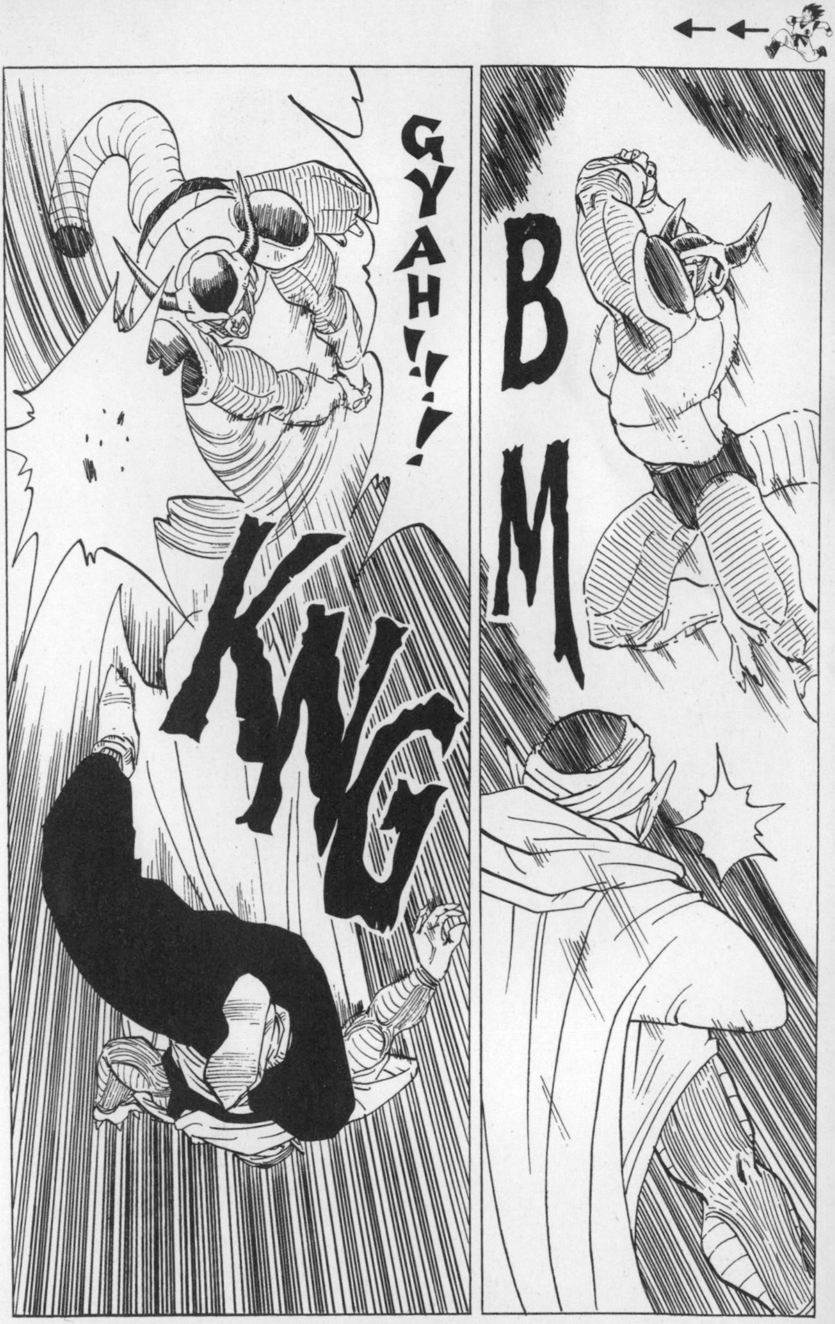
BM
GYAH!!!
KNG

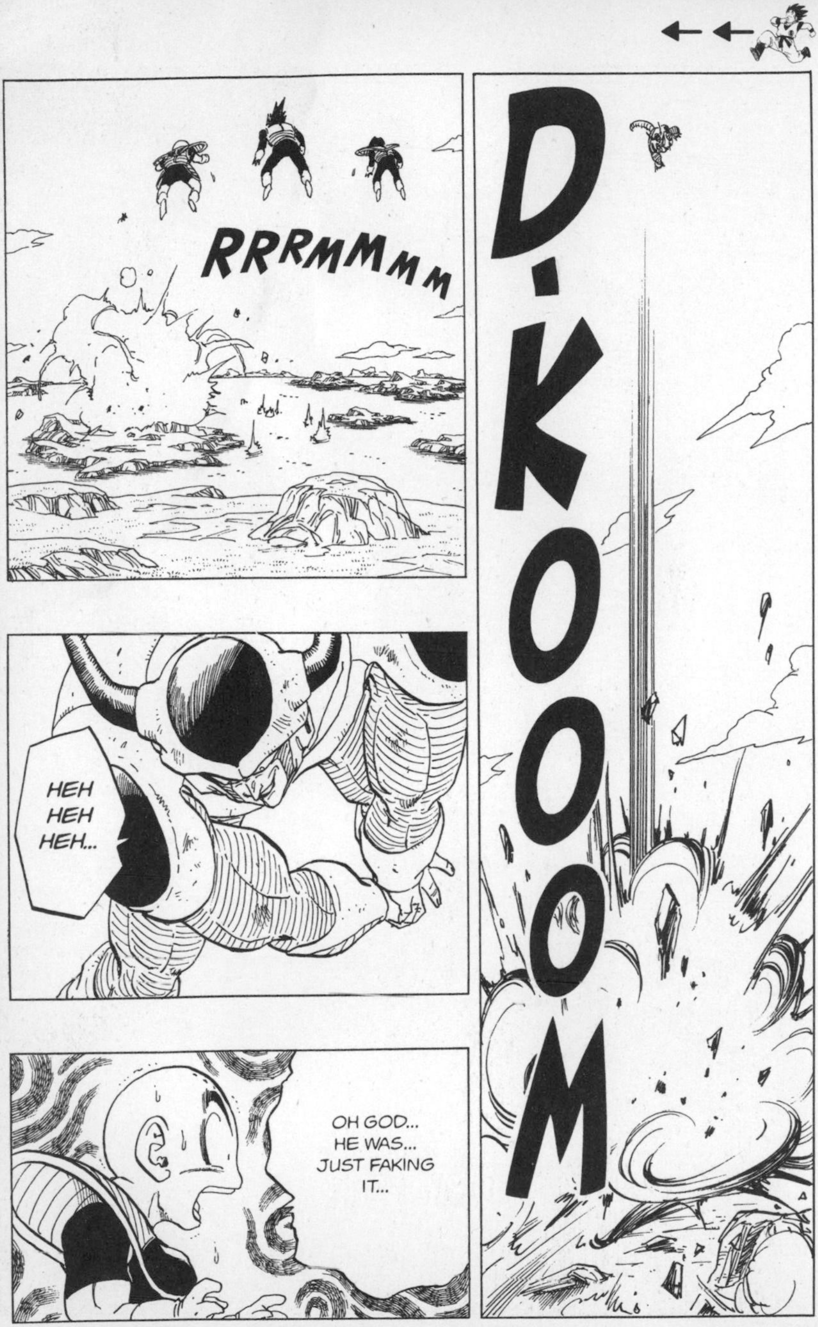
DOKOOM
RRRMMMM
HEH HEH HEH...
OH GOD... HE WAS... JUST FAKING IT...

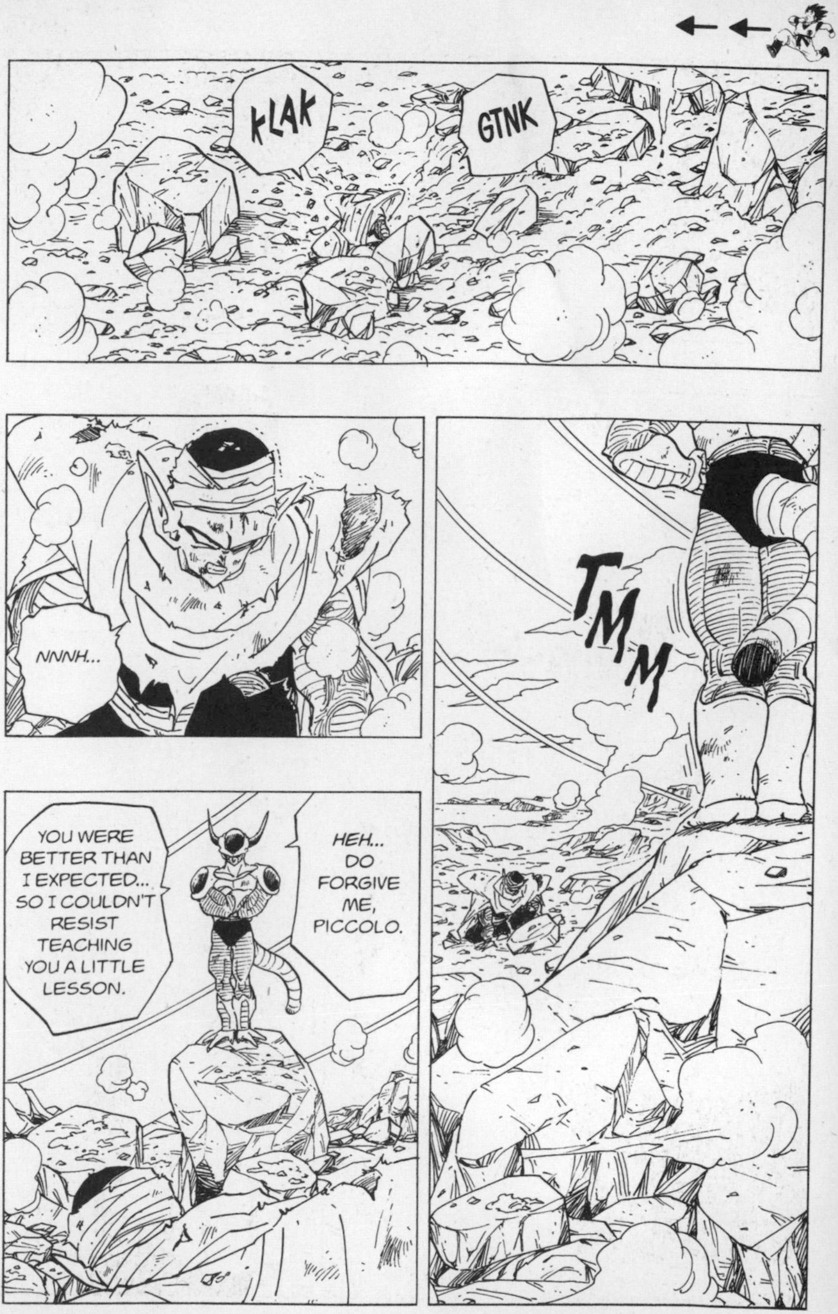
GTNK
KLAK
TMM
NNNH...
HEH... DO FORGIVE ME, PICCOLO.
YOU WERE BETTER THAN I EXPECTED... SO I COULDN'T RESIST TEACHING YOU A LITTLE LESSON.

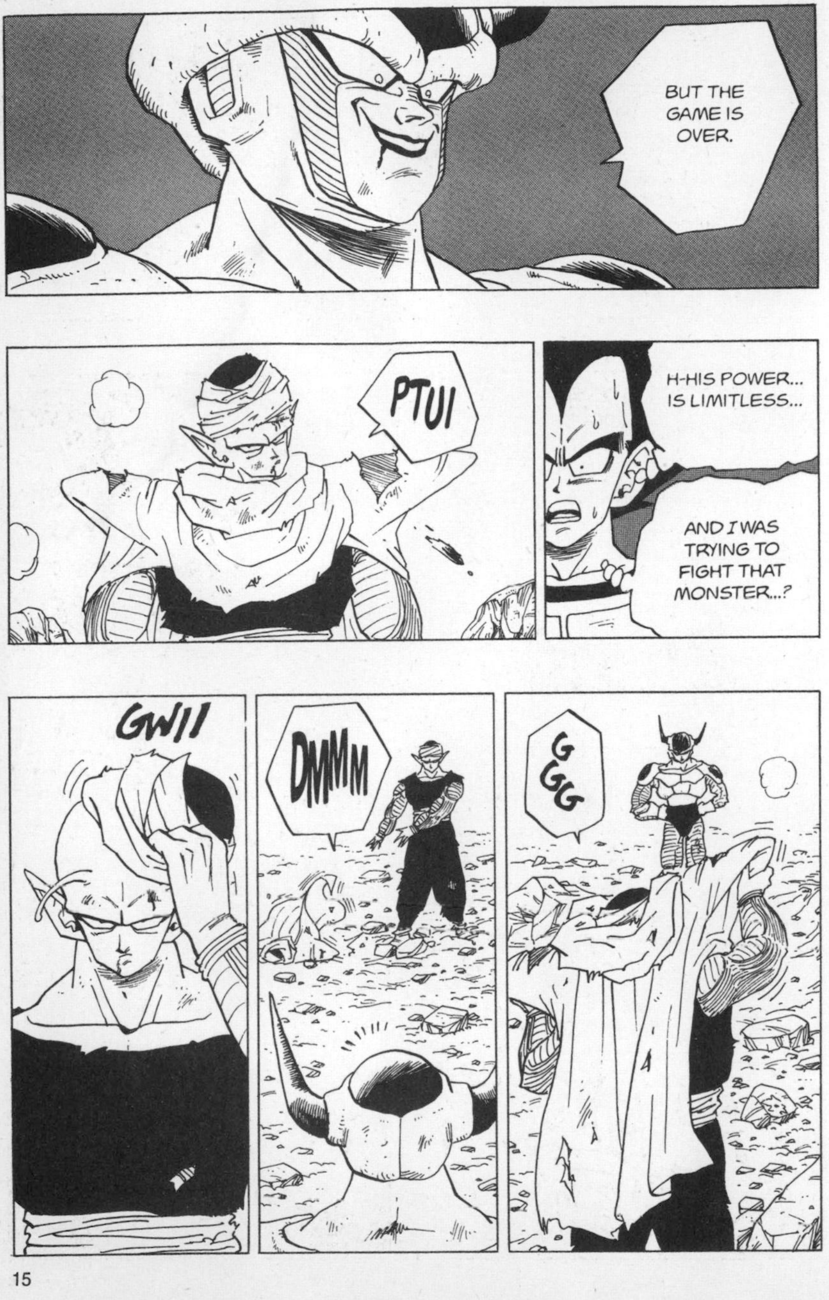
BUT THE GAME IS OVER.
H-HIS POWER... IS LIMITLESS...
AND I WAS TRYING TO FIGHT THAT MONSTER...?
PTUI
GGG
DMMM
GWII

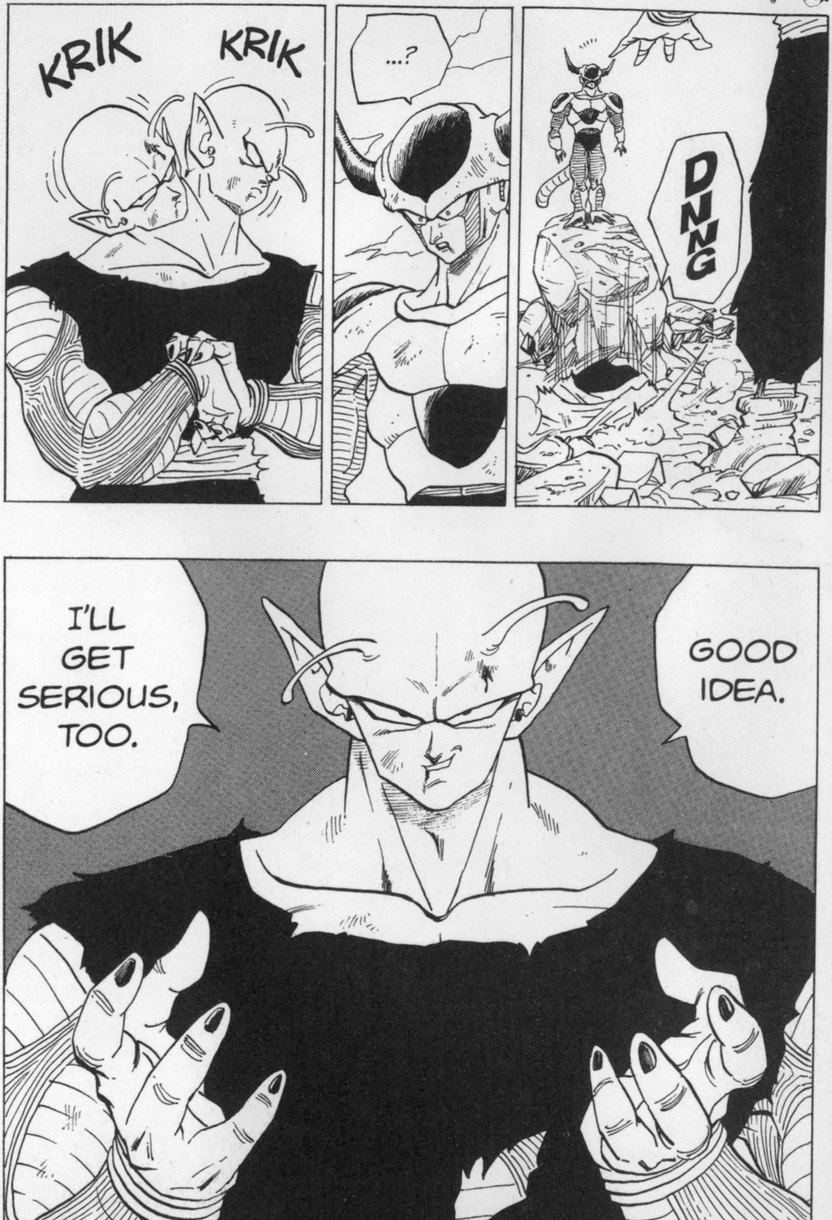
DNNG
...?
KRIK KRIK
GOOD IDEA.
I'LL GET SERIOUS, TOO.

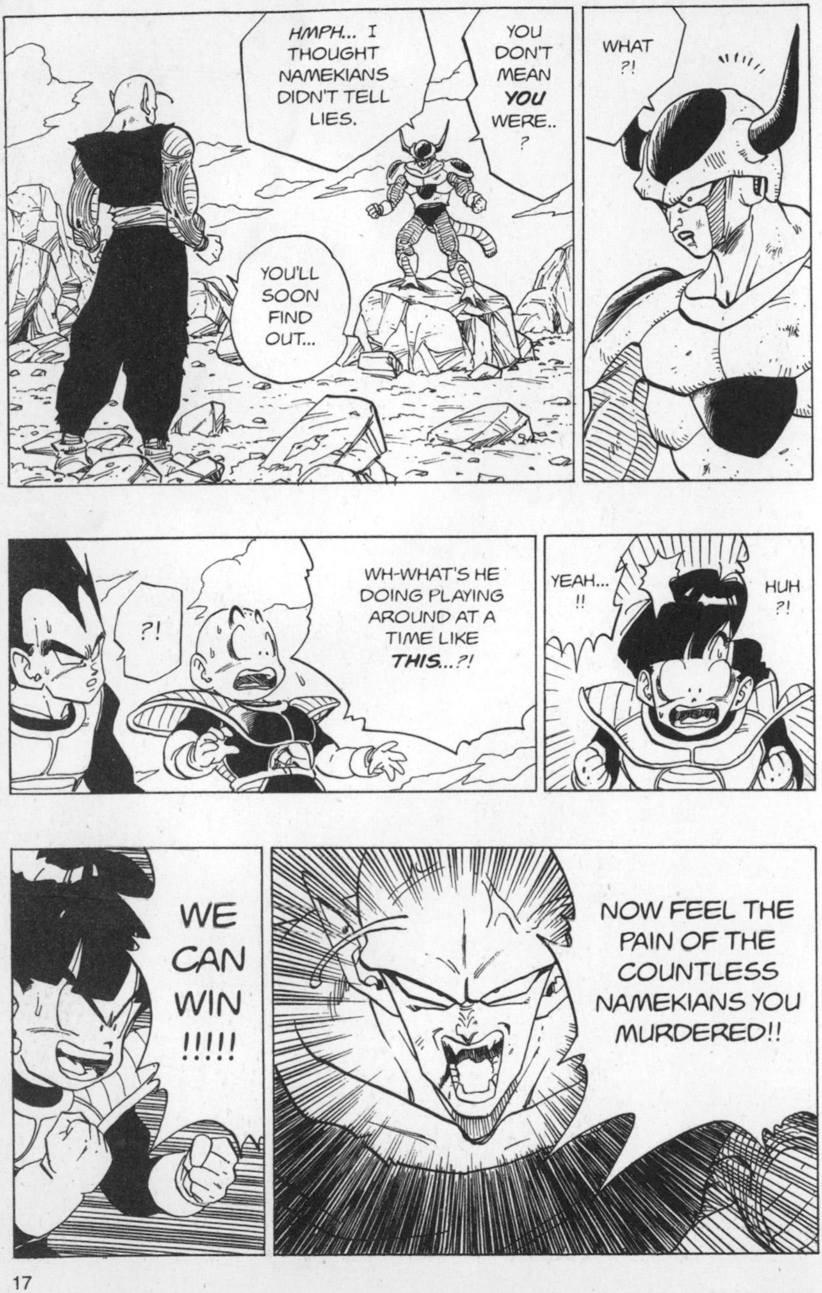
WHAT ?!
YOU DON'T MEAN YOU WERE.. ?
HMPH... I THOUGHT NAMEKIANS DIDN'T TELL LIES.
YOU'LL SOON FIND OUT...
HUH ?!
YEAH... !!
WH-WHAT'S HE DOING PLAYING AROUND AT A TIME LIKE THIS...?!
?!
NOW FEEL THE PAIN OF THE COUNTLESS NAMEKIANS YOU MURDERED!!
WE CAN WIN !!!!!

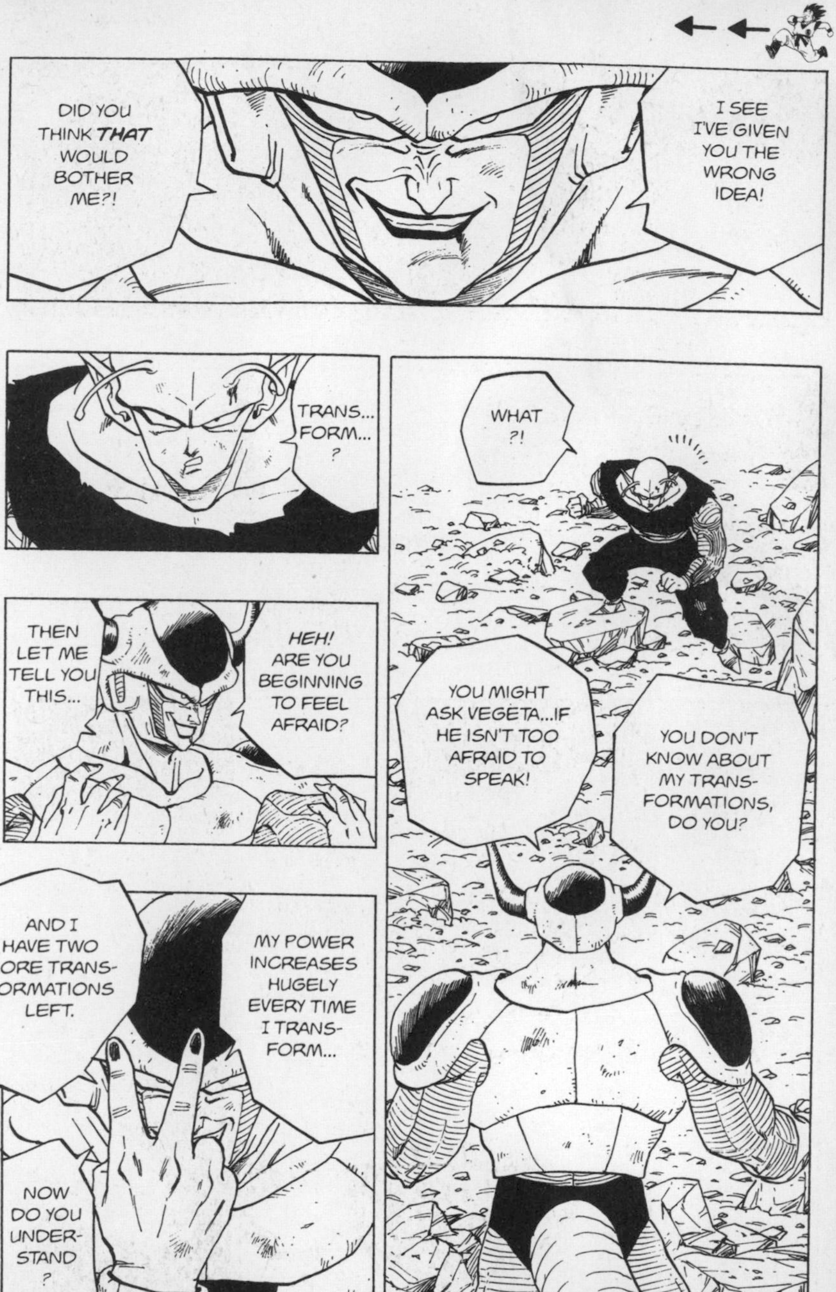
I SEE I'VE GIVEN YOU THE WRONG IDEA!
DID YOU THINK *THAT* WOULD BOTHER ME?!
WHAT ?!
YOU DON'T KNOW ABOUT MY TRANS-FORMATIONS, DO YOU?
YOU MIGHT ASK VEGETA...IF HE ISN'T TOO AFRAID TO SPEAK!
TRANS... FORM... ?
HEH! ARE YOU BEGINNING TO FEEL AFRAID?
THEN LET ME TELL YOU THIS...
MY POWER INCREASES HUGELY EVERY TIME I TRANS-FORM...
AND I HAVE TWO MORE TRANS-FORMATIONS LEFT.
NOW DO YOU UNDER-STAND ?

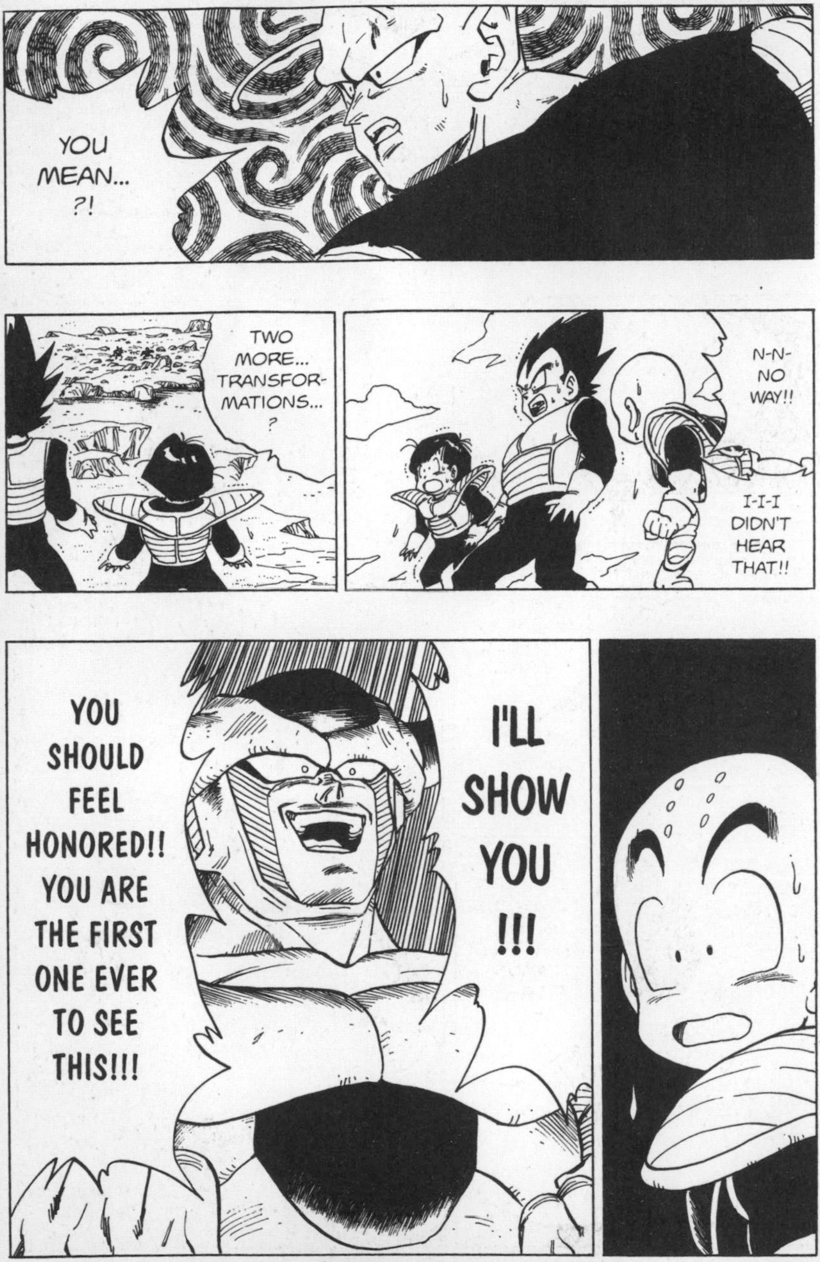
YOU MEAN... ?!
N-N-NO WAY!!
I-I-I DIDN'T HEAR THAT!!
TWO MORE... TRANSFORMATIONS... ?
I'LL SHOW YOU !!!
YOU SHOULD FEEL HONORED!! YOU ARE THE FIRST ONE EVER TO SEE THIS!!!

***NEXT*: The Second Transformation!**

DBZ:108 • Freeza's Third Form

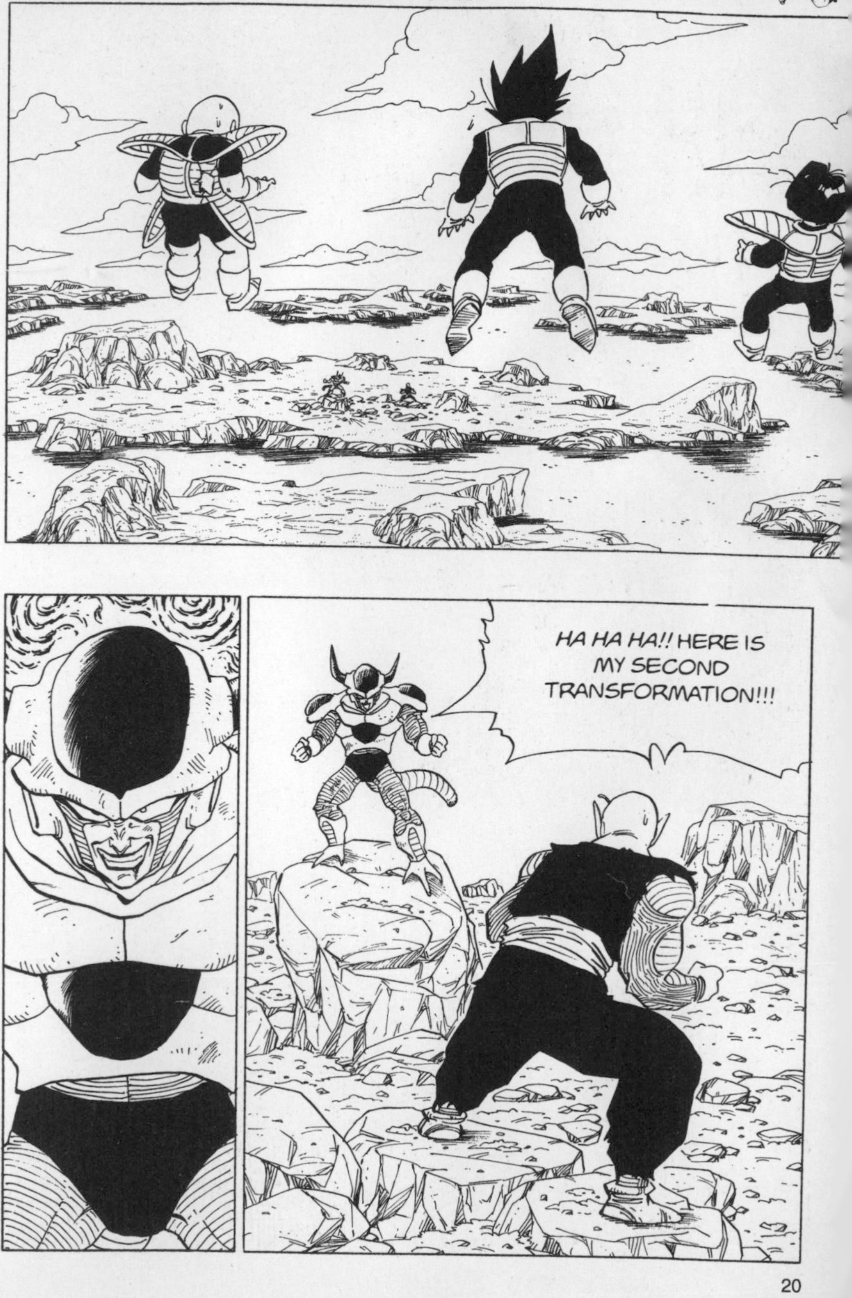
HA HA HA!! HERE IS MY SECOND TRANSFORMATION!!!

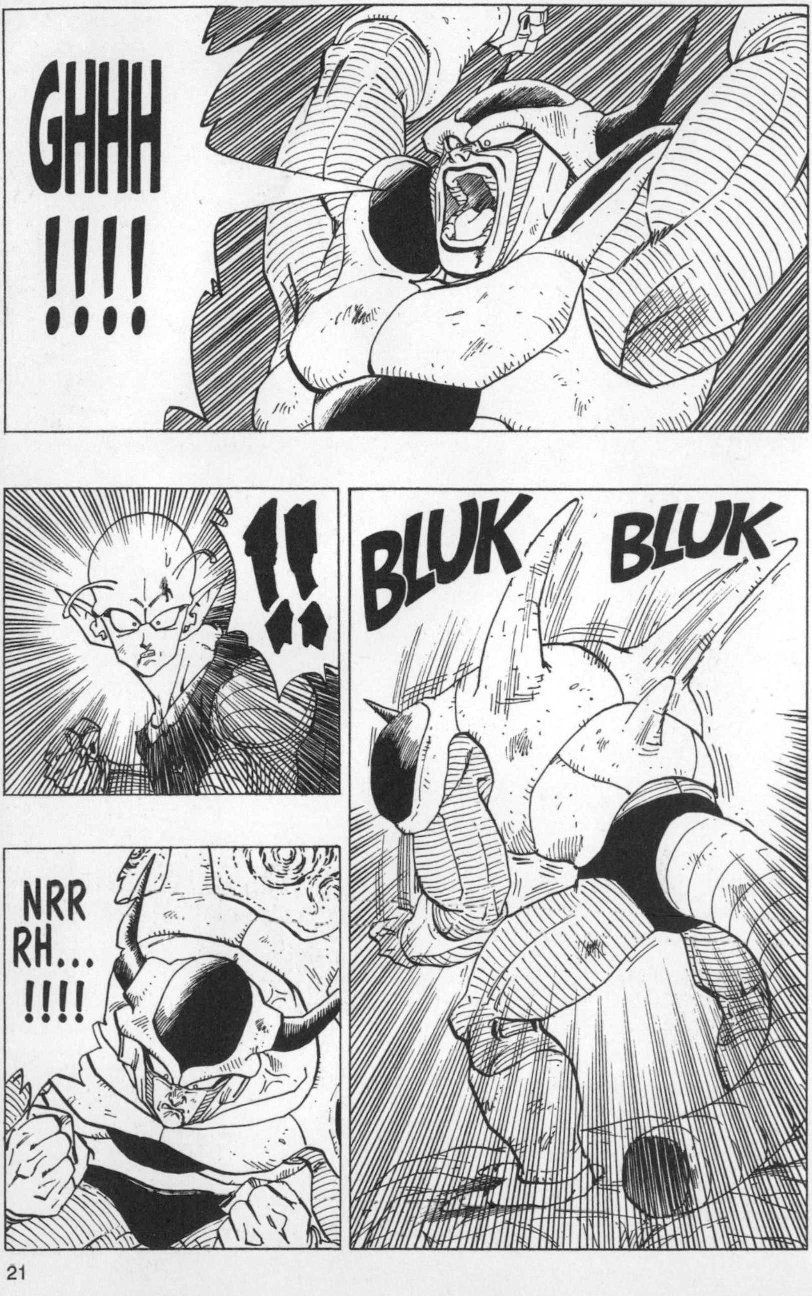
GHHH!!!!
BLUK BLUK
!!
NRRRH...!!!!

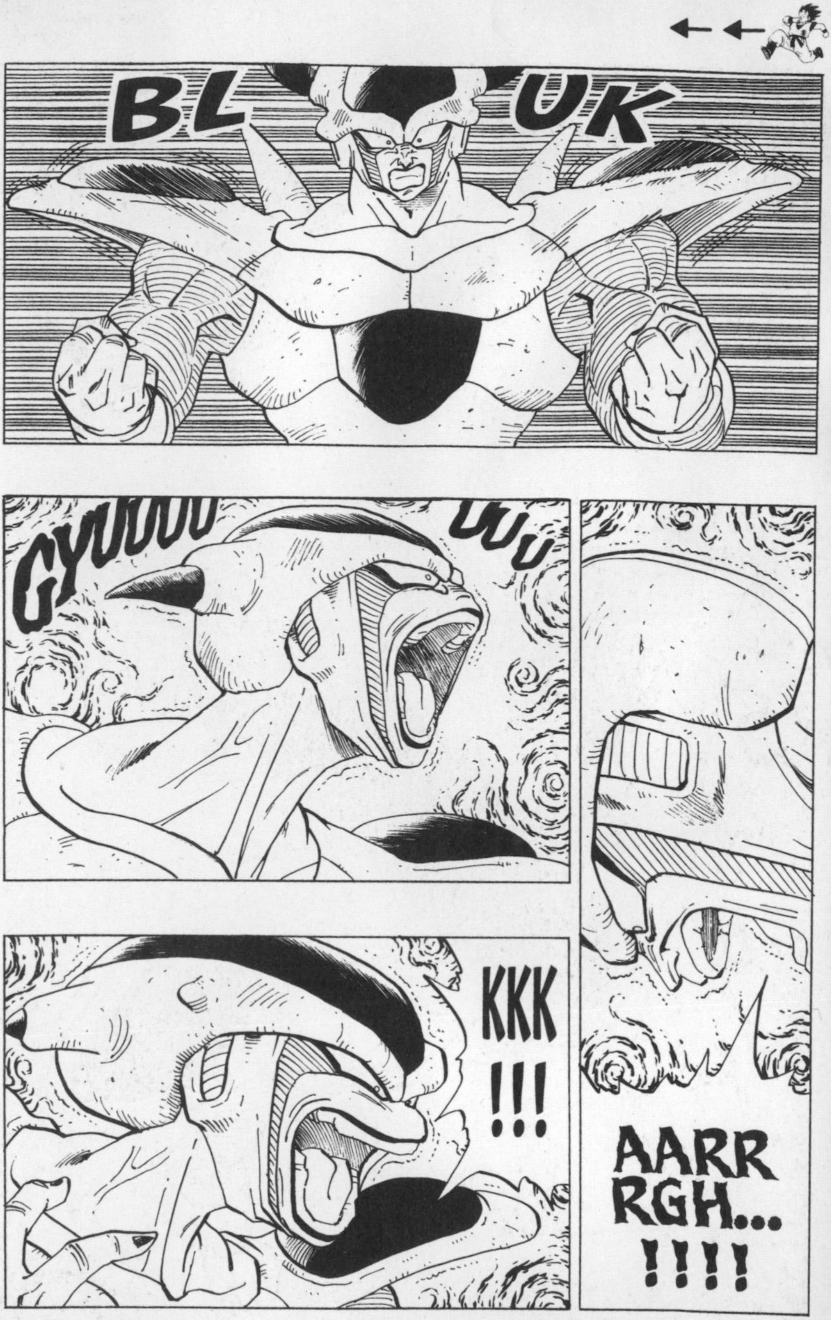
BL UK
AARR
RGH...
!!!!
GYUUUU UUU
KKK
!!!

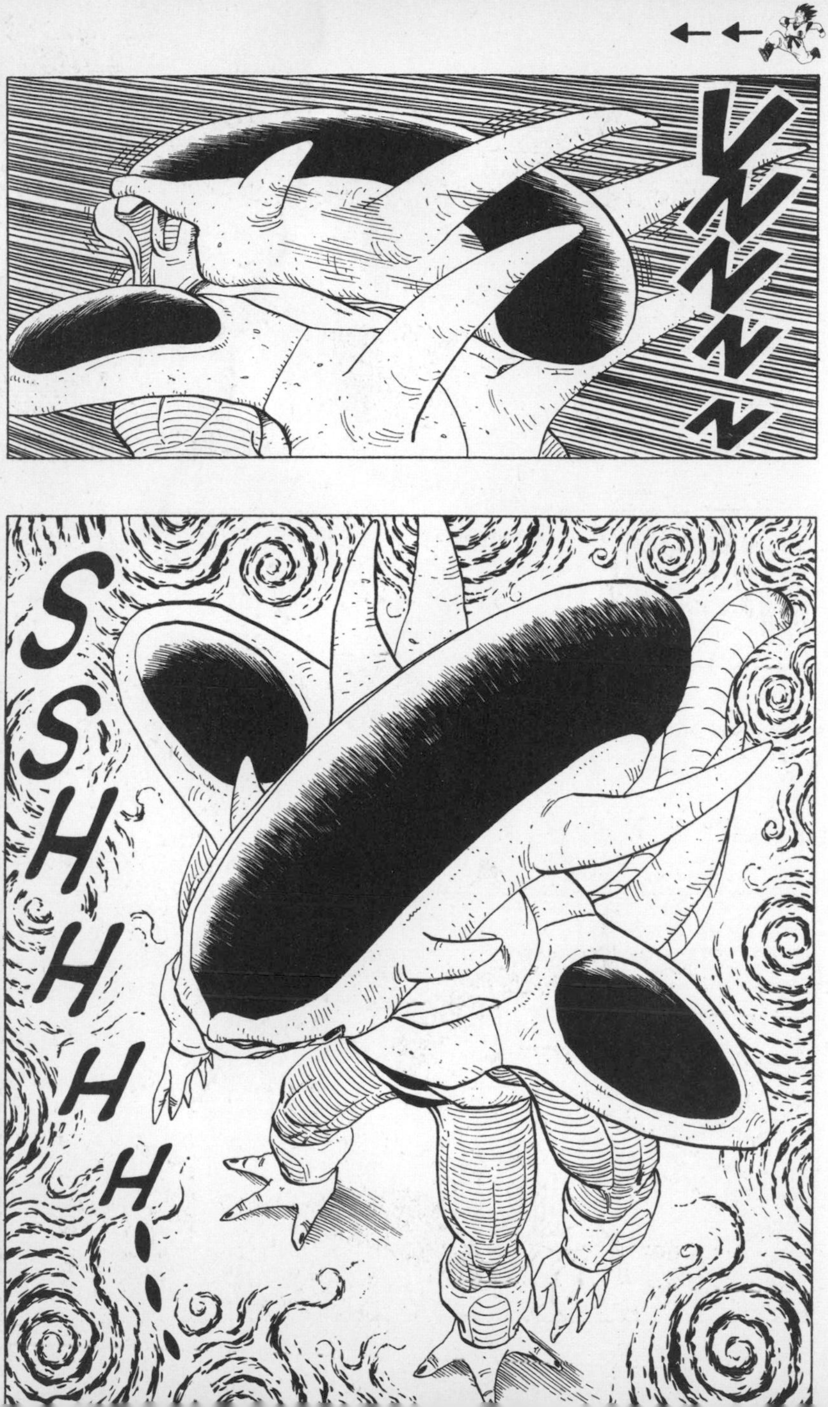
VNNNN
SSHHHH...

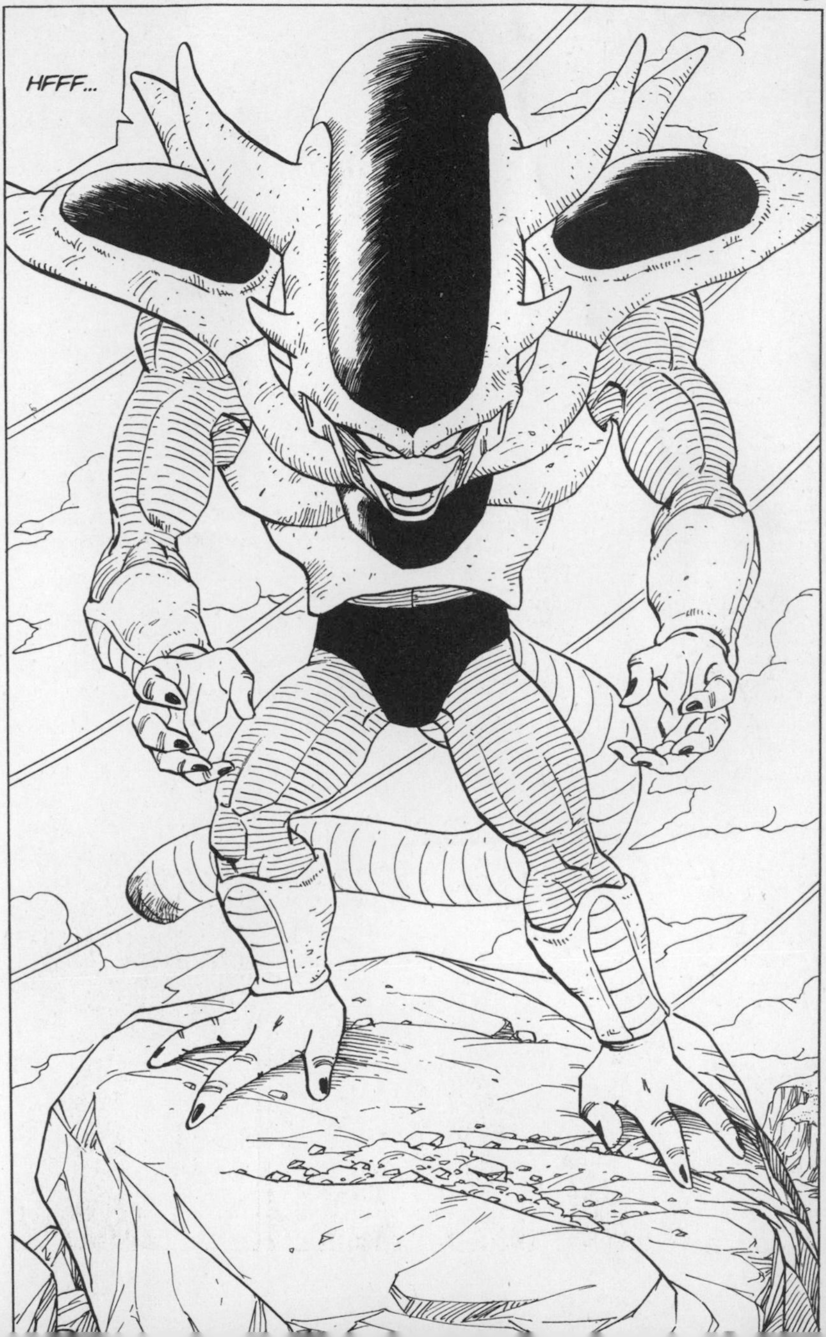
HFFF...

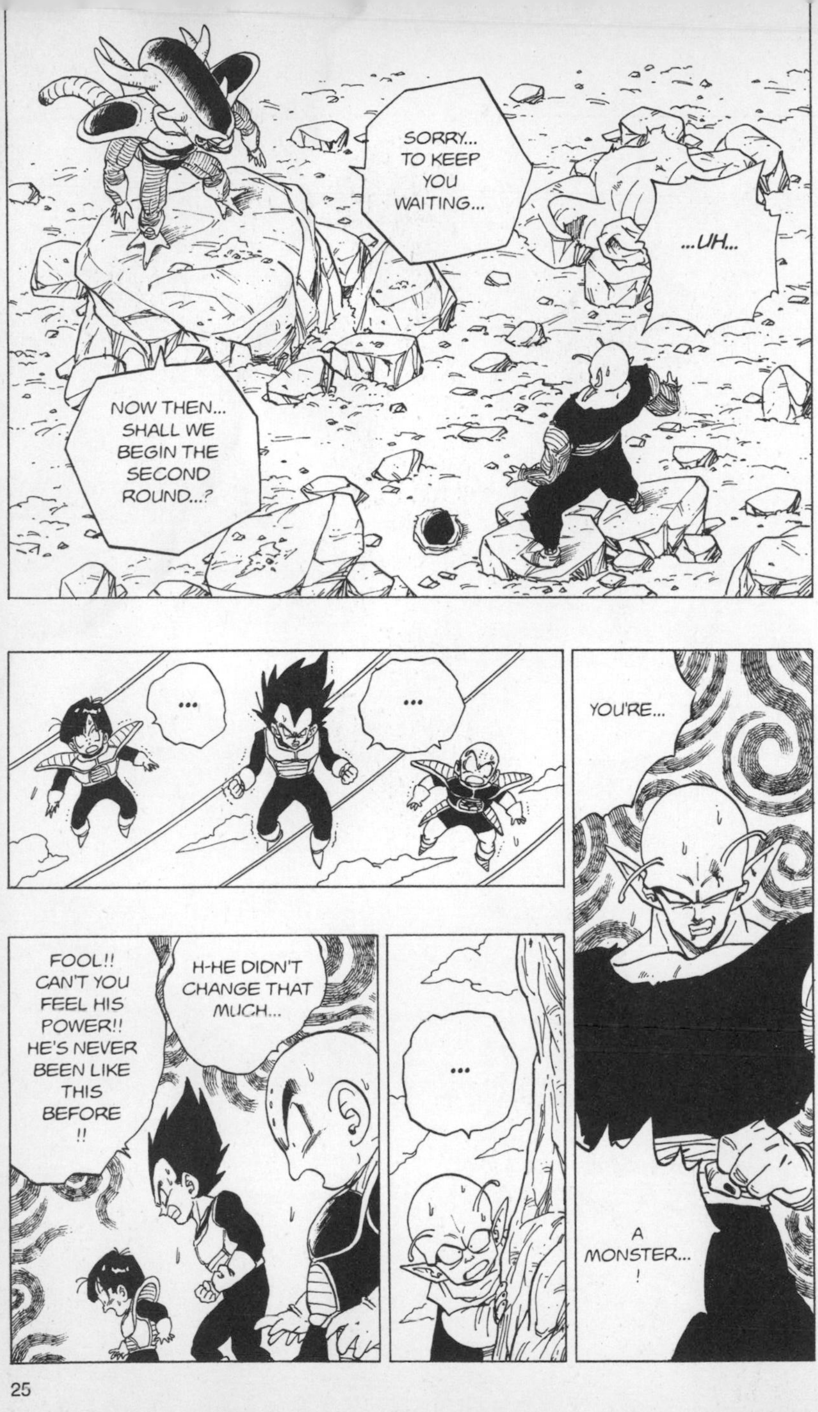
SORRY... TO KEEP YOU WAITING...
...UH...
NOW THEN... SHALL WE BEGIN THE SECOND ROUND...?
YOU'RE...
A MONSTER...!
...
...
...
H-HE DIDN'T CHANGE THAT MUCH...
FOOL!! CAN'T YOU FEEL HIS POWER!! HE'S NEVER BEEN LIKE THIS BEFORE!!

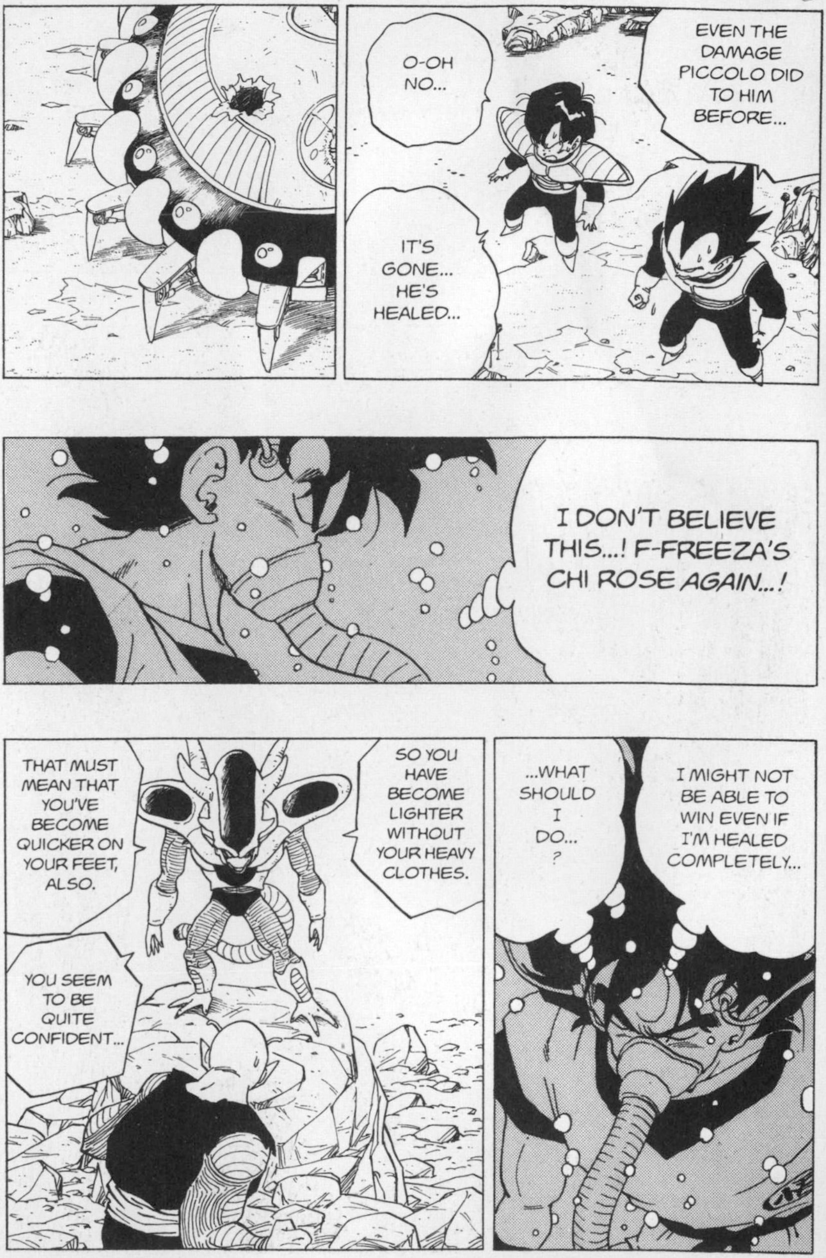
EVEN THE DAMAGE PICCOLO DID TO HIM BEFORE...
O-OH NO...
IT'S GONE... HE'S HEALED...
I DON'T BELIEVE THIS...! F-FREEZA'S CHI ROSE *AGAIN*...!
I MIGHT NOT BE ABLE TO WIN EVEN IF I'M HEALED COMPLETELY...
...WHAT SHOULD I DO...?
SO YOU HAVE BECOME LIGHTER WITHOUT YOUR HEAVY CLOTHES.
THAT MUST MEAN THAT YOU'VE BECOME QUICKER ON YOUR FEET, ALSO.
YOU SEEM TO BE QUITE CONFIDENT...

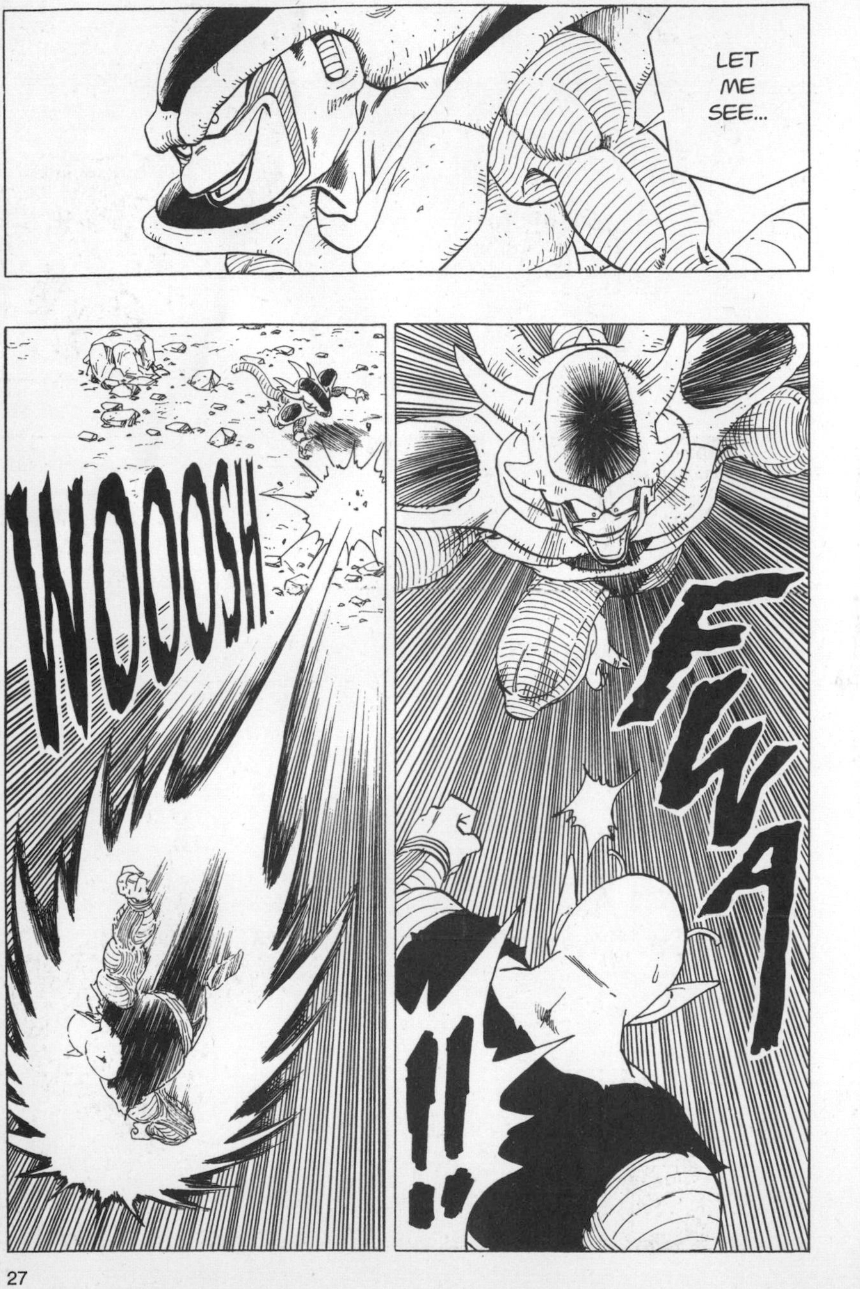
LET ME SEE...
FWA
!!
WOOOSH

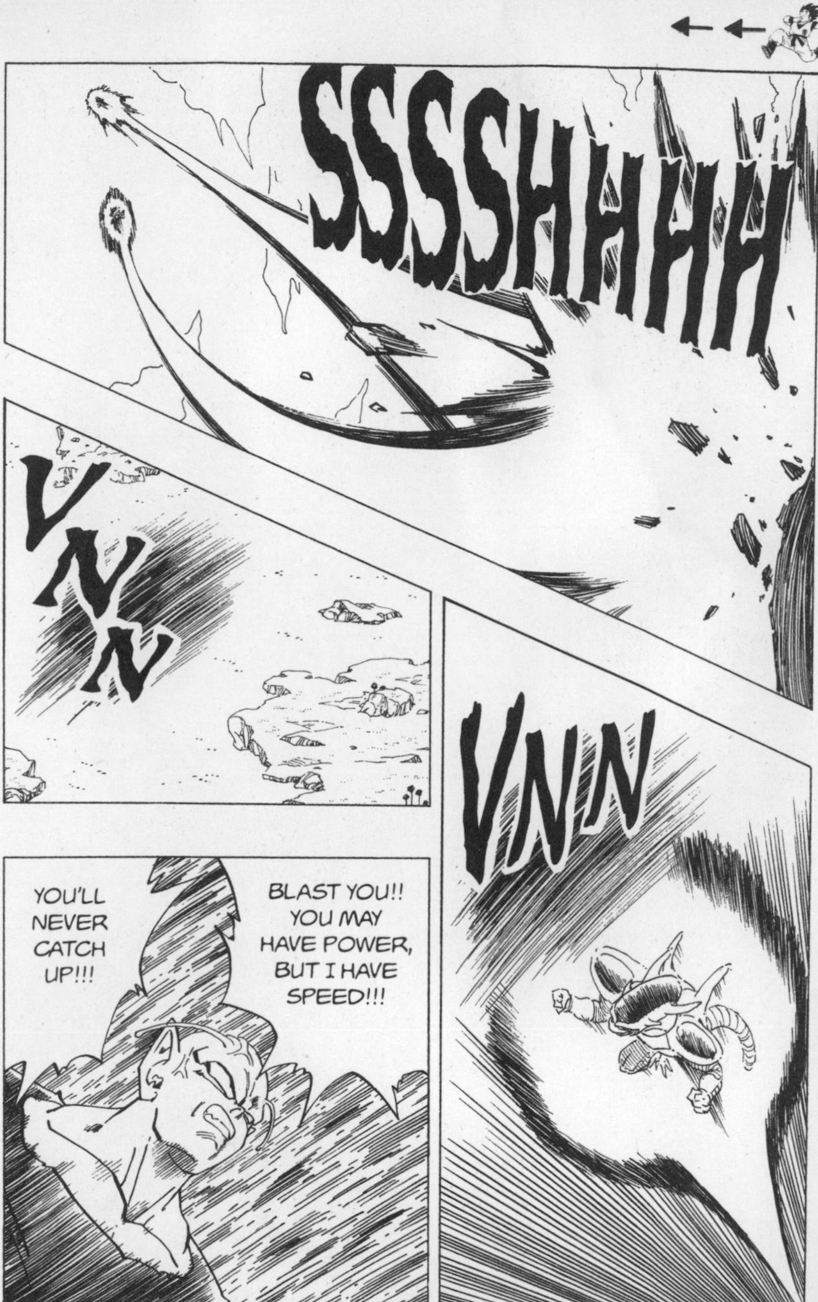
SSSSHHHH
VNN
VNN
BLAST YOU!! YOU MAY HAVE POWER, BUT I HAVE SPEED!!!
YOU'LL NEVER CATCH UP!!!

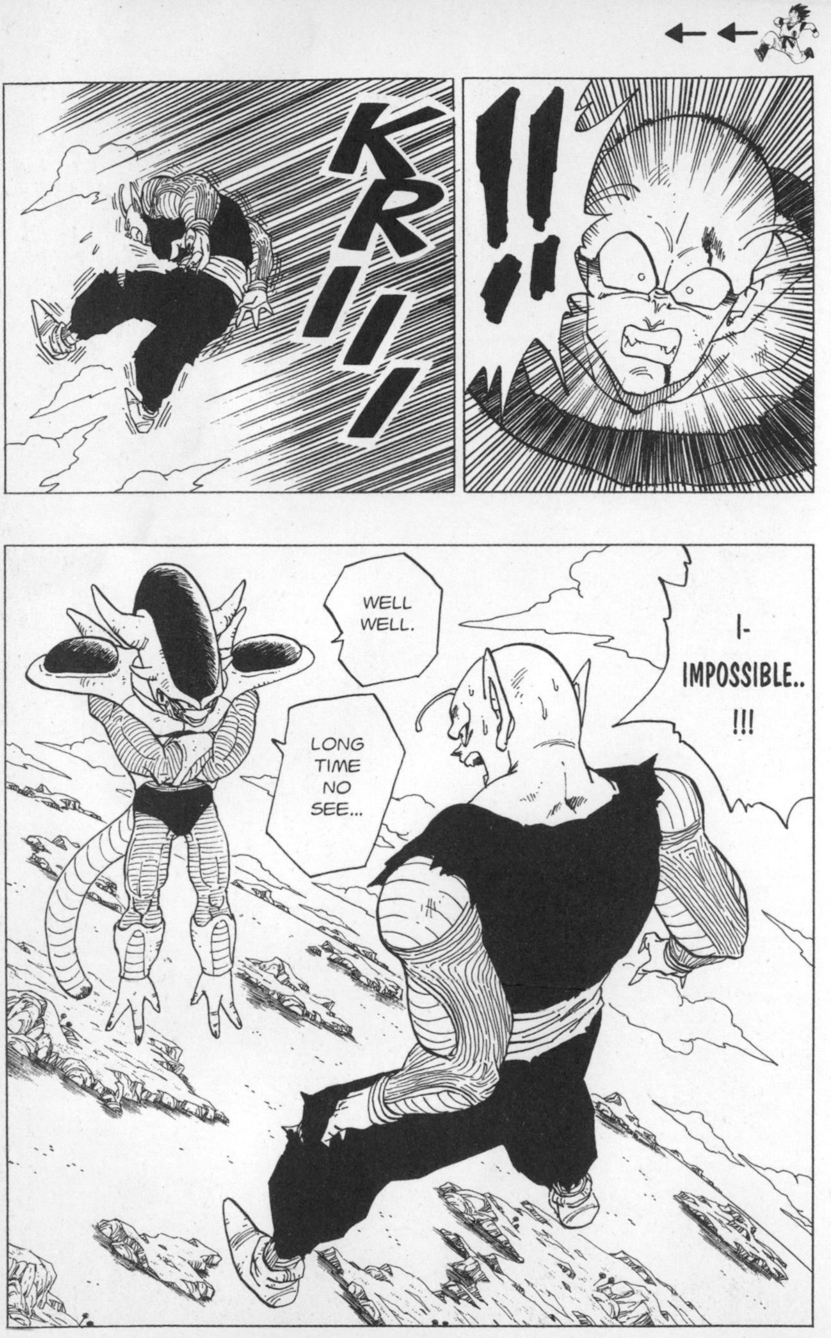
!!
KRIIII
I- IMPOSSIBLE.. !!!
WELL WELL.
LONG TIME NO SEE...

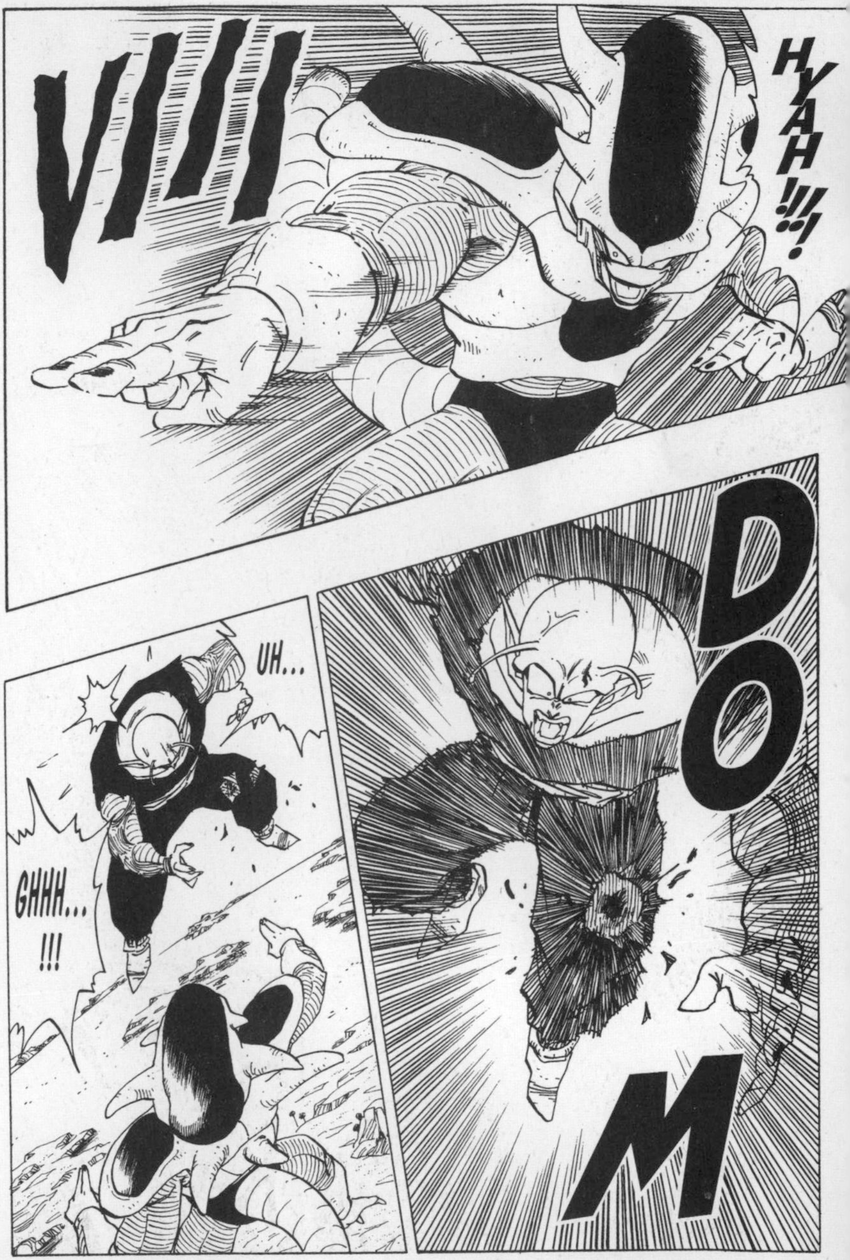
HYAH!!!!
VIIII
DOM
UH...
GHHH... !!!

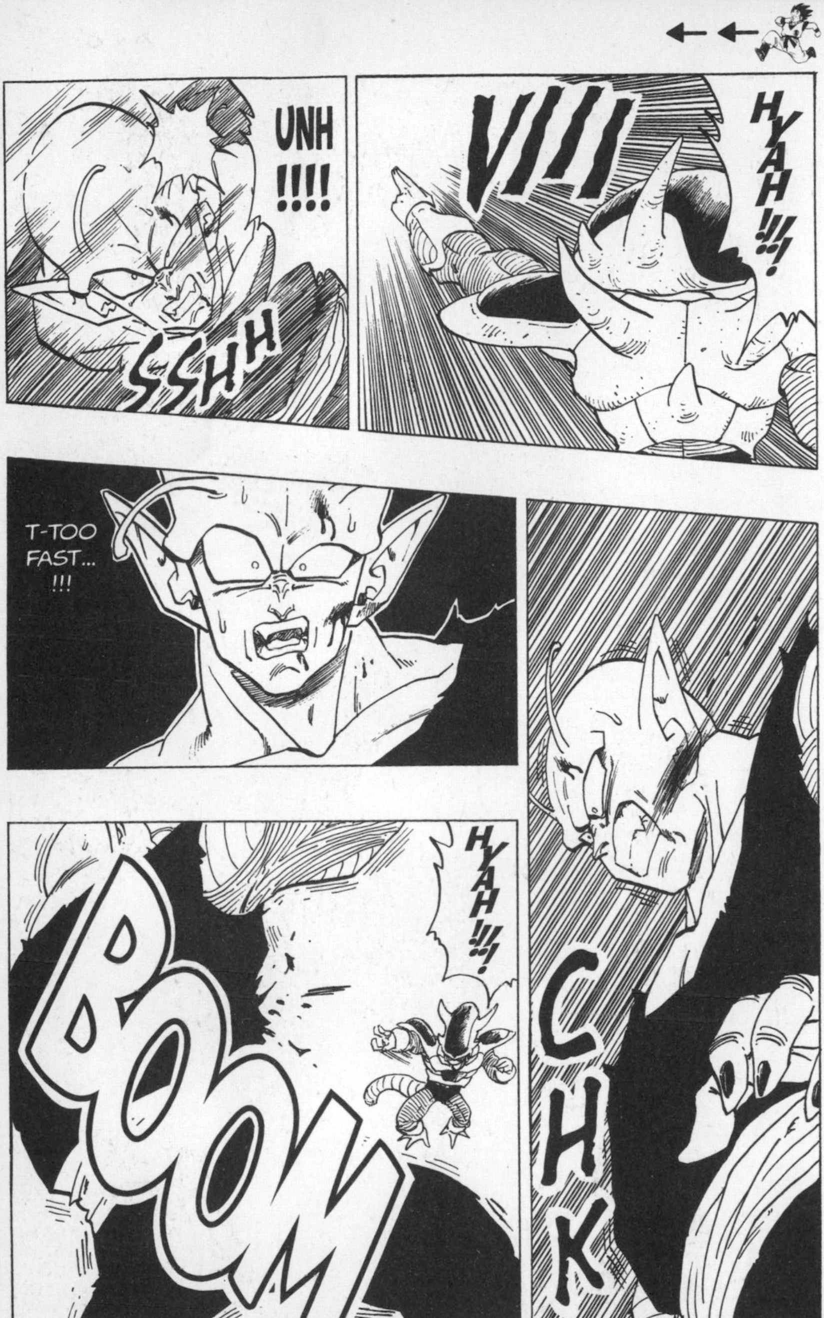
HYAH!!!
VIII
UNH !!!!
SSHH
CHK
T-TOO FAST... !!!
HYAH!!!
BOOM

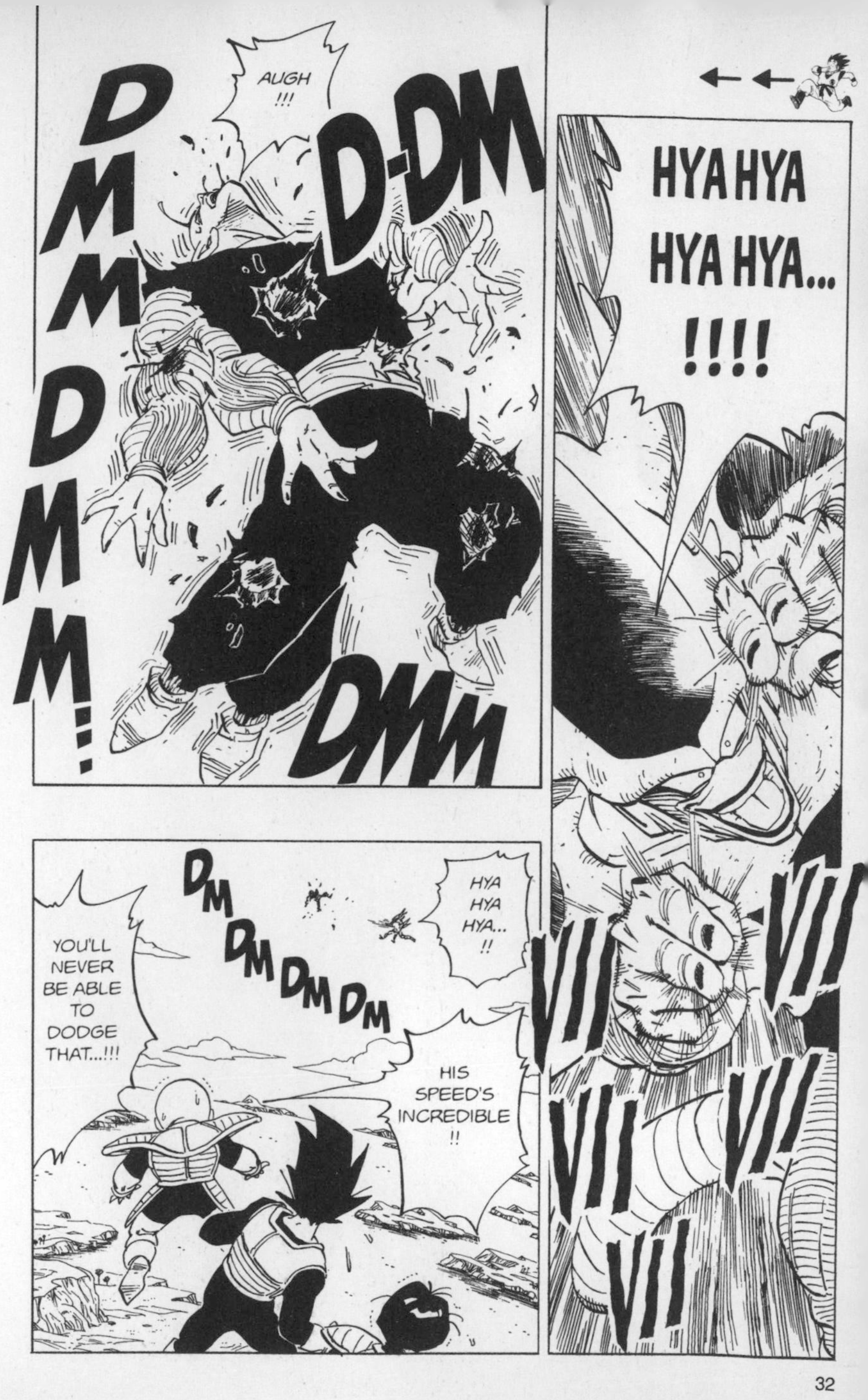

HYA HYA HYA HYA... !!!!
VII-VII
VII VII VII
VII VII
D-DM
AUGH !!!
DMMMDMMMM!!
DMM
HYA HYA HYA... !!
DMDMDMDMDM
YOU'LL NEVER BE ABLE TO DODGE THAT...!!!
HIS SPEED'S INCREDIBLE !!

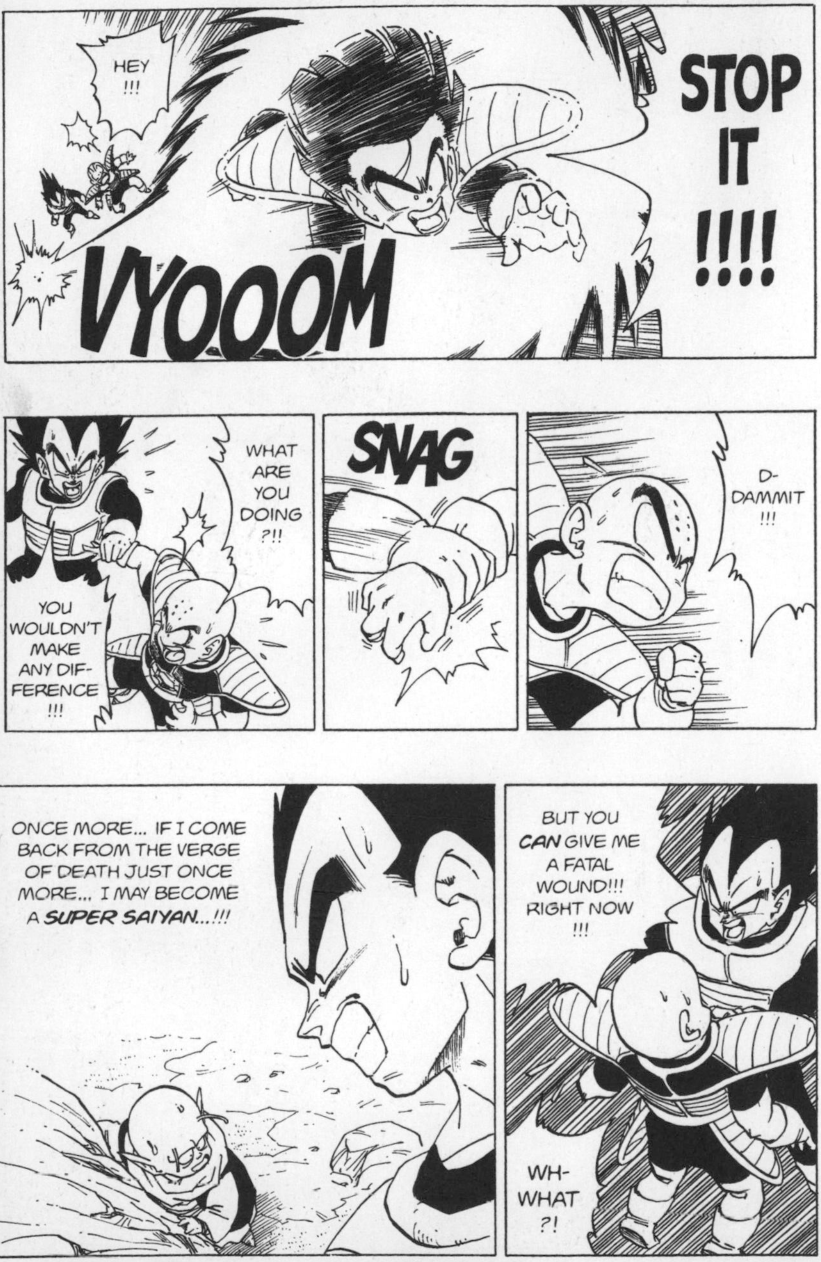
STOP IT !!!!
HEY !!!
VYOOOM
D-DAMMIT !!!
SNAG
WHAT ARE YOU DOING ?!!
YOU WOULDN'T MAKE ANY DIF-FERENCE !!!
BUT YOU CAN GIVE ME A FATAL WOUND!!! RIGHT NOW !!!
WH-WHAT ?!
ONCE MORE... IF I COME BACK FROM THE VERGE OF DEATH JUST ONCE MORE... I MAY BECOME A SUPER SAIYAN...!!!

NEXT: The Last Transformation!

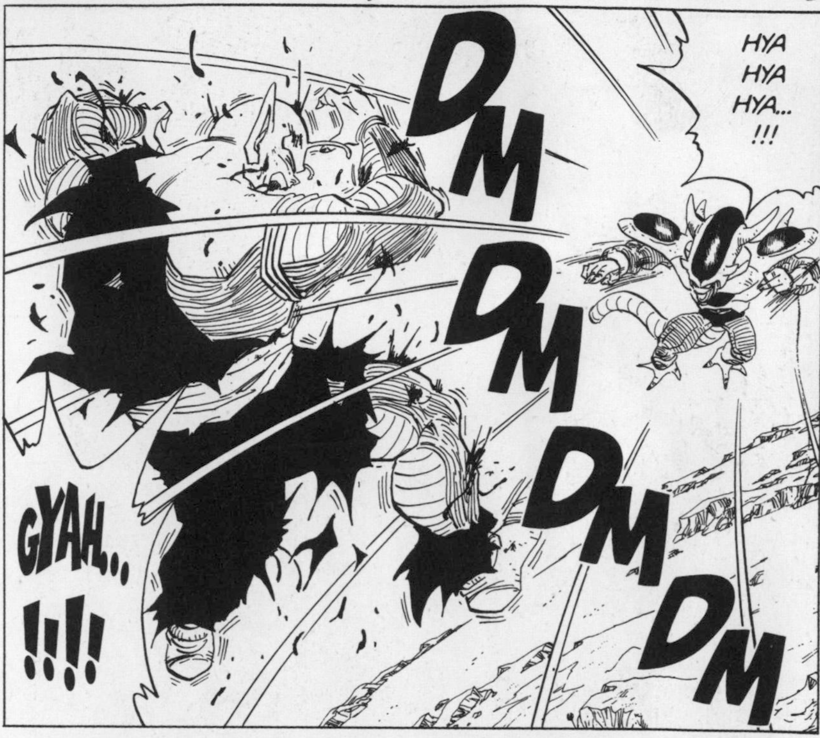
HYA
HYA
HYA...
!!!
DM DM DM DM DM
GYAH...
!!!!

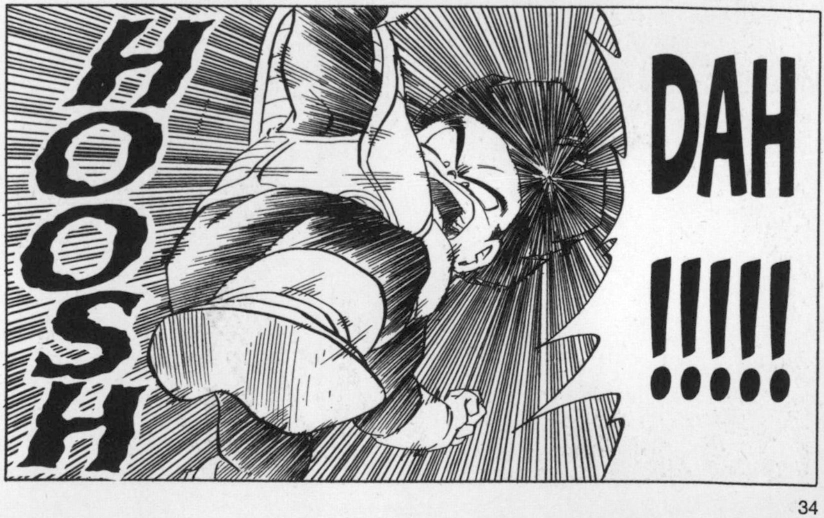
DAH
!!!!!
HOOSH

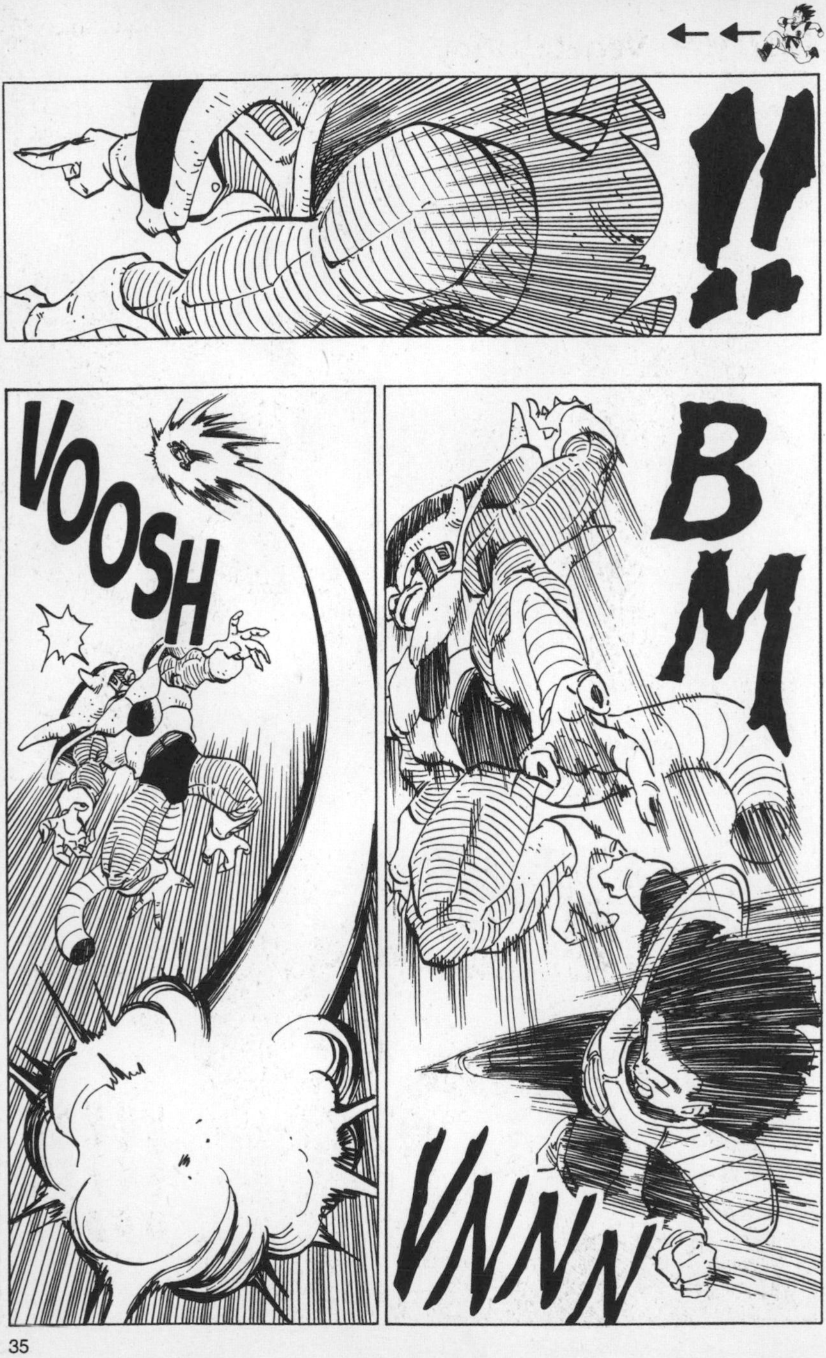
!!
BM
VNNN
VOOSH

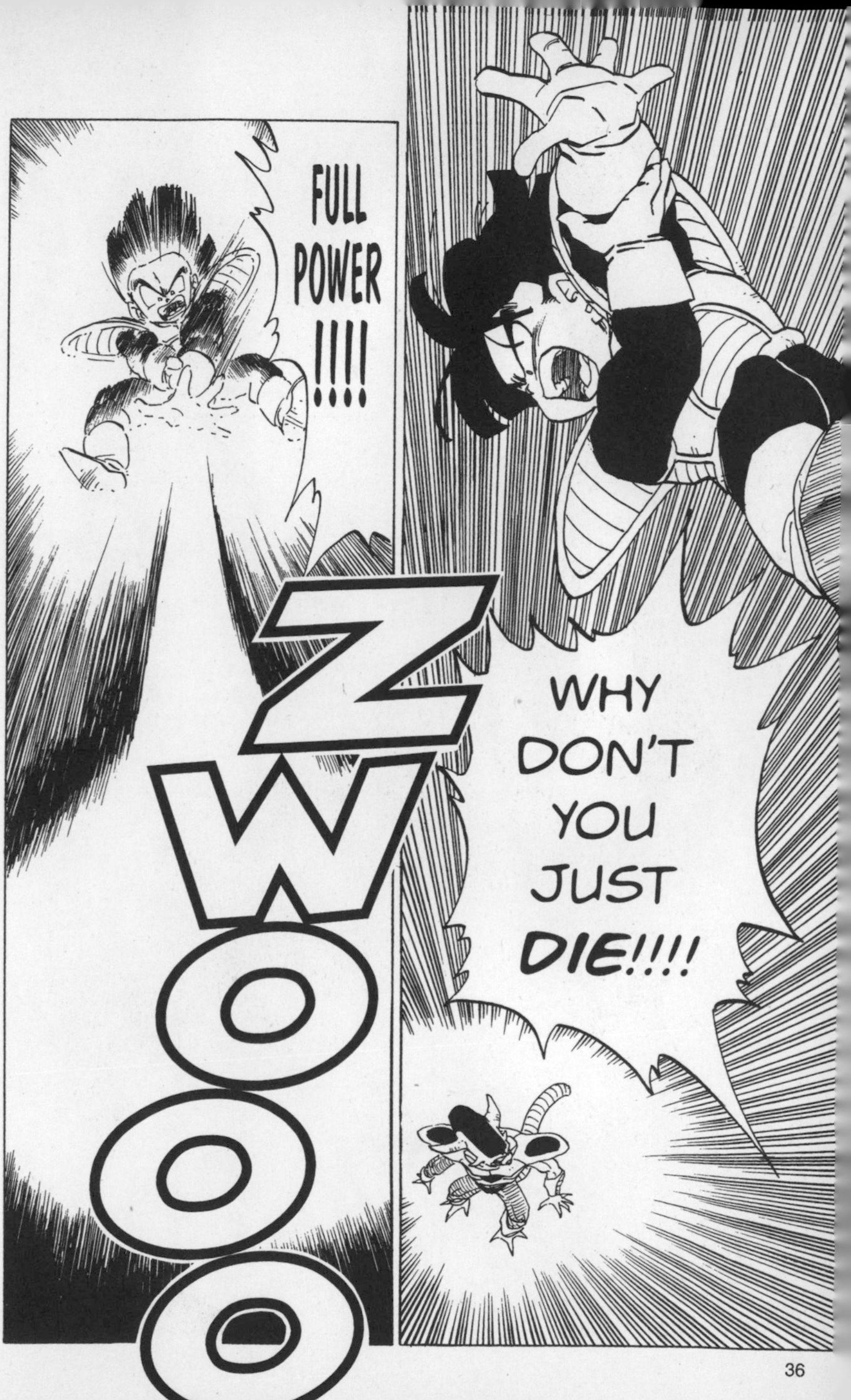
WHY DON'T YOU JUST DIE!!!!
FULL POWER!!!!
ZWOOOO

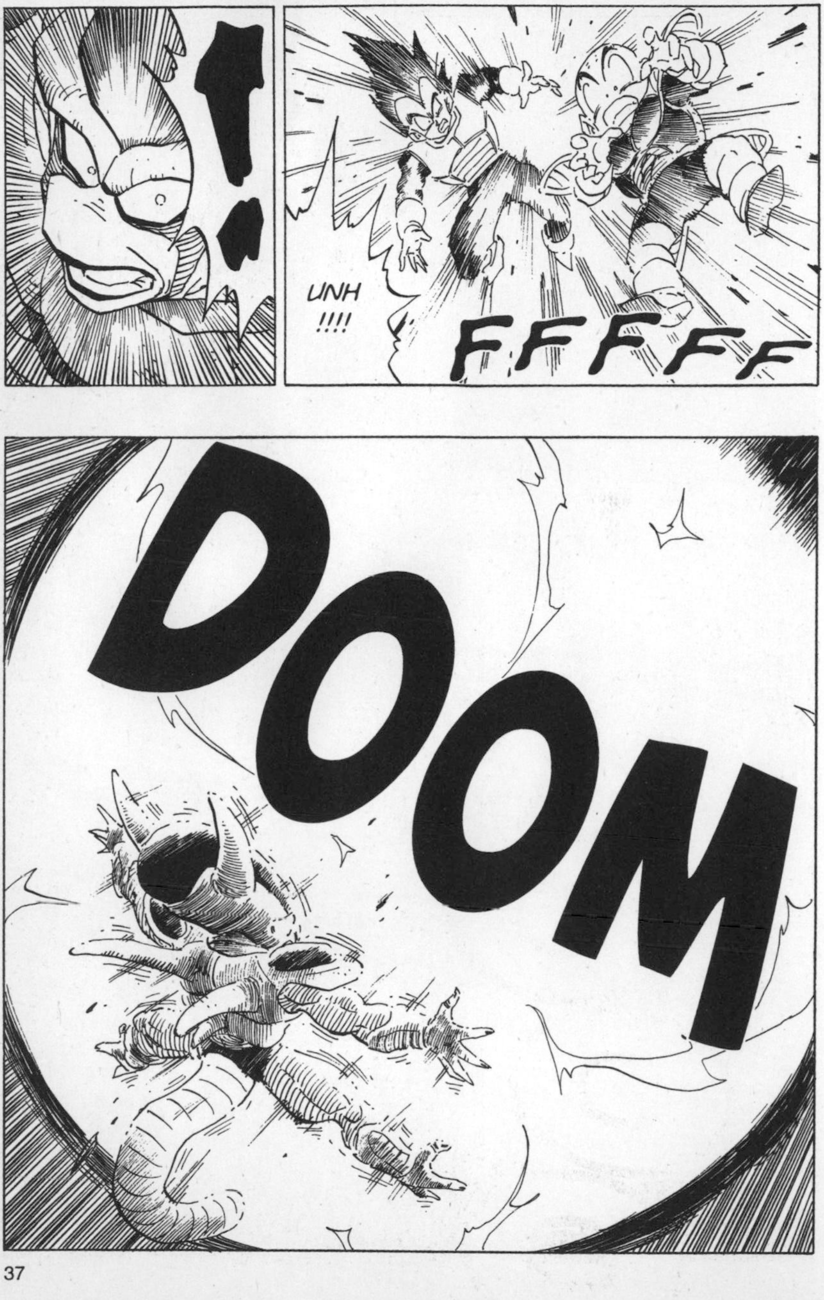
UNH !!!!
FFFFFF
!
DOOM

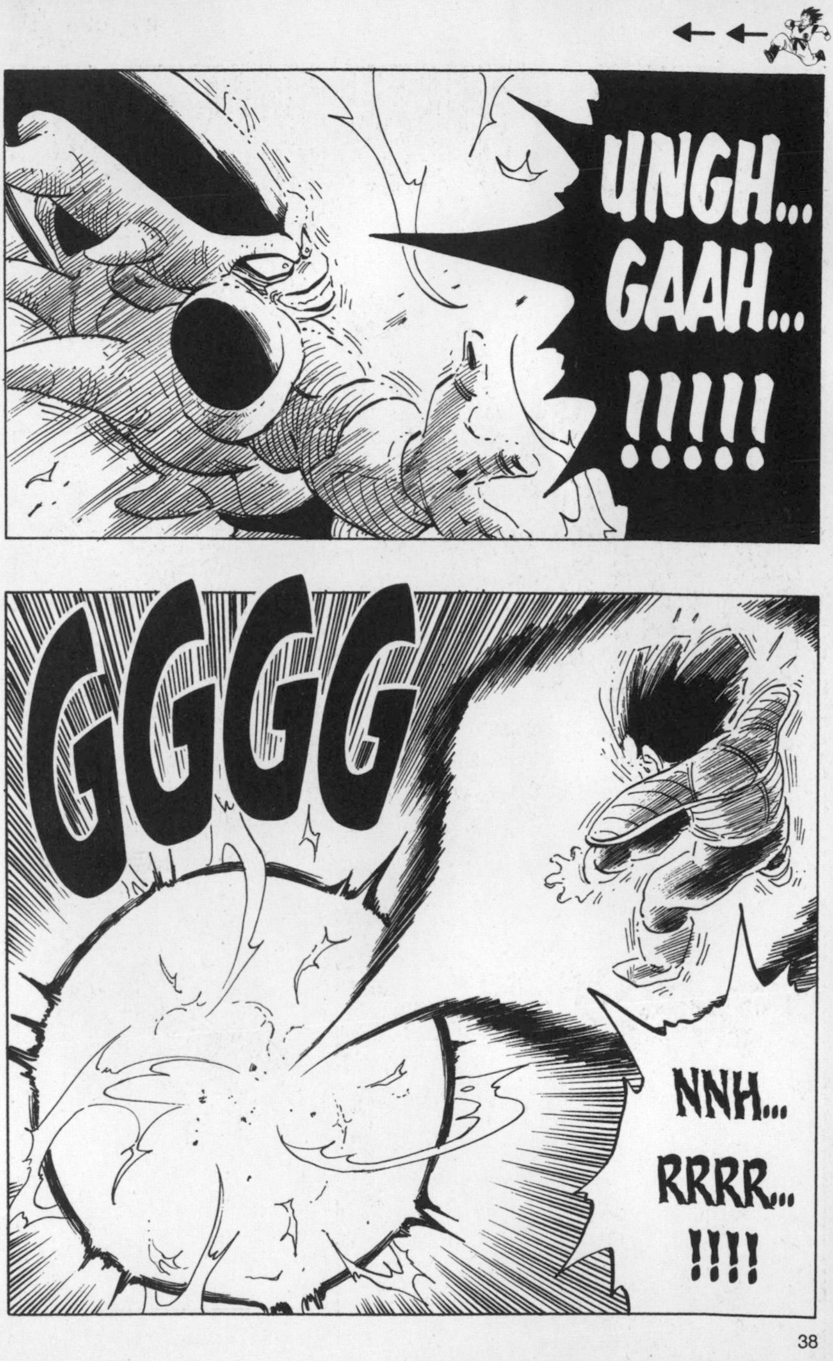
UNGH... GAAH... !!!!!
GGGG
NNH... RRRR... !!!!

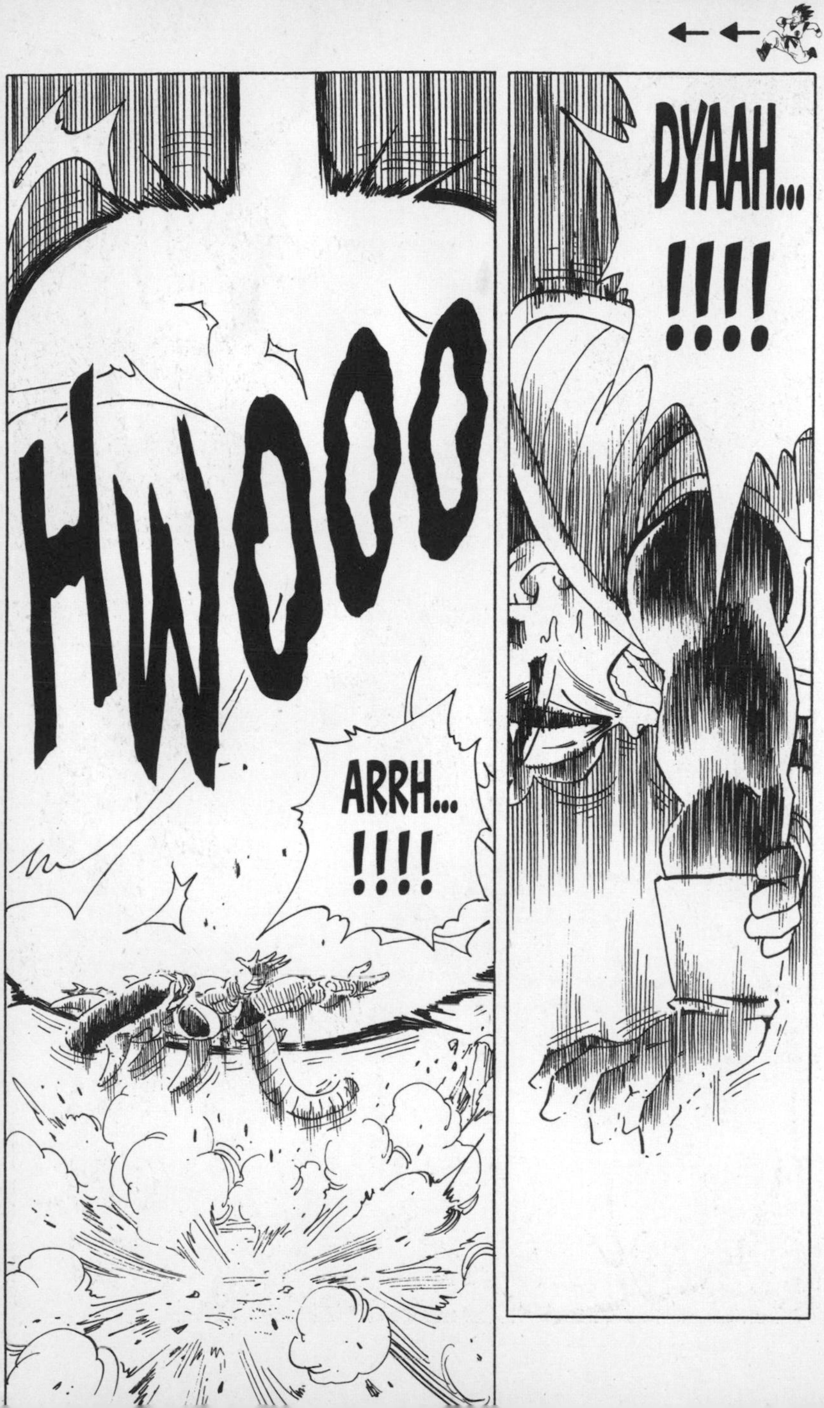
DYAAH...
!!!!
HWOOO
ARRH...
!!!!

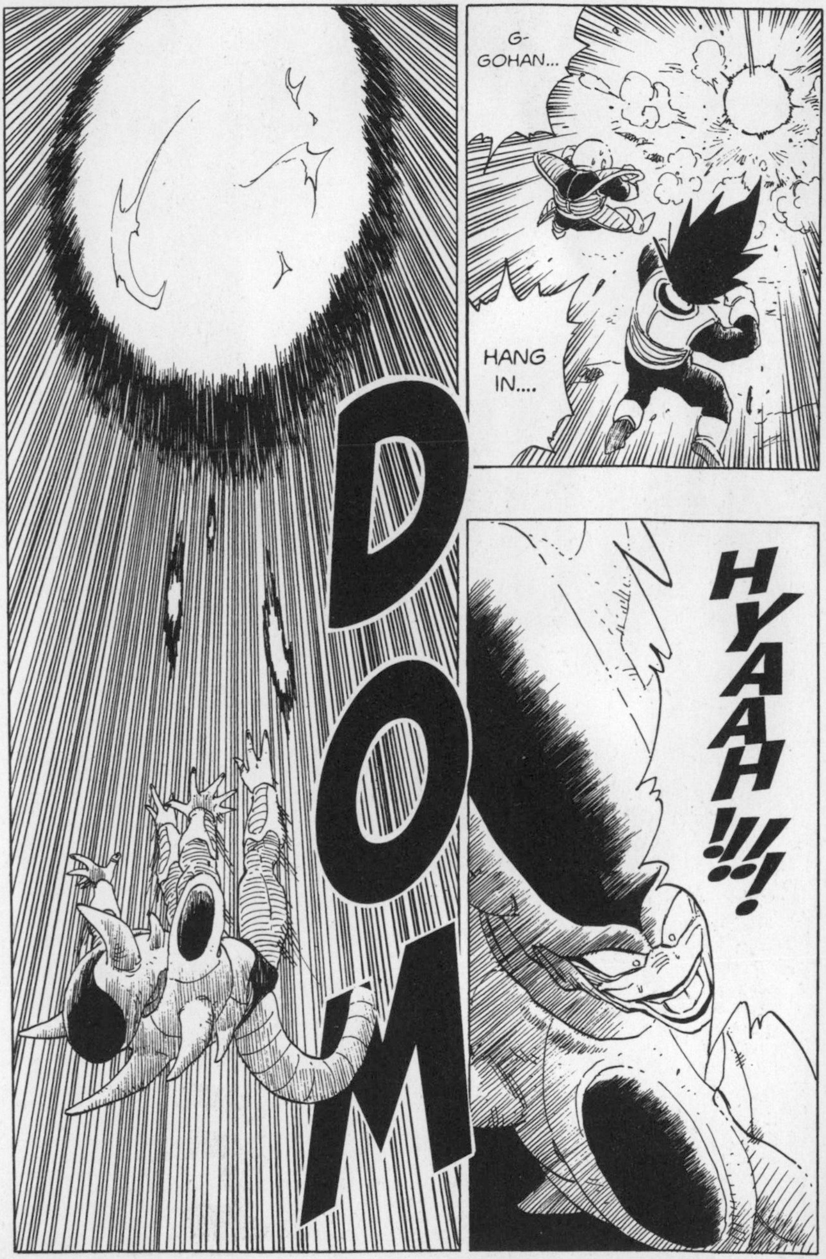
G-
GOHAN...
HANG
IN....
HYAAH!!!!
DOM

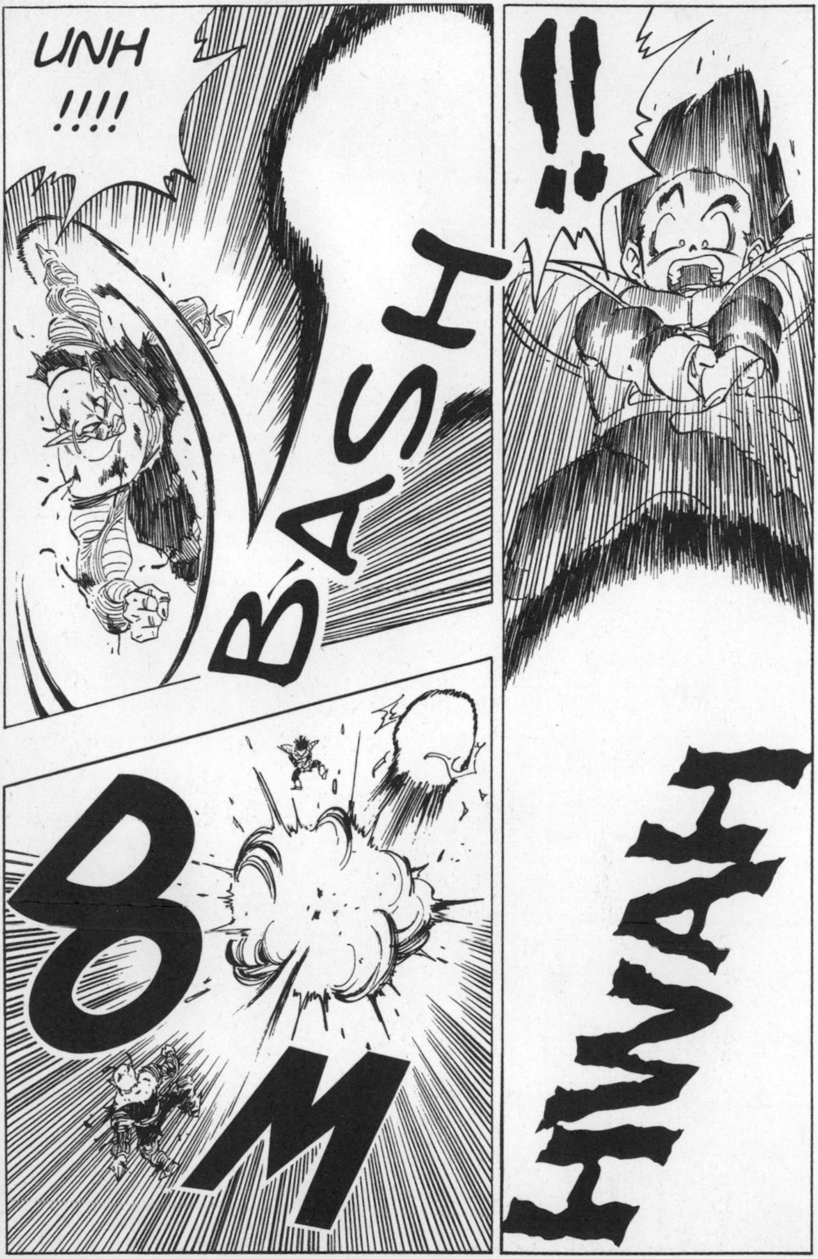
!!
HWAH
UNH !!!!
BASH
BOM

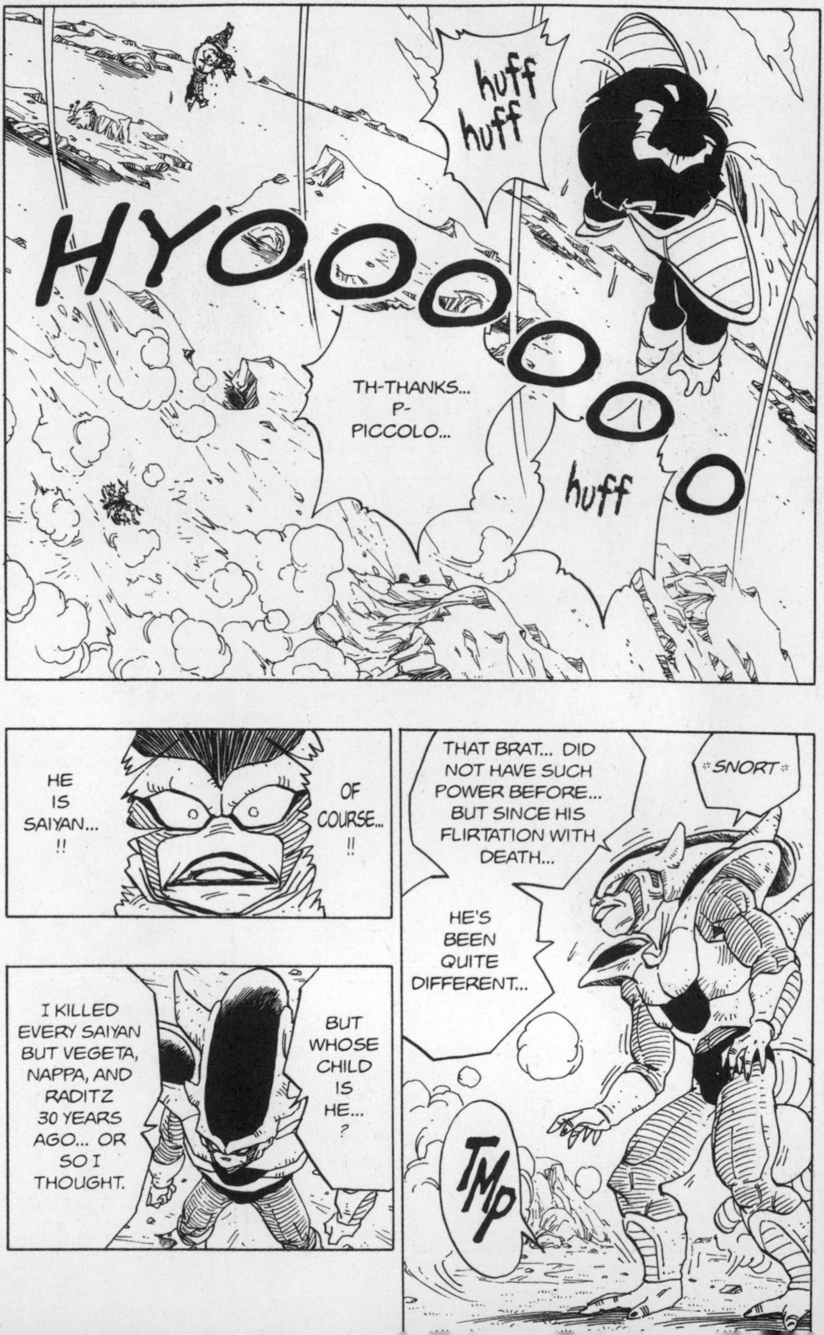
huff huff
HYOOOOOOOO
TH-THANKS... P-PICCOLO...
huff
SNORT
THAT BRAT... DID NOT HAVE SUCH POWER BEFORE... BUT SINCE HIS FLIRTATION WITH DEATH...
HE'S BEEN QUITE DIFFERENT...
TMP
OF COURSE... !!
HE IS SAIYAN... !!
BUT WHOSE CHILD IS HE... ?
I KILLED EVERY SAIYAN BUT VEGETA, NAPPA, AND RADITZ 30 YEARS AGO... OR SO I THOUGHT.

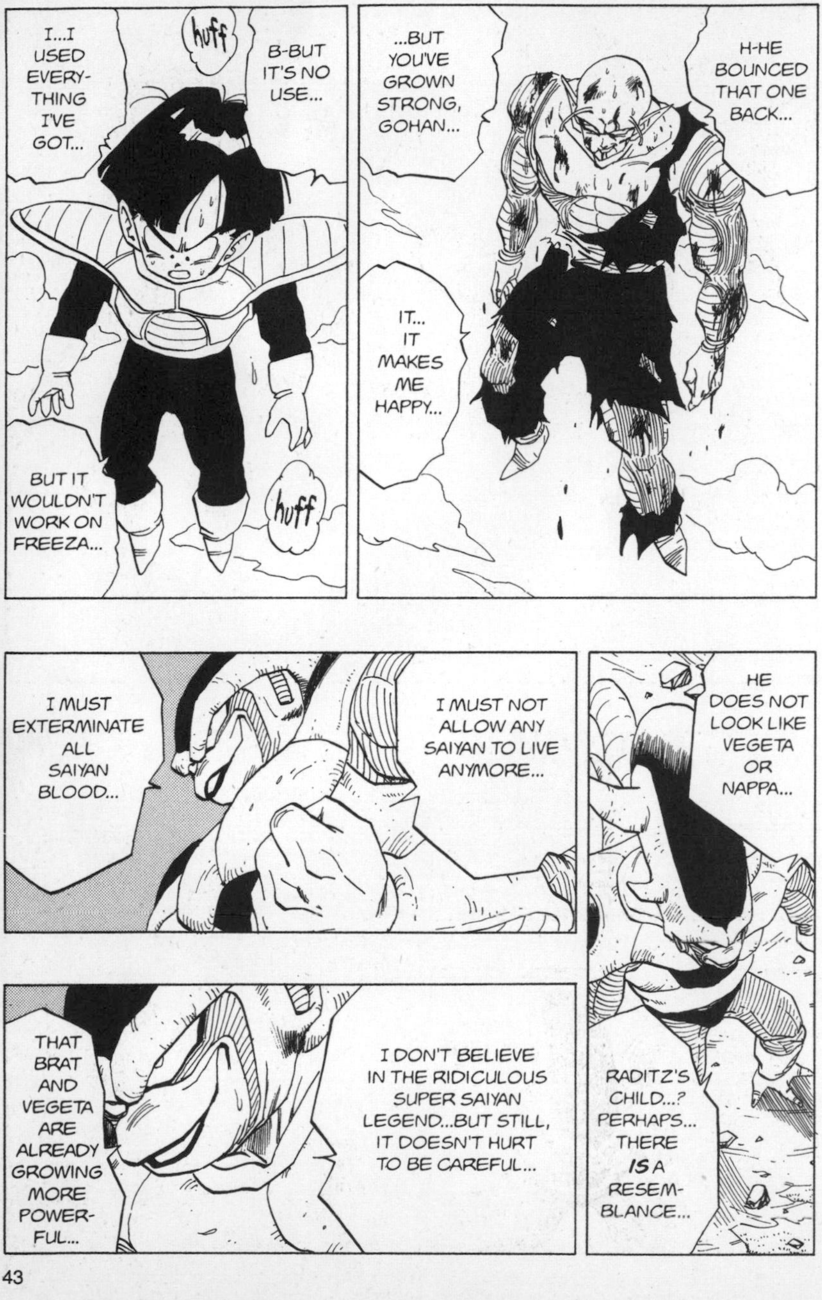
H-HE BOUNCED THAT ONE BACK...
...BUT YOU'VE GROWN STRONG, GOHAN...
IT... IT MAKES ME HAPPY...
B-BUT IT'S NO USE...
huff
I...I USED EVERY-THING I'VE GOT...
huff
BUT IT WOULDN'T WORK ON FREEZA...
HE DOES NOT LOOK LIKE VEGETA OR NAPPA...
RADITZ'S CHILD...? PERHAPS... THERE *IS* A RESEM-BLANCE...
I MUST NOT ALLOW ANY SAIYAN TO LIVE ANYMORE...
I MUST EXTERMINATE ALL SAIYAN BLOOD...
I DON'T BELIEVE IN THE RIDICULOUS SUPER SAIYAN LEGEND...BUT STILL, IT DOESN'T HURT TO BE CAREFUL...
THAT BRAT AND VEGETA ARE ALREADY GROWING MORE POWER-FUL...

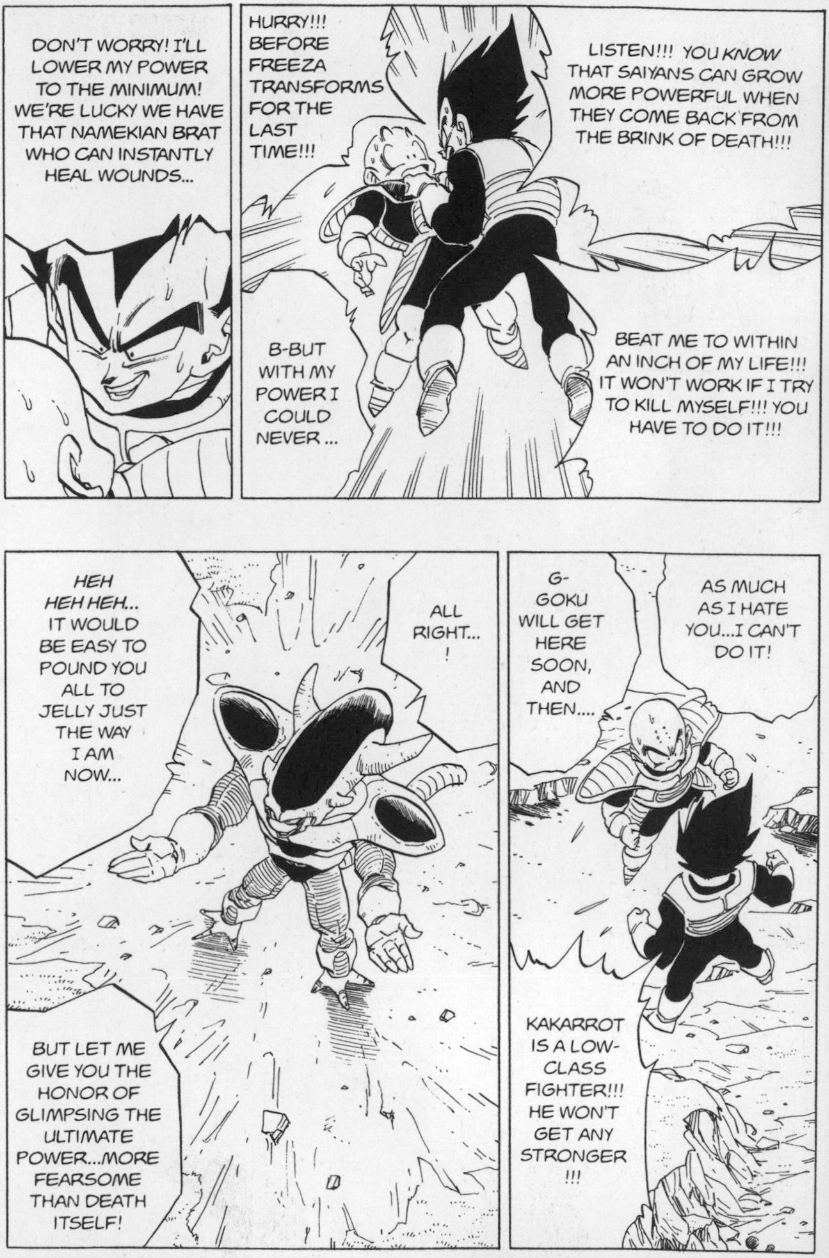
LISTEN!!! YOU KNOW THAT SAIYANS CAN GROW MORE POWERFUL WHEN THEY COME BACK FROM THE BRINK OF DEATH!!!
HURRY!!! BEFORE FREEZA TRANSFORMS FOR THE LAST TIME!!!
BEAT ME TO WITHIN AN INCH OF MY LIFE!!! IT WON'T WORK IF I TRY TO KILL MYSELF!!! YOU HAVE TO DO IT!!!
B-BUT WITH MY POWER I COULD NEVER ...
DON'T WORRY! I'LL LOWER MY POWER TO THE MINIMUM! WE'RE LUCKY WE HAVE THAT NAMEKIAN BRAT WHO CAN INSTANTLY HEAL WOUNDS...
AS MUCH AS I HATE YOU...I CAN'T DO IT!
G-GOKU WILL GET HERE SOON, AND THEN....
KAKARROT IS A LOW-CLASS FIGHTER!!! HE WON'T GET ANY STRONGER !!!
ALL RIGHT... !
HEH HEH HEH... IT WOULD BE EASY TO POUND YOU ALL TO JELLY JUST THE WAY I AM NOW...
BUT LET ME GIVE YOU THE HONOR OF GLIMPSING THE ULTIMATE POWER...MORE FEARSOME THAN DEATH ITSELF!

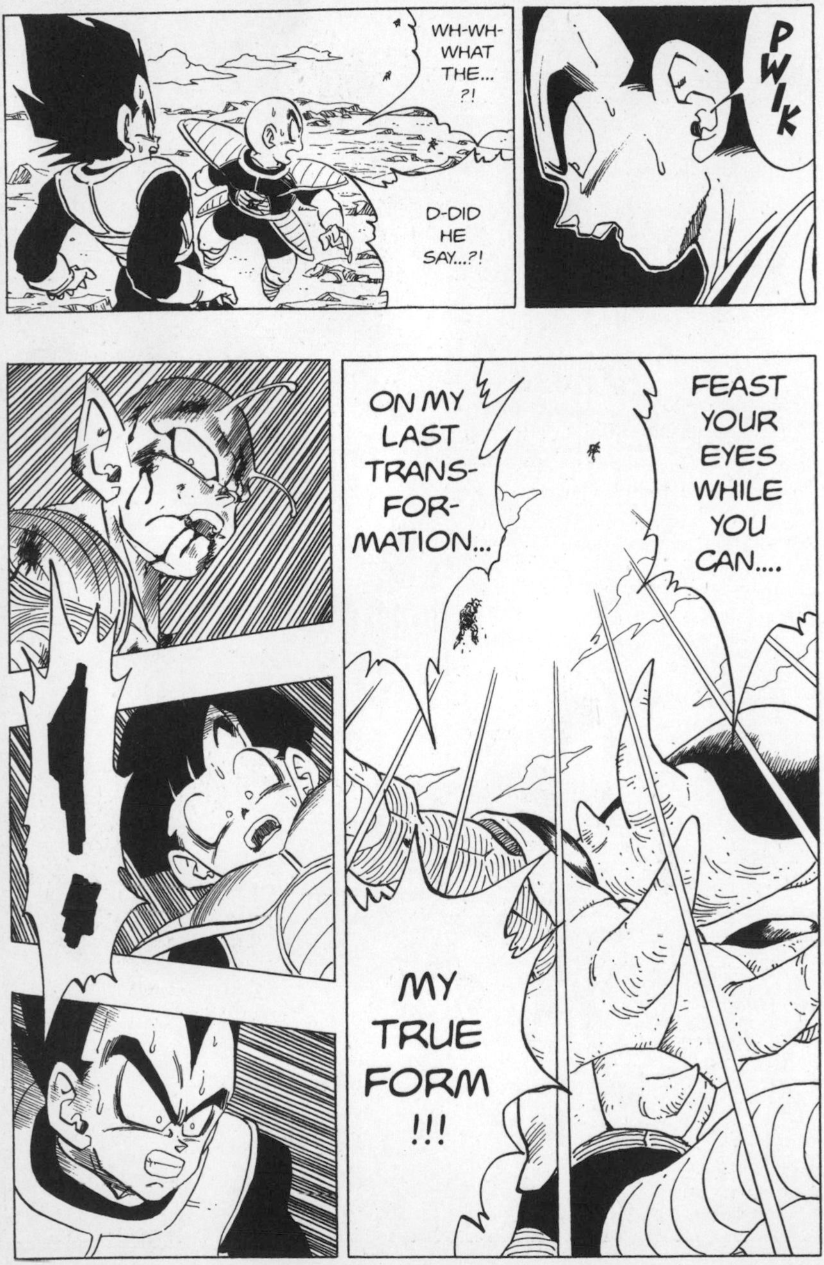
PWIK
WH-WH-WHAT THE... ?!
D-DID HE SAY...?!
FEAST YOUR EYES WHILE YOU CAN....
ON MY LAST TRANS-FOR-MATION...
MY TRUE FORM !!!
!

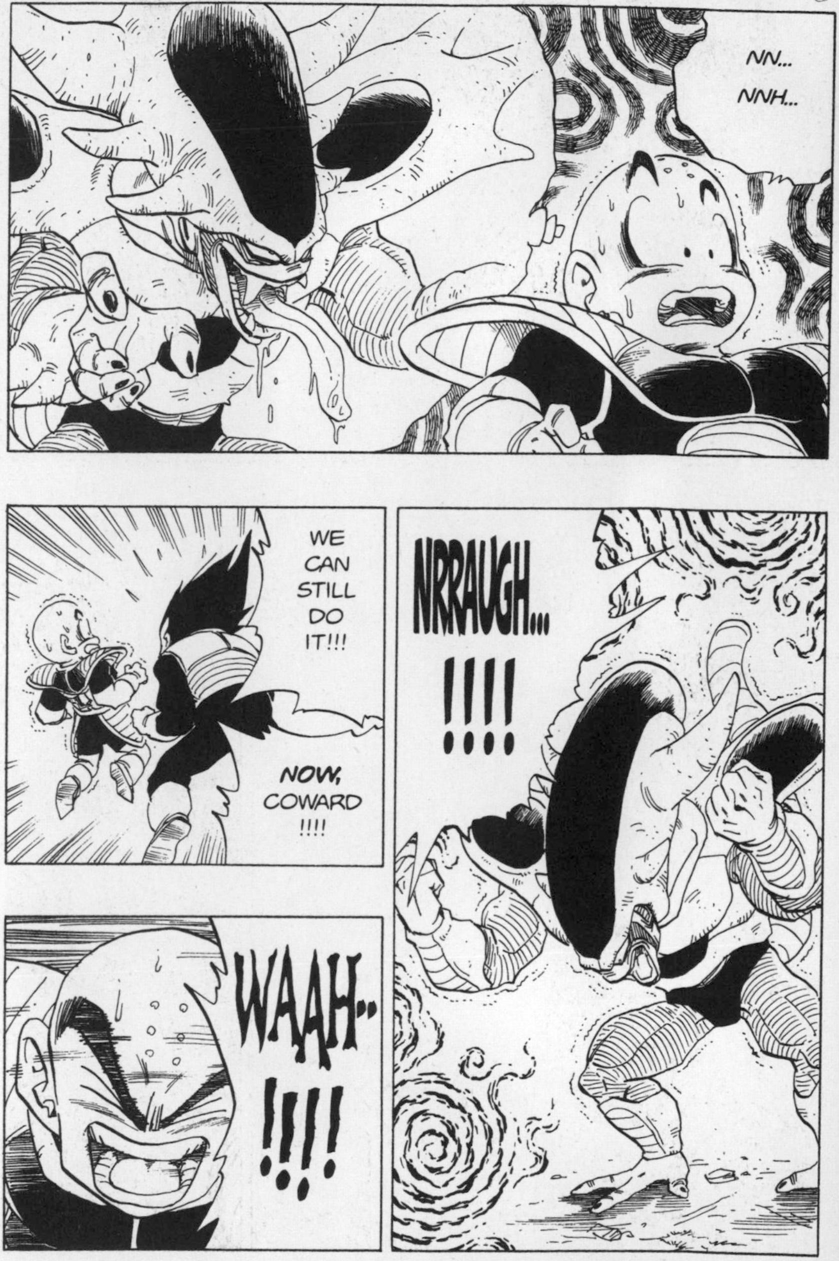
NN...
NNH...
NRRAUGH...
!!!!
WE CAN STILL DO IT!!!
NOW, COWARD!!!!
WAAH..
!!!!

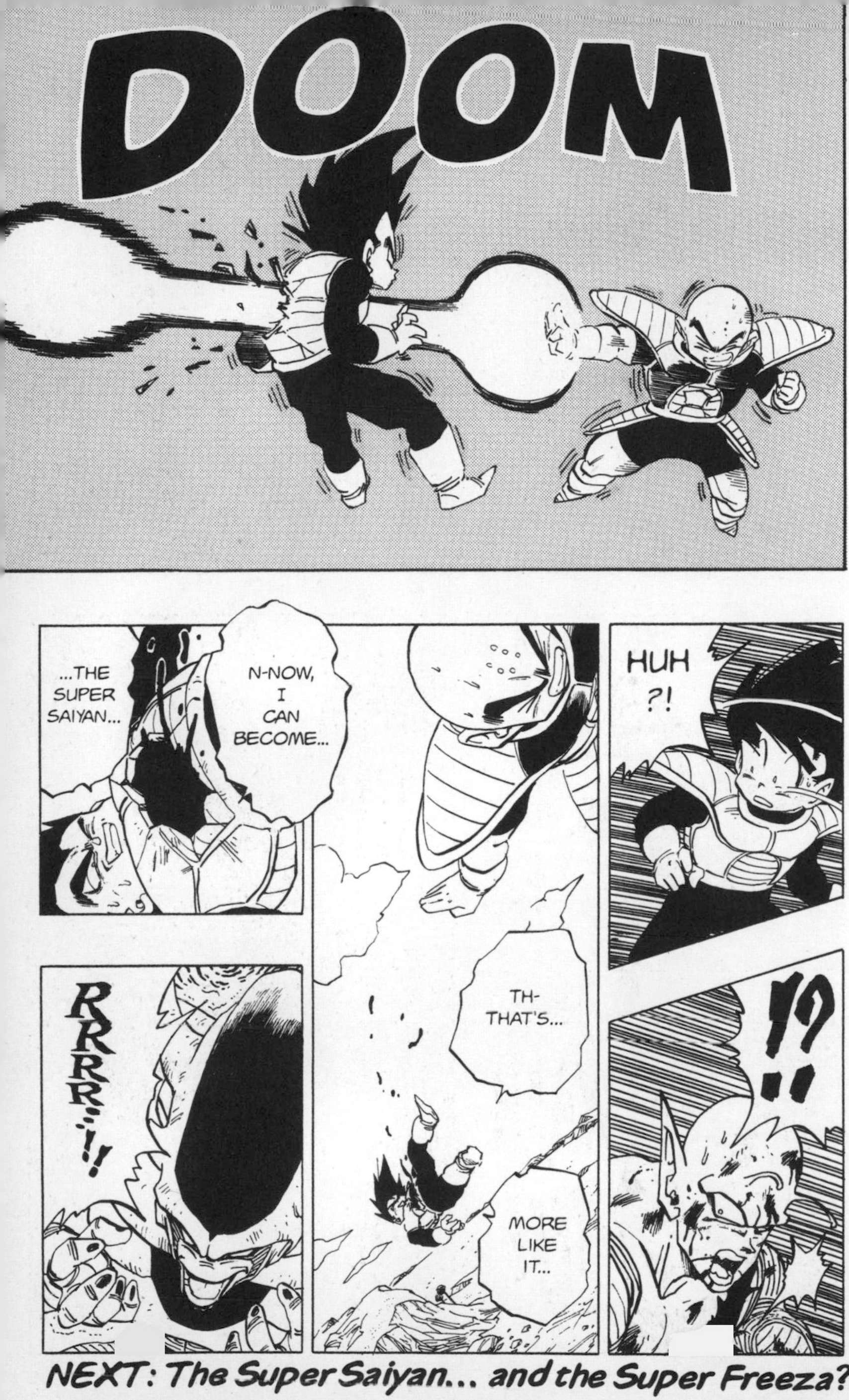
DOOM
HUH ?!
N-NOW, I CAN BECOME...
...THE SUPER SAIYAN...
!?!!
TH- THAT'S...
MORE LIKE IT...
RRRR...!!

NEXT: The Super Saiyan... and the Super Freeza?!

DBZ:110 • The Final Transformation

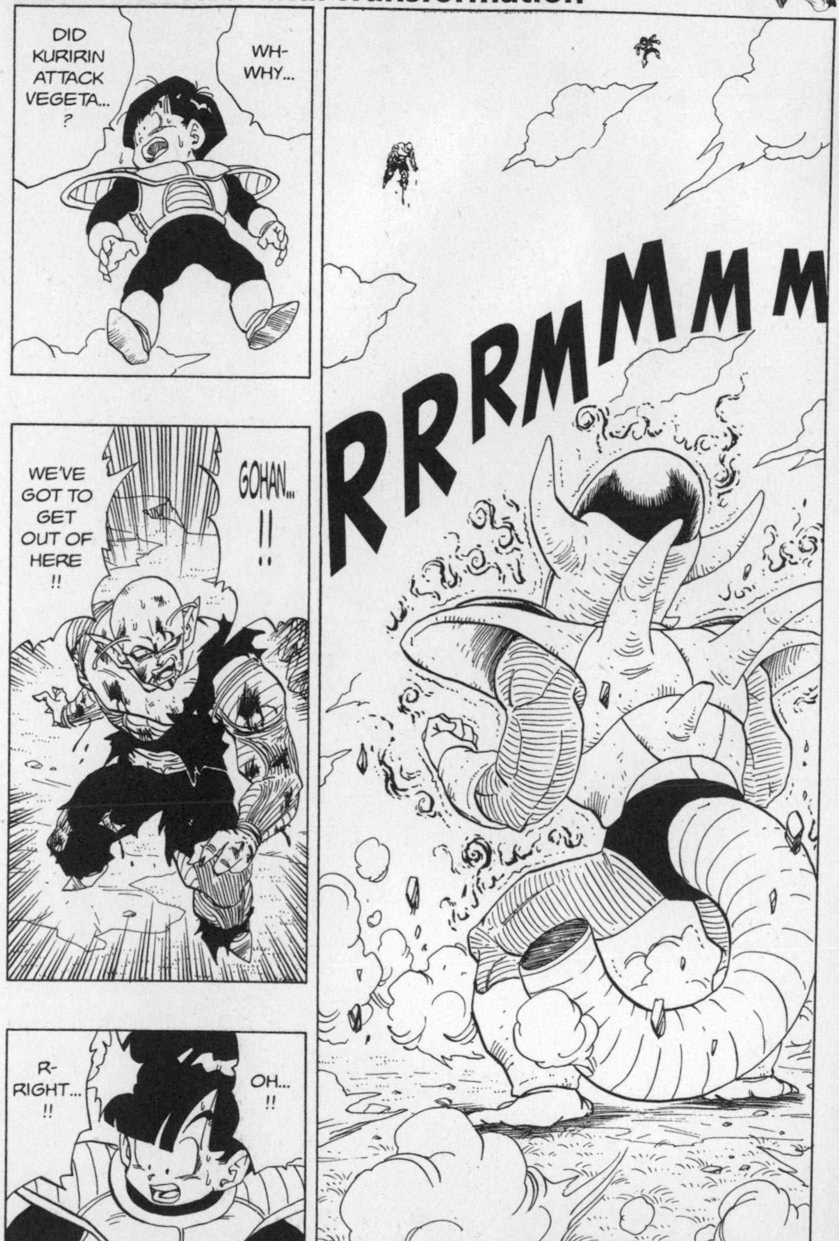
RRRMMMMM
WH-WHY...
DID KURIRIN ATTACK VEGETA...?
GOHAN...!!
WE'VE GOT TO GET OUT OF HERE!!
OH...!!
R-RIGHT...!!

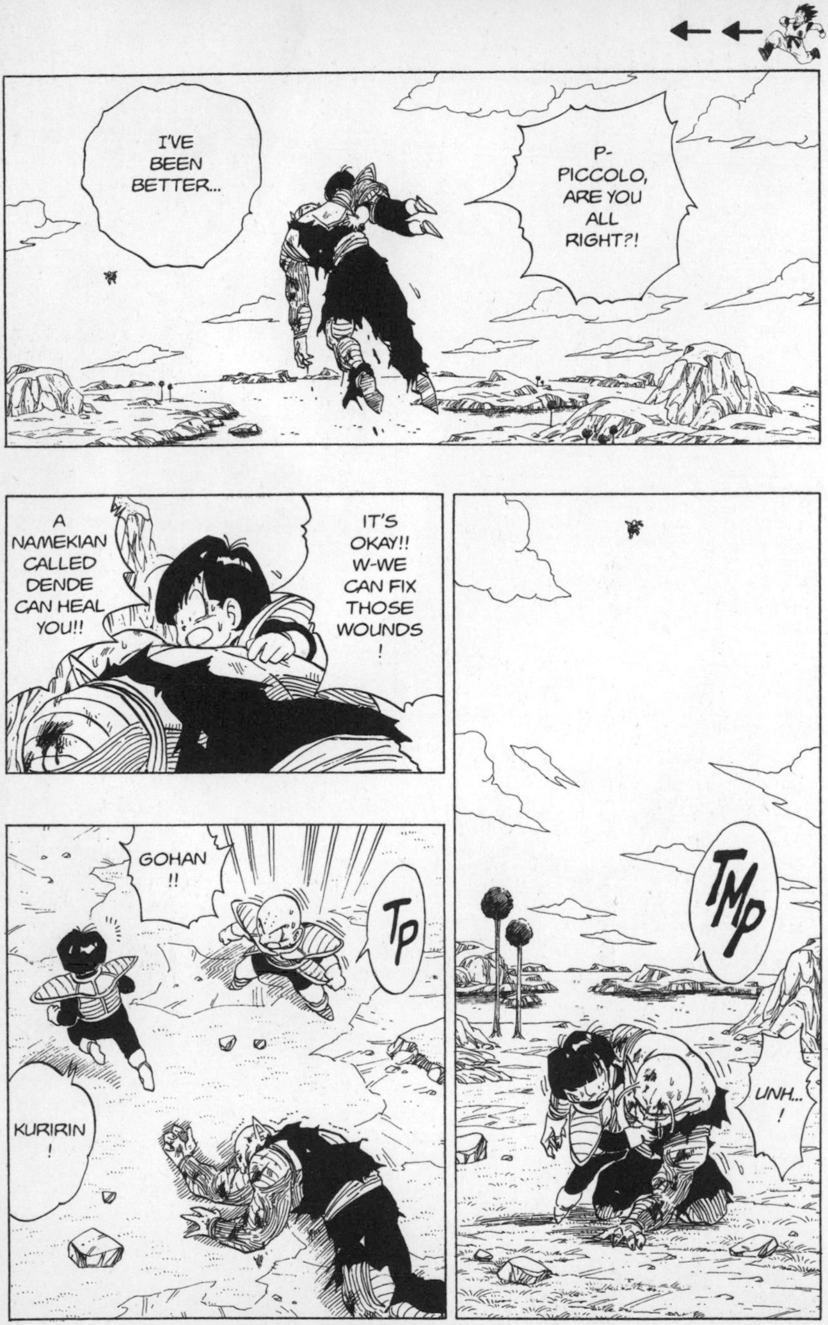
P-PICCOLO, ARE YOU ALL RIGHT?!
I'VE BEEN BETTER...
TMP
UNH...!
IT'S OKAY!! W-WE CAN FIX THOSE WOUNDS!
A NAMEKIAN CALLED DENDE CAN HEAL YOU!!
GOHAN!!
TP
KURIRIN!

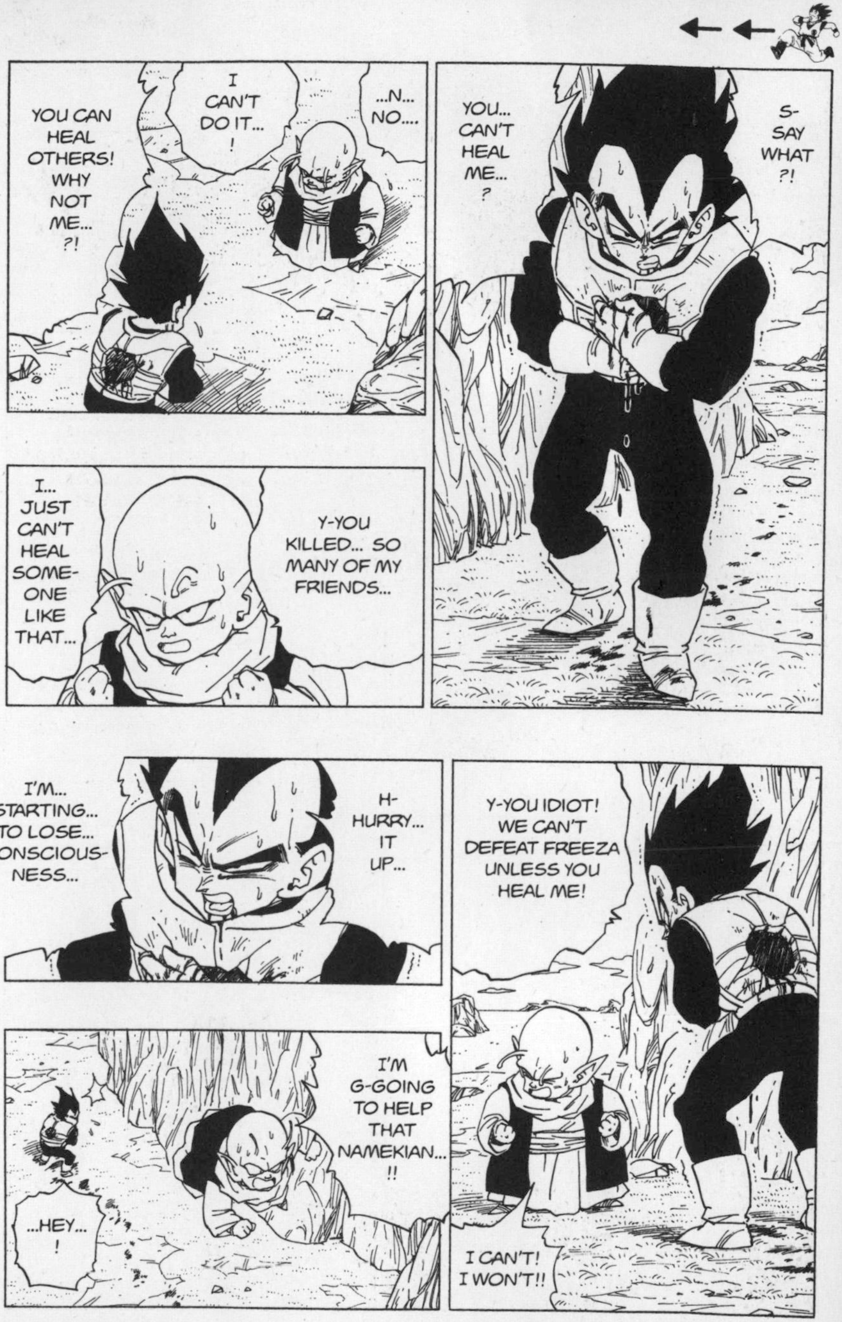
S-SAY WHAT?!
YOU... CAN'T HEAL ME...?
...N... NO....
I CAN'T DO IT...!
YOU CAN HEAL OTHERS! WHY NOT ME...?!
Y-YOU KILLED... SO MANY OF MY FRIENDS...
I... JUST CAN'T HEAL SOMEONE LIKE THAT...
Y-YOU IDIOT! WE CAN'T DEFEAT FREEZA UNLESS YOU HEAL ME!
I CAN'T! I WON'T!!
H-HURRY... IT UP...
I'M... STARTING... TO LOSE... CONSCIOUSNESS...
I'M G-GOING TO HELP THAT NAMEKIAN...!!
...HEY...!

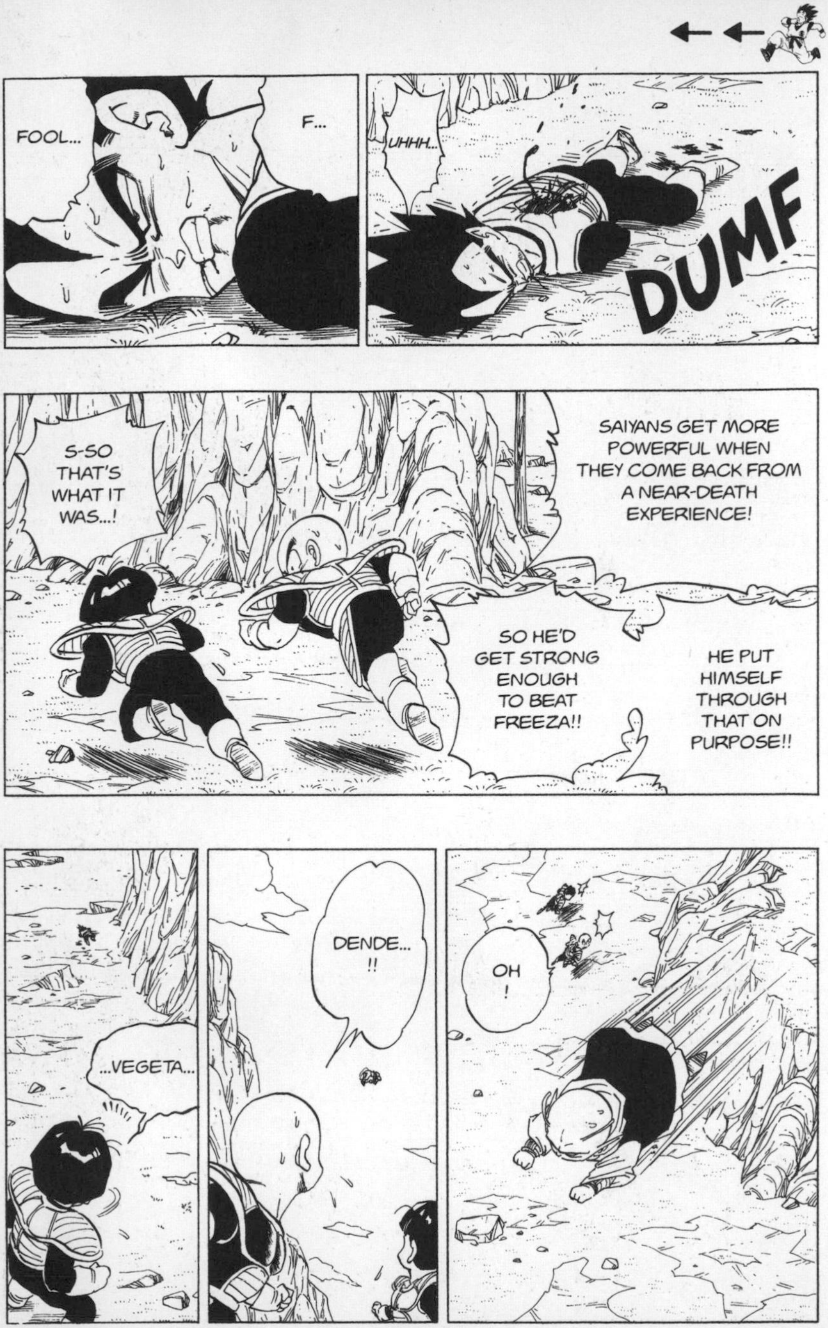
UHHH...
DUMF
F...
FOOL...
SAIYANS GET MORE POWERFUL WHEN THEY COME BACK FROM A NEAR-DEATH EXPERIENCE!
HE PUT HIMSELF THROUGH THAT ON PURPOSE!!
SO HE'D GET STRONG ENOUGH TO BEAT FREEZA!!
S-SO THAT'S WHAT IT WAS...!
OH !
DENDE... !!
...VEGETA...

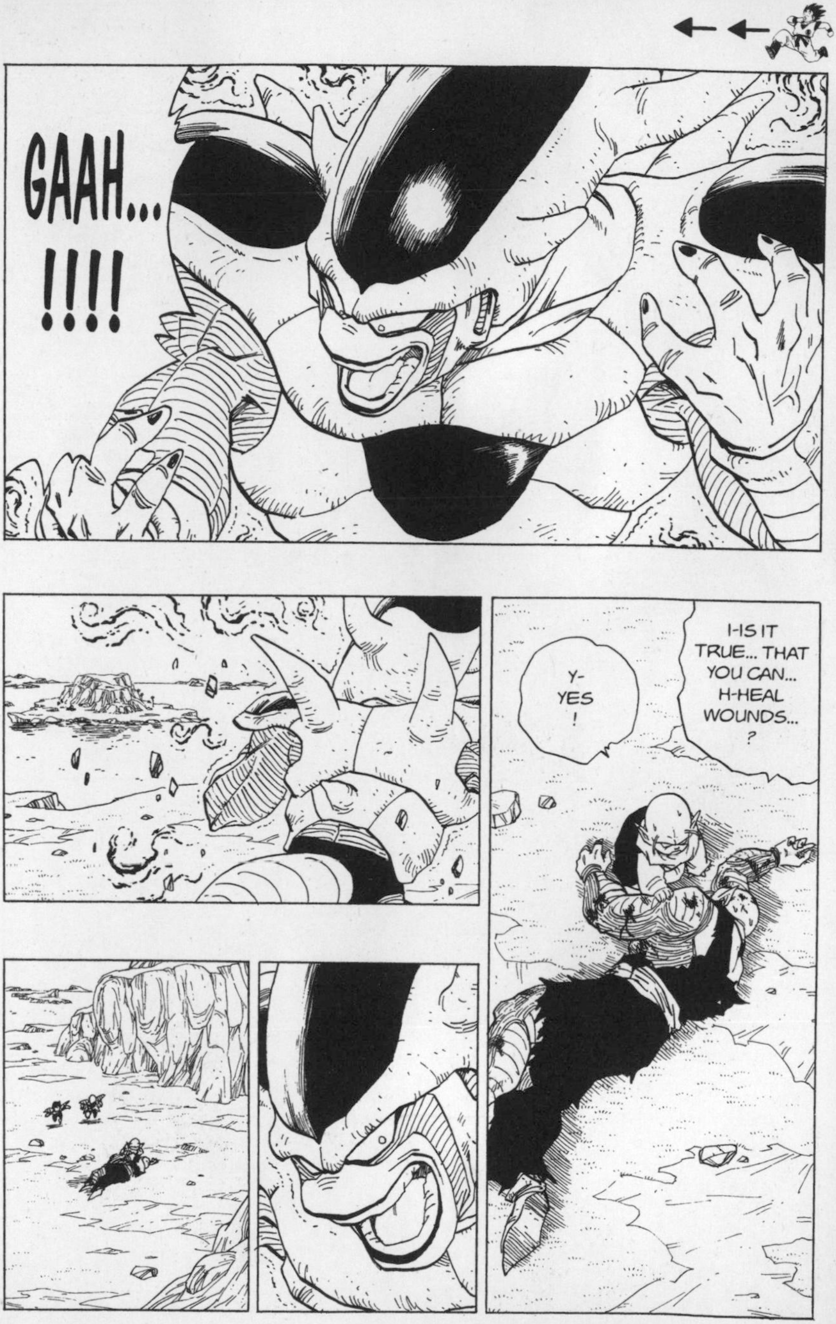
GAAH... !!!!
I-IS IT TRUE... THAT YOU CAN... H-HEAL WOUNDS...?
Y-YES!

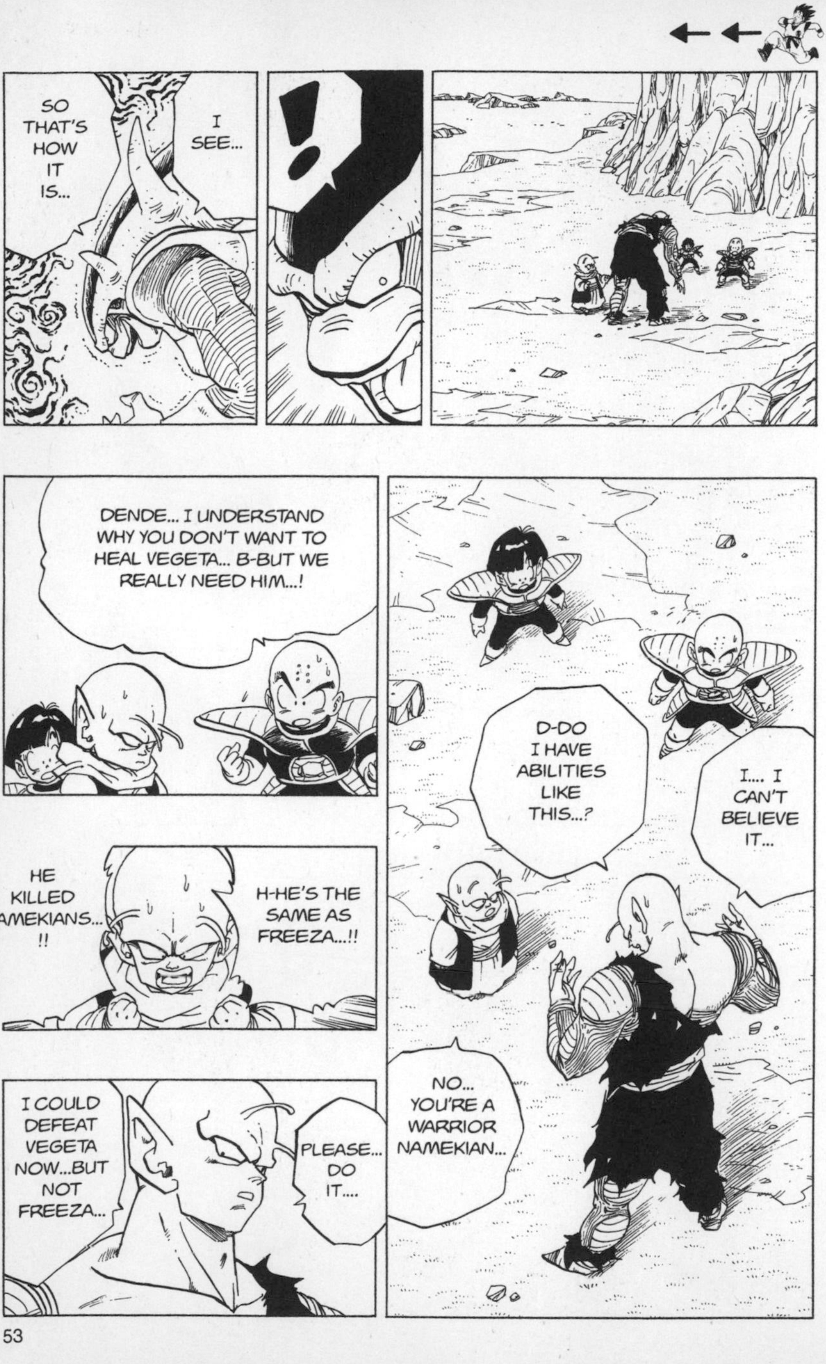
!
I SEE...
SO THAT'S HOW IT IS...
I.... I CAN'T BELIEVE IT...
D-DO I HAVE ABILITIES LIKE THIS...?
NO... YOU'RE A WARRIOR NAMEKIAN...
DENDE... I UNDERSTAND WHY YOU DON'T WANT TO HEAL VEGETA... B-BUT WE REALLY NEED HIM...!
H-HE'S THE SAME AS FREEZA...!!
HE KILLED NAMEKIANS... !!
PLEASE... DO IT....
I COULD DEFEAT VEGETA NOW...BUT NOT FREEZA...

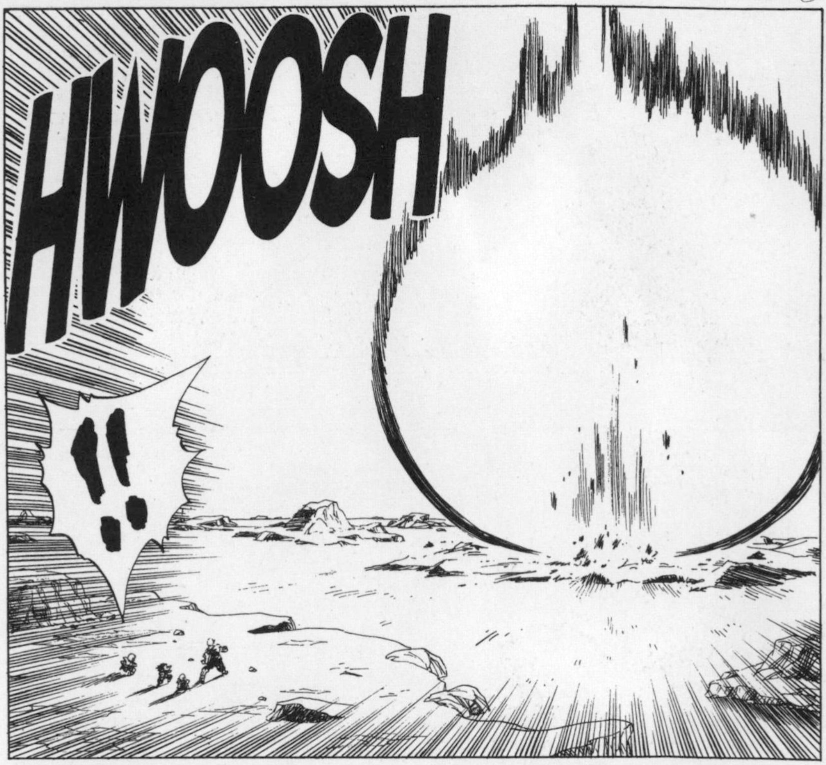
HWOOSH
!!

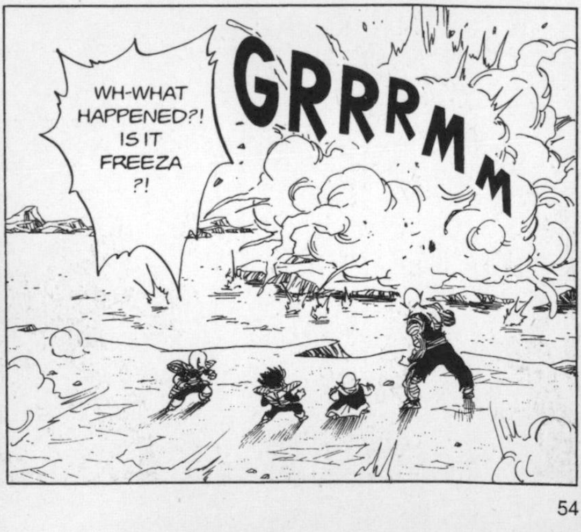
GRRRMM
WH-WHAT HAPPENED?! IS IT FREEZA ?!

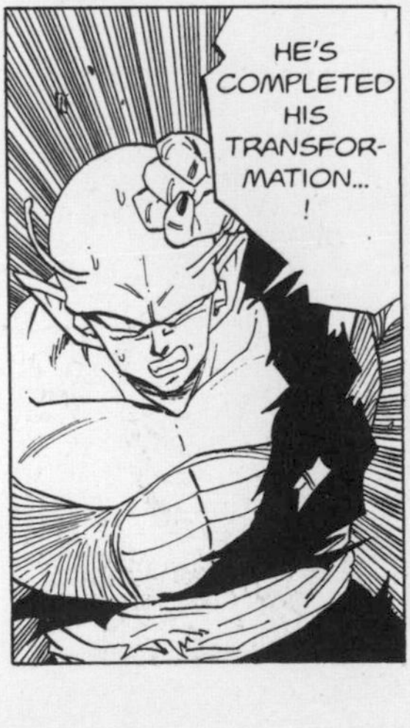
HE'S COMPLETED HIS TRANSFOR-MATION... !

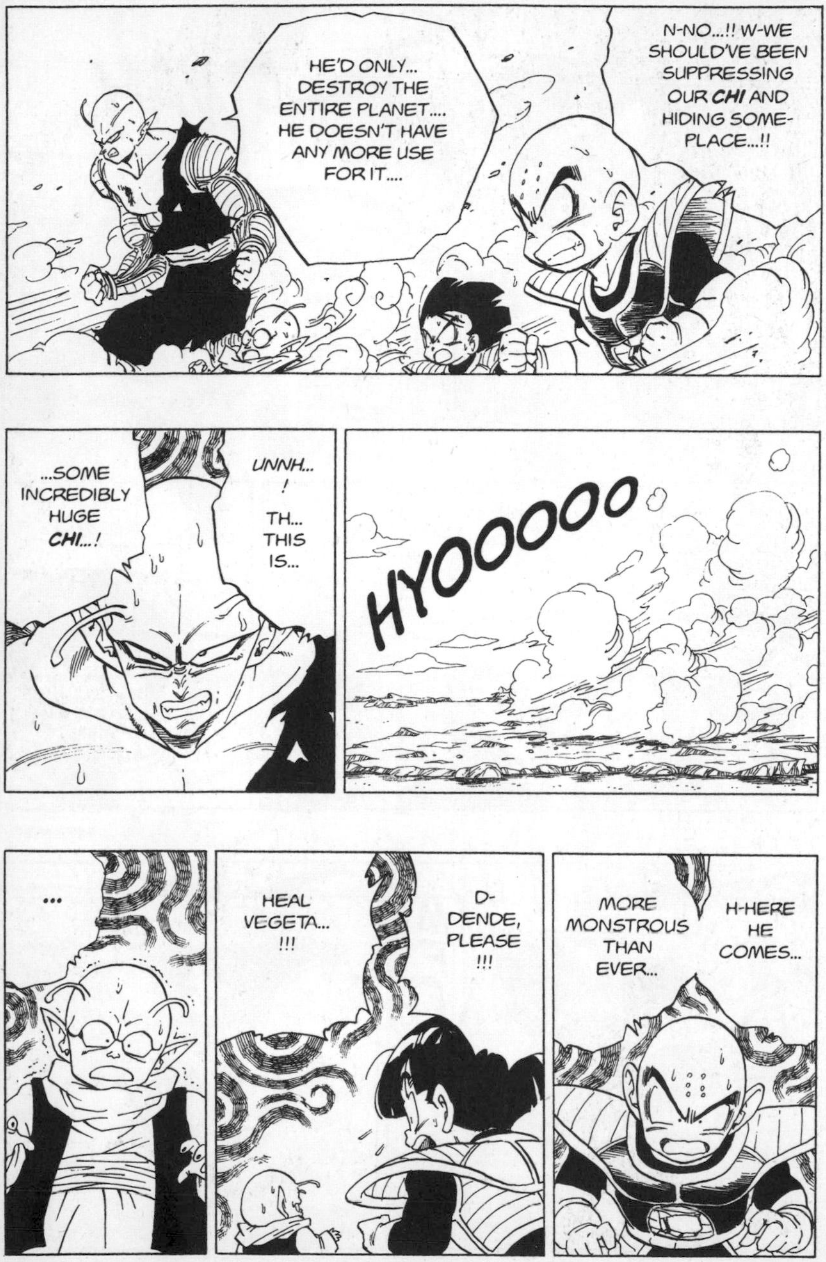
N-NO...!! W-WE SHOULD'VE BEEN SUPPRESSING OUR **CHI** AND HIDING SOME-PLACE...!!
HE'D ONLY... DESTROY THE ENTIRE PLANET.... HE DOESN'T HAVE ANY MORE USE FOR IT....
HYOOOOO
UNNH... !
TH... THIS IS...
...SOME INCREDIBLY HUGE **CHI**...!
H-HERE HE COMES...
MORE MONSTROUS THAN EVER...
D-DENDE, PLEASE !!!
HEAL VEGETA... !!!
...

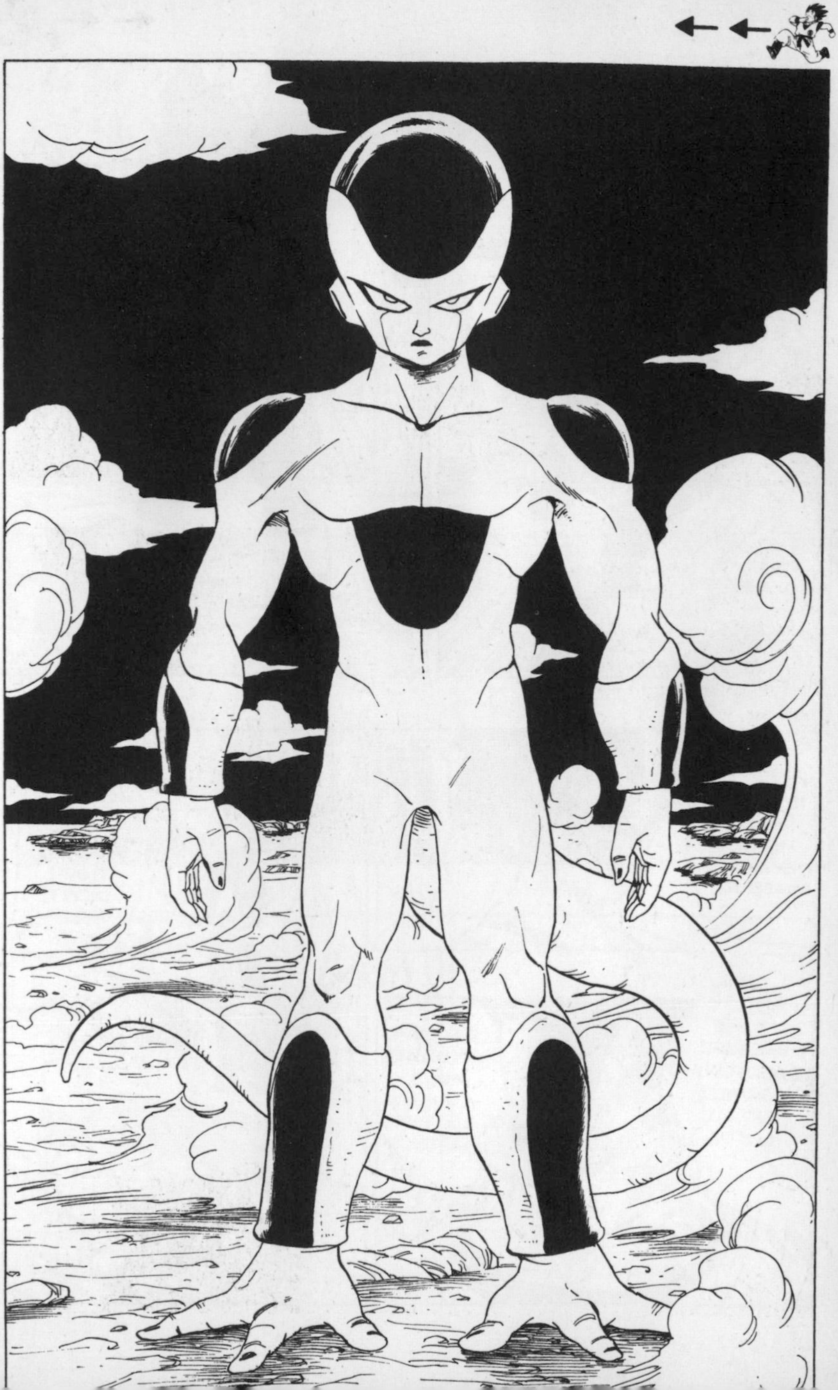

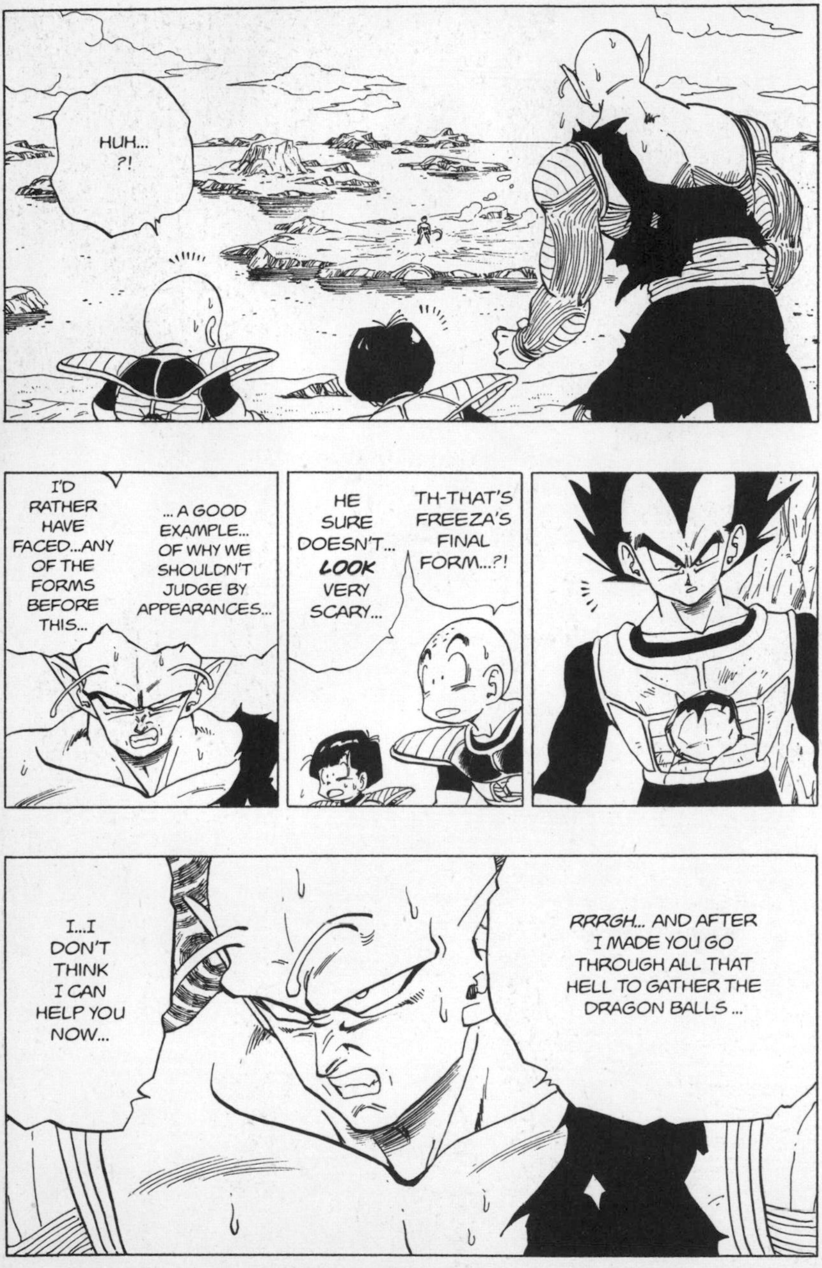
HUH... ?!
TH-THAT'S FREEZA'S FINAL FORM...?!
HE SURE DOESN'T... **LOOK** VERY SCARY...
... A GOOD EXAMPLE... OF WHY WE SHOULDN'T JUDGE BY APPEARANCES...
I'D RATHER HAVE FACED...ANY OF THE FORMS BEFORE THIS...
RRRGH... AND AFTER I MADE YOU GO THROUGH ALL THAT HELL TO GATHER THE DRAGON BALLS ...
I...I DON'T THINK I CAN HELP YOU NOW...

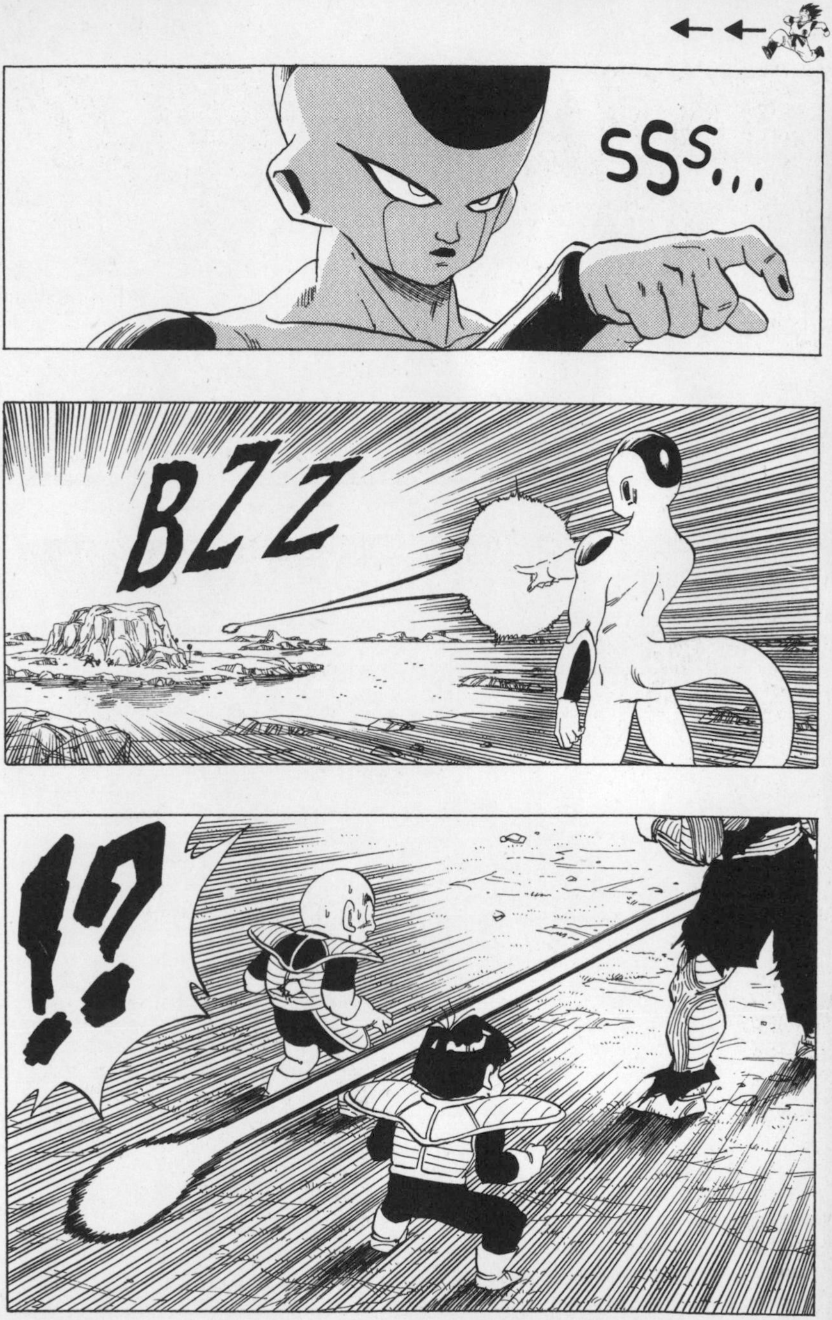
SSS...
BZZ
!?

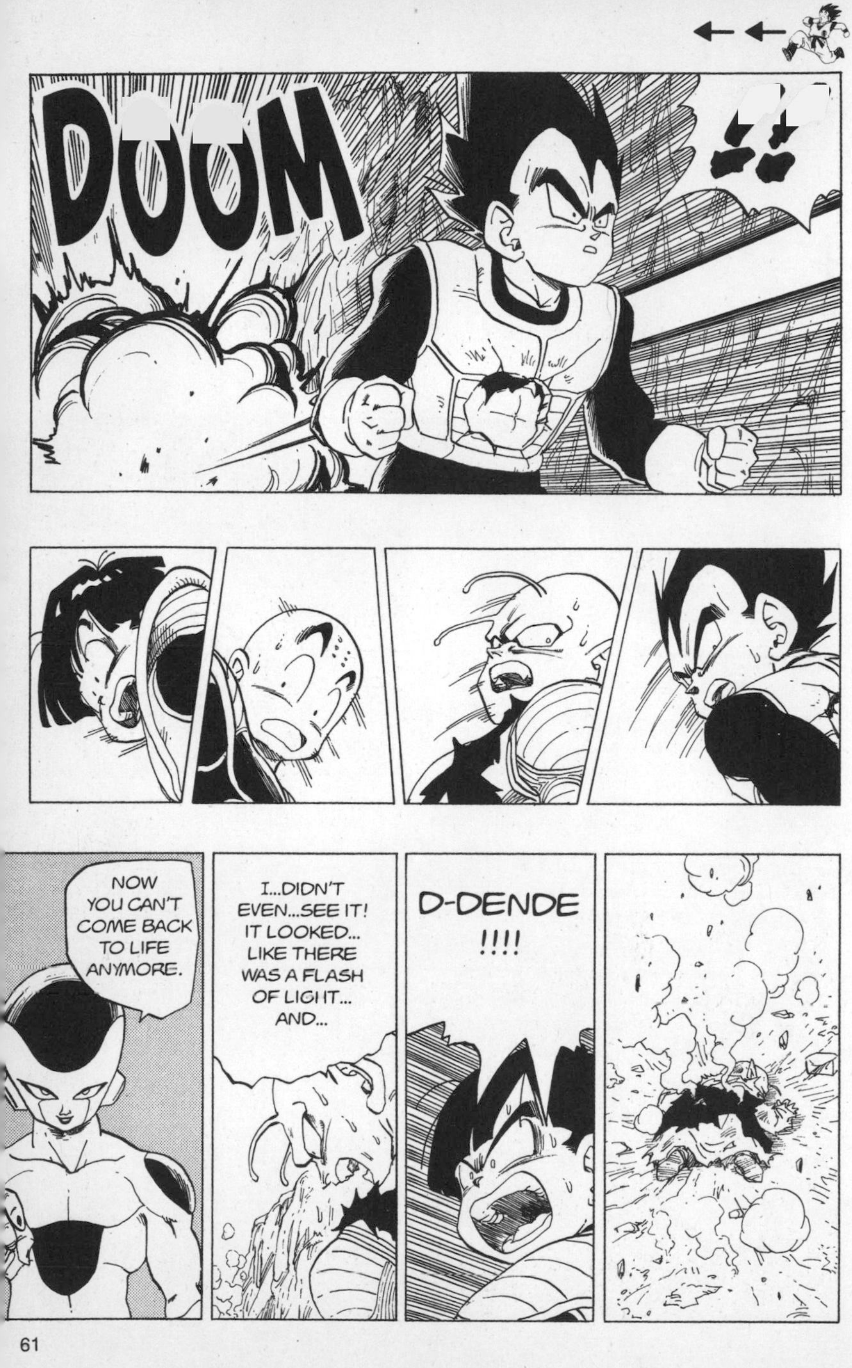
DOOM
!!
D-DENDE !!!!
I...DIDN'T EVEN...SEE IT! IT LOOKED... LIKE THERE WAS A FLASH OF LIGHT... AND...
NOW YOU CAN'T COME BACK TO LIFE ANYMORE.

DBZ:111 • Will It Be Freeza? Or Vegeta?

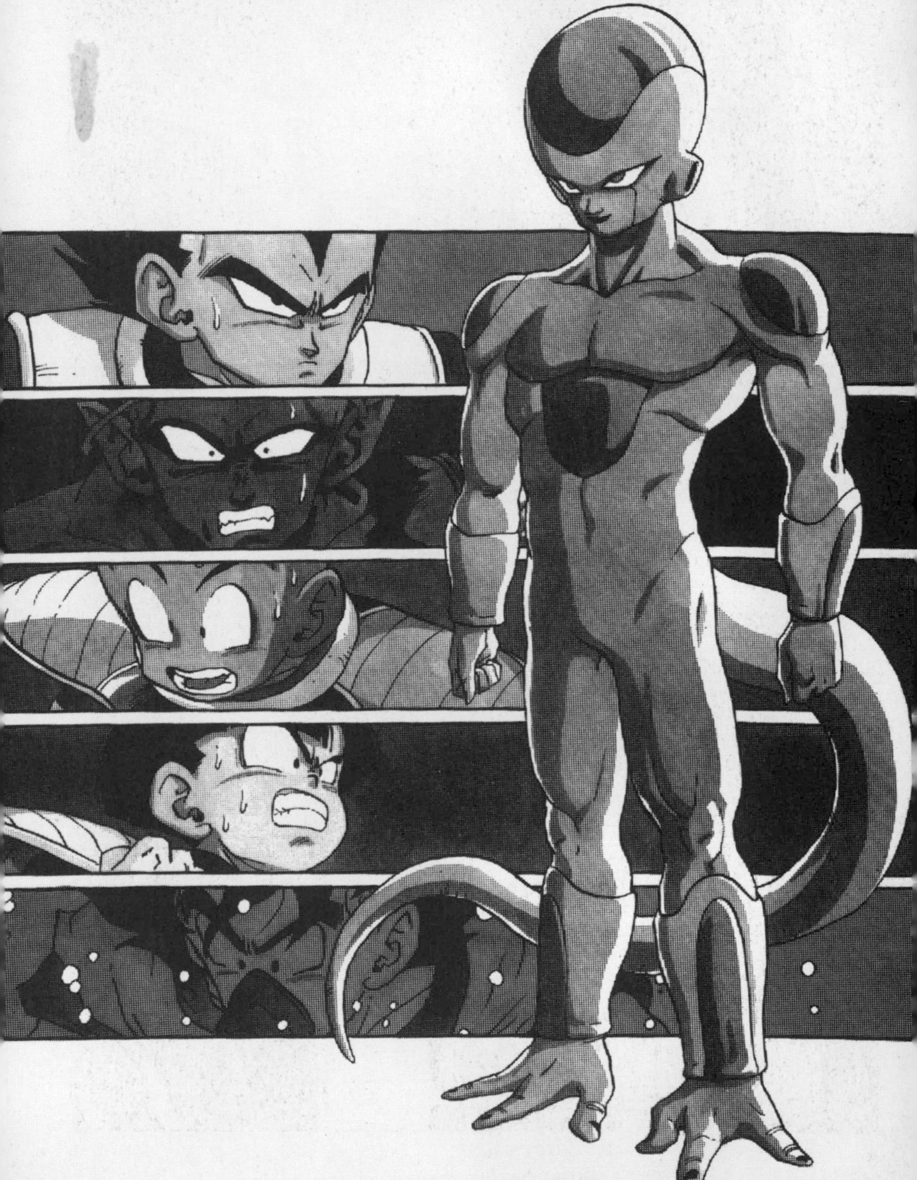

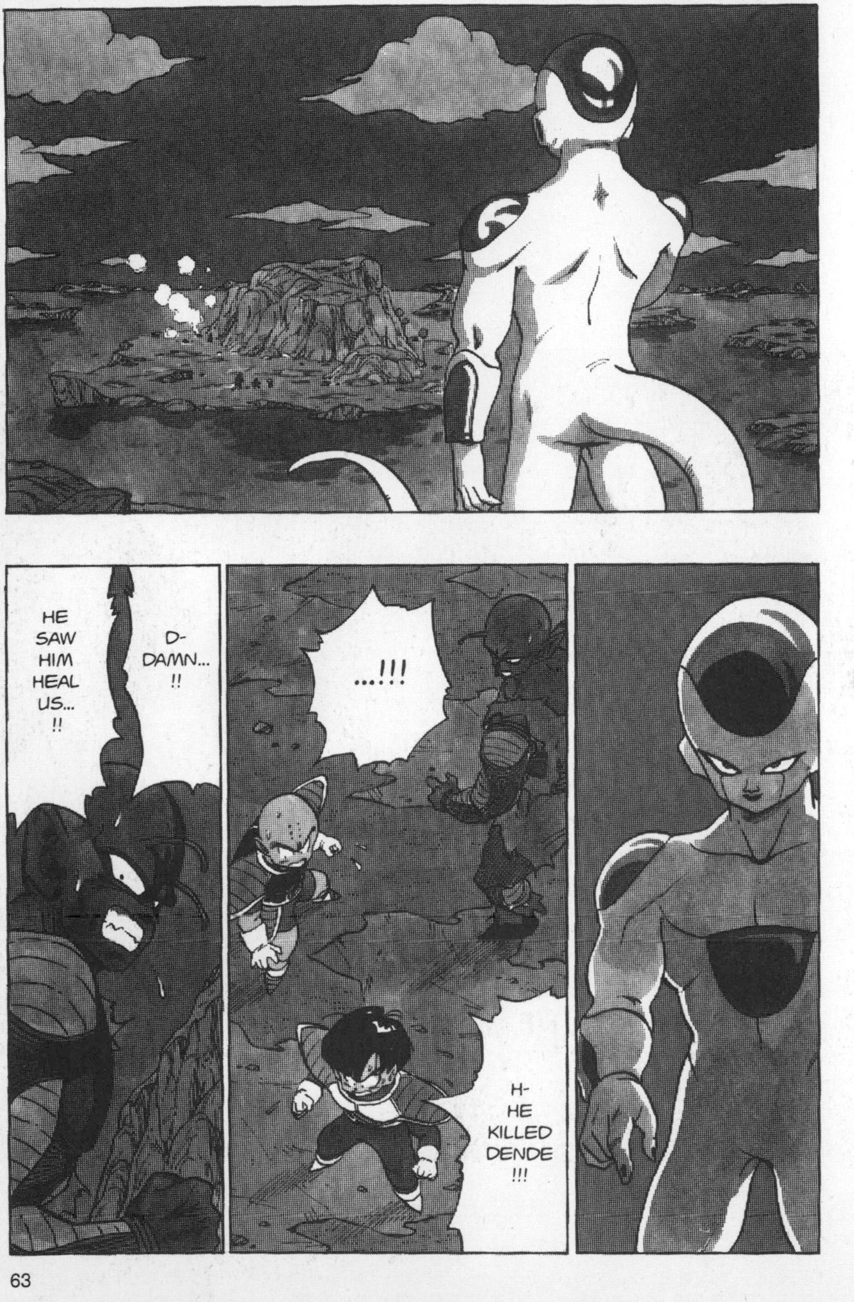
...!!!
H-HE KILLED DENDE!!!
D-DAMN...!!
HE SAW HIM HEAL US...!!

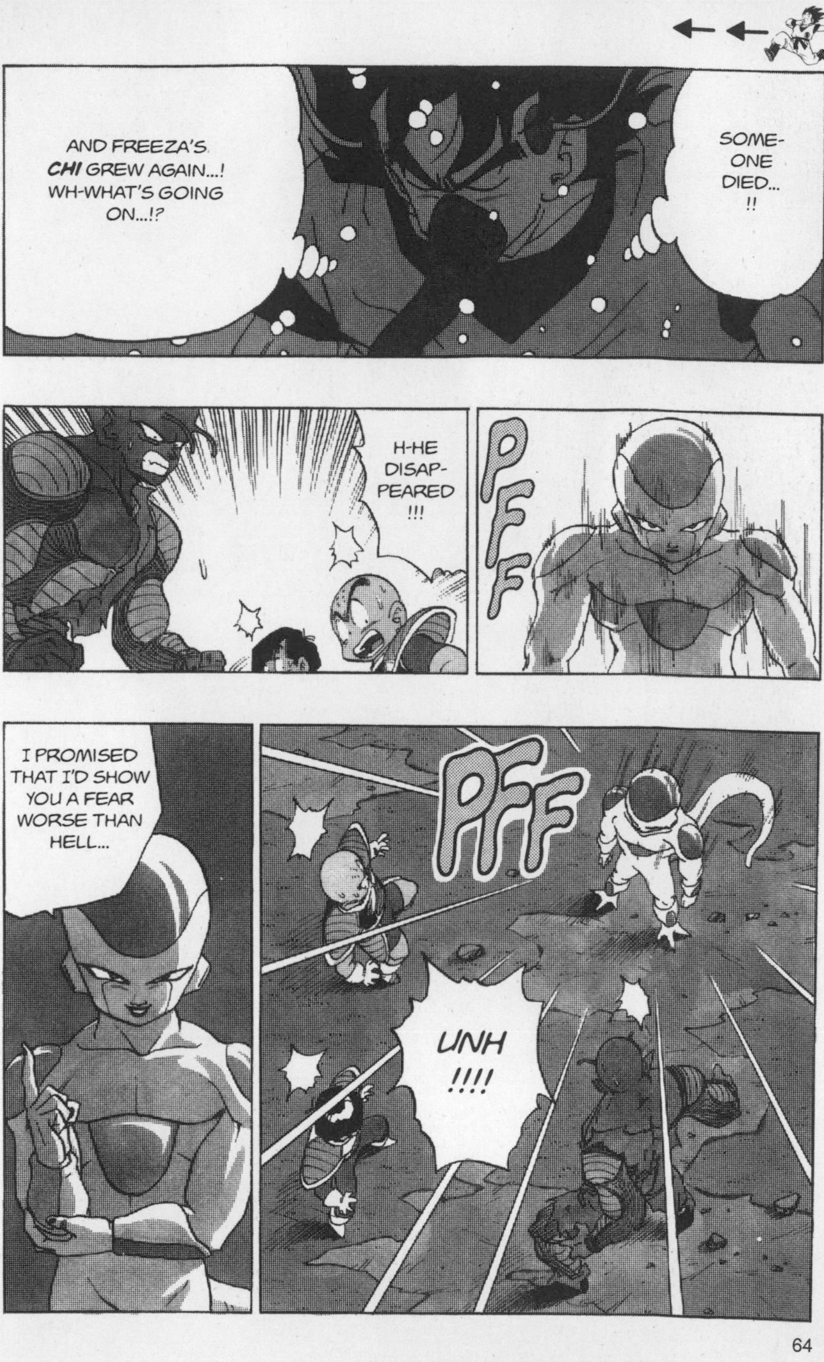

SOME-ONE DIED... !!
AND FREEZA'S CHI GREW AGAIN...! WH-WHAT'S GOING ON...!?
PFF
H-HE DISAP-PEARED !!!
PFF
UNH !!!!
I PROMISED THAT I'D SHOW YOU A FEAR WORSE THAN HELL...

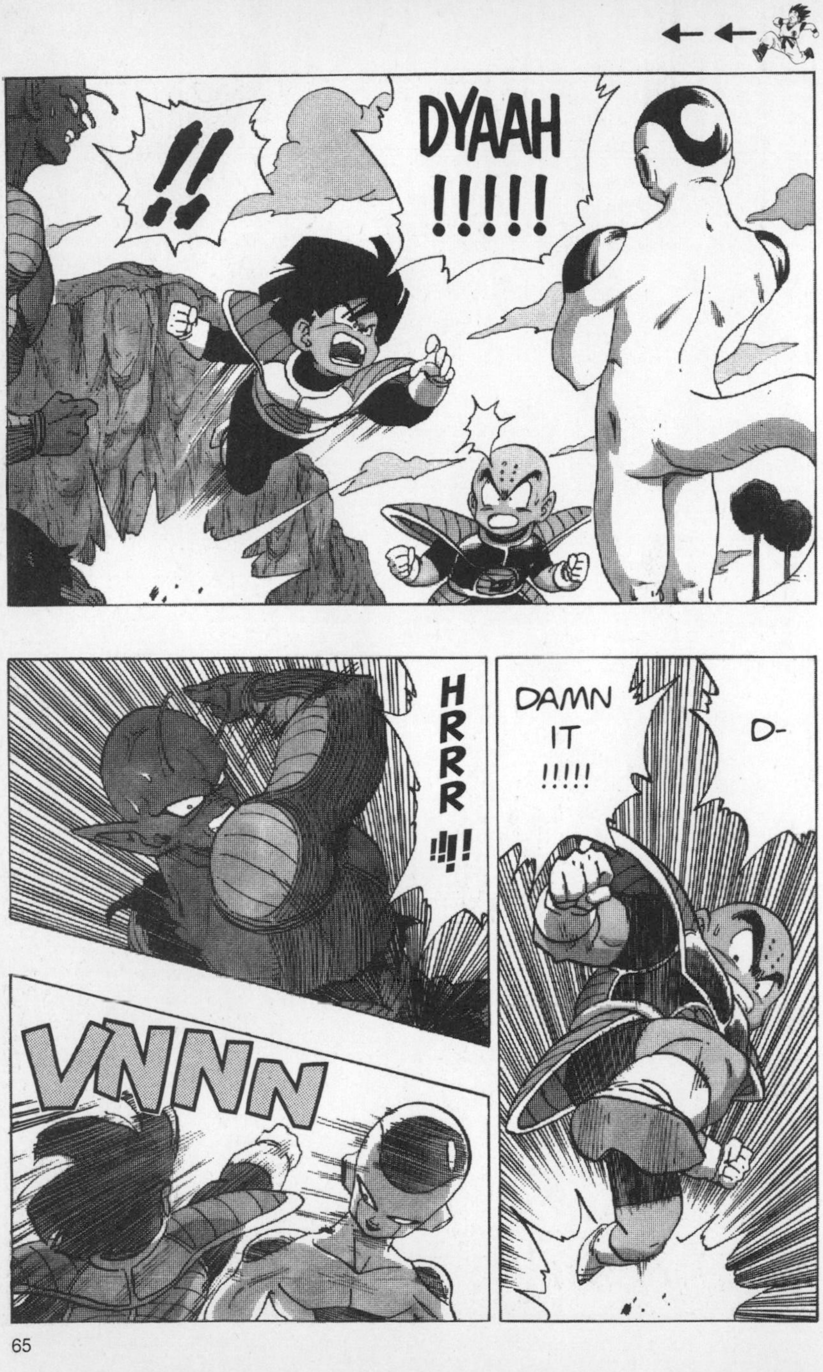
DYAAH !!!!!
!!
D-
DAMN IT !!!!!
HRRR !!!!
VNNN

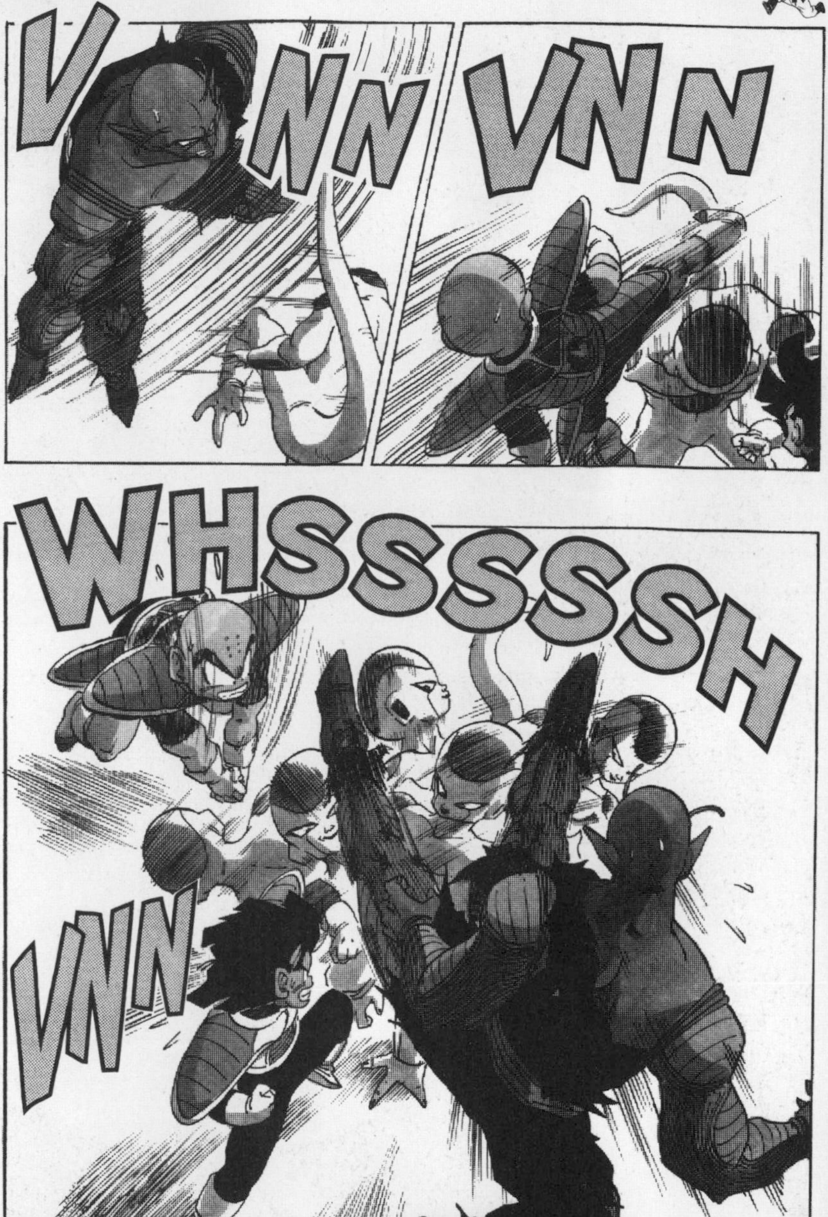
VNN
VNN
WHSSSSSH
VNN

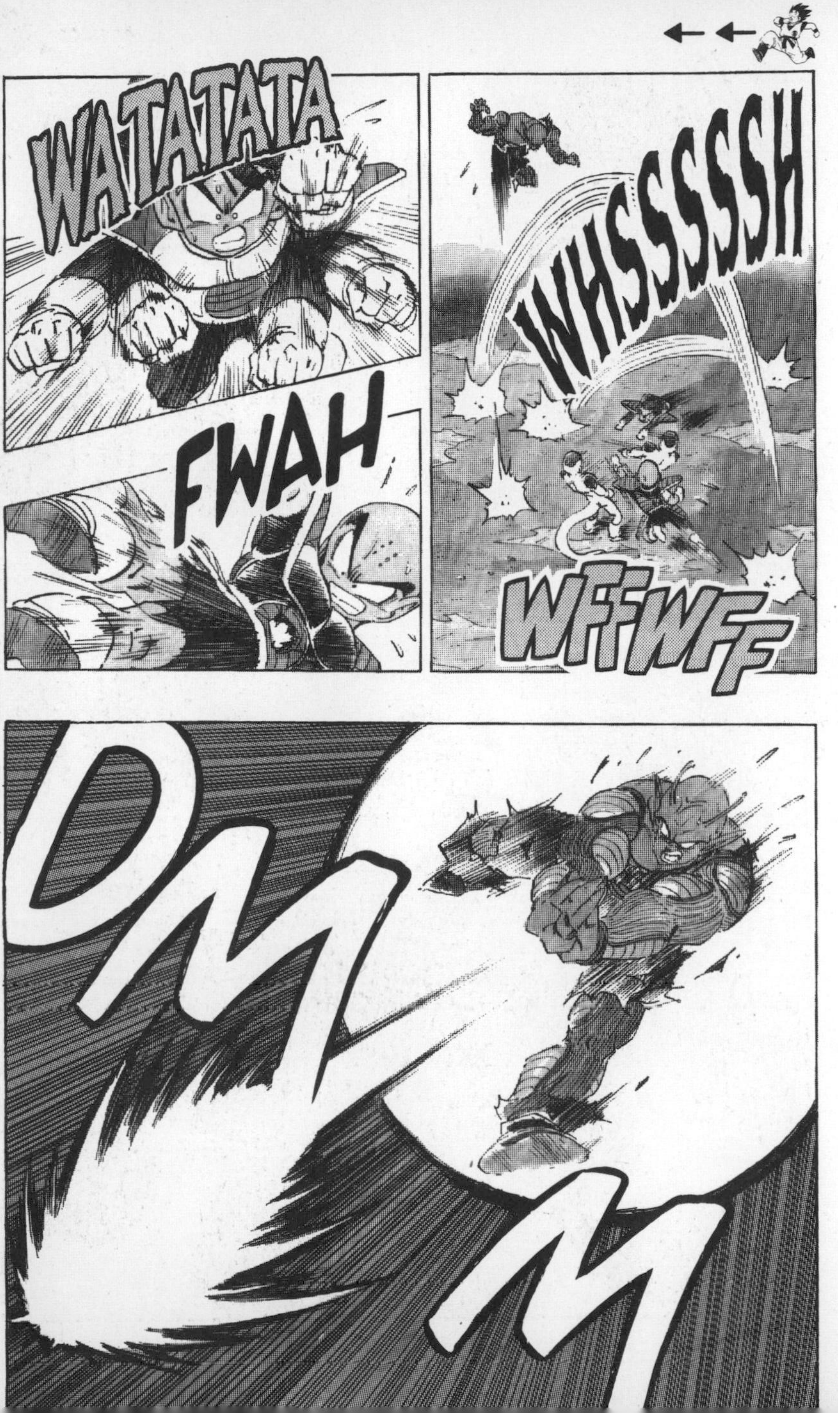
WHSSSSSH
WFFWFF
WATATATA
FWAH
DMMM

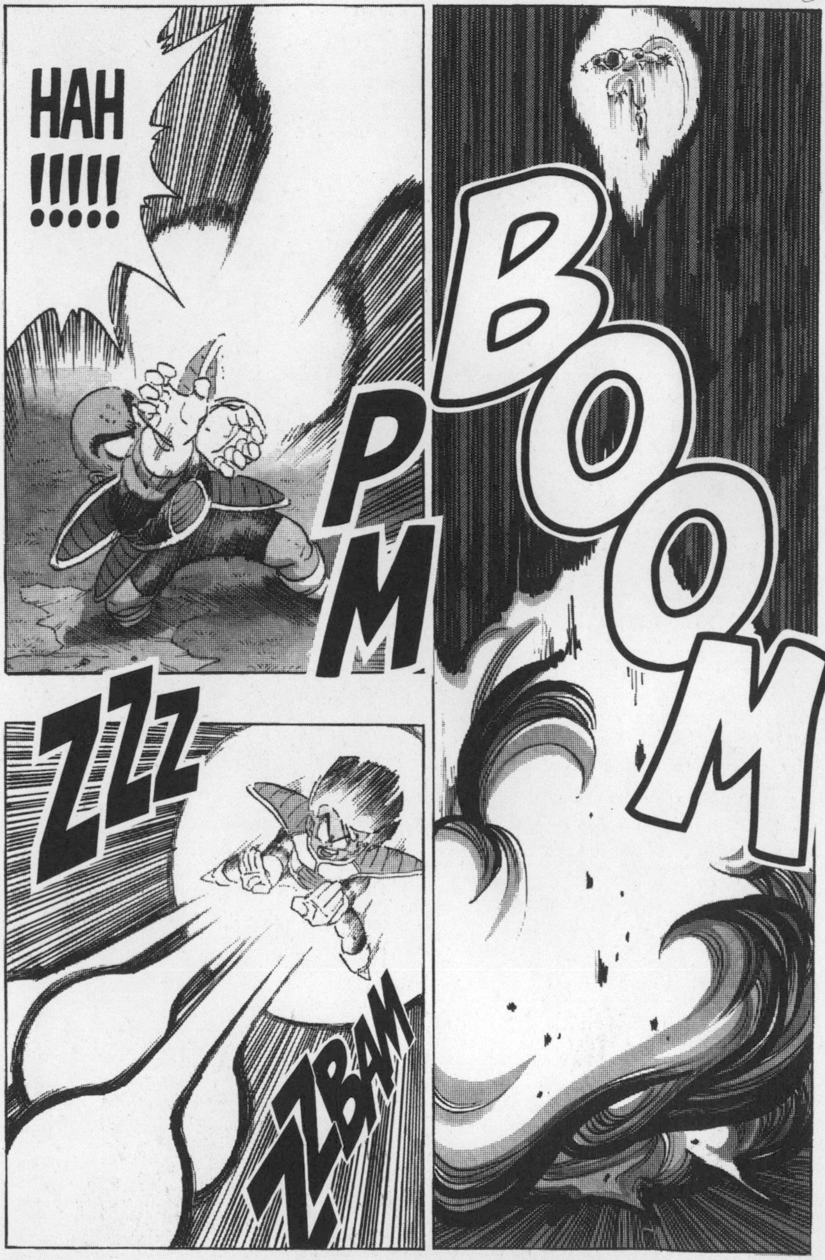
BOOOM
HAH!!!!!
PM
ZZZ
ZBAM

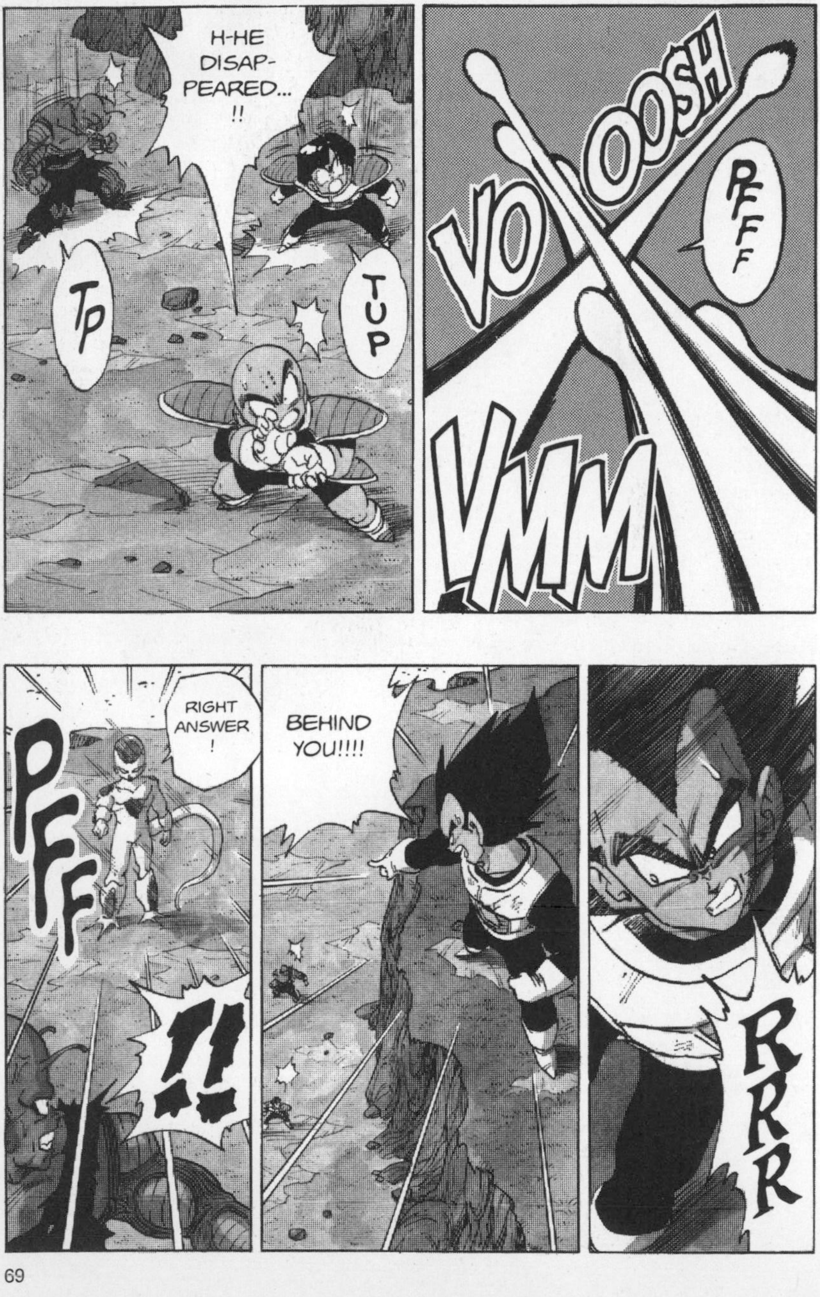
VOOOSH
RFFF
VMM
H-HE DISAP-PEARED...!!
TUP
TP
RRR
BEHIND YOU!!!!
RIGHT ANSWER!
PFF
!!

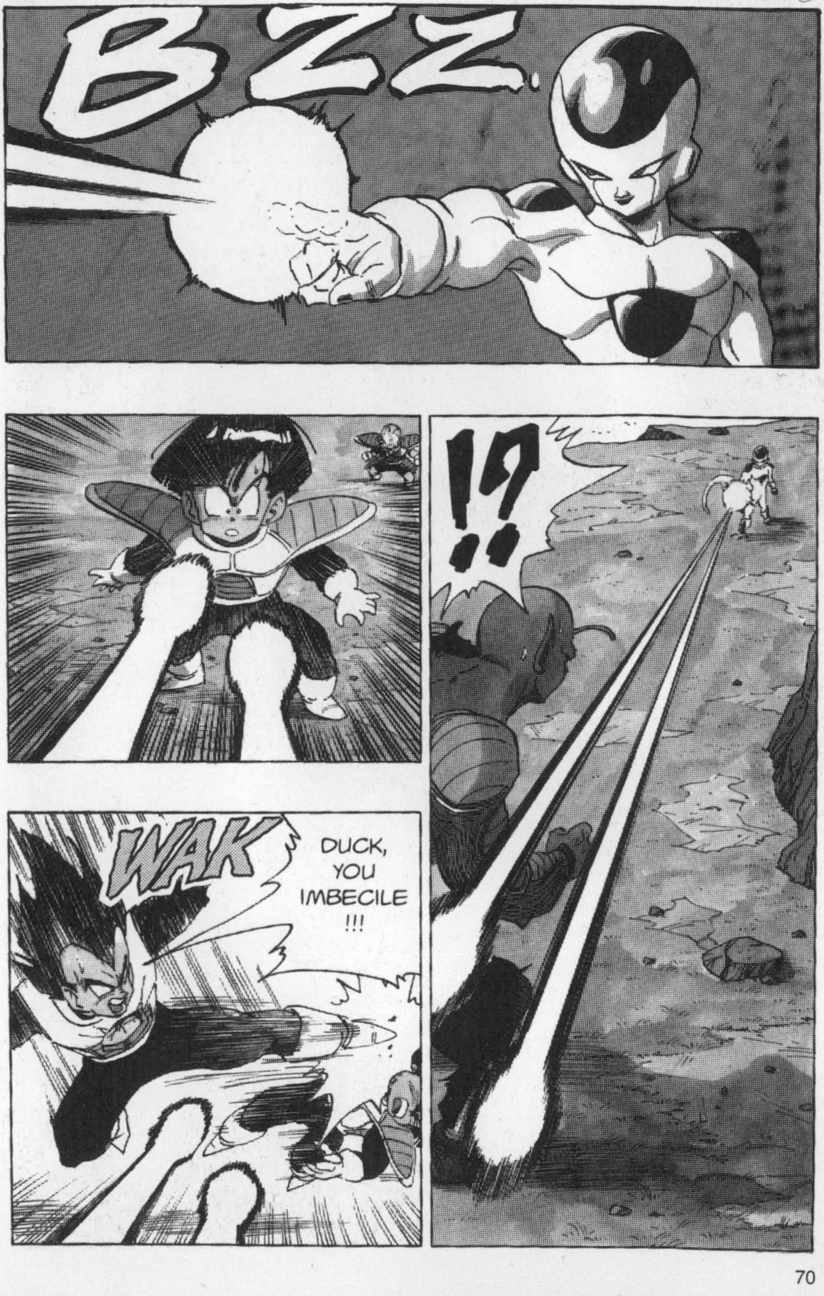
BZZ.
!?
!!
WAK
DUCK, YOU IMBECILE !!!

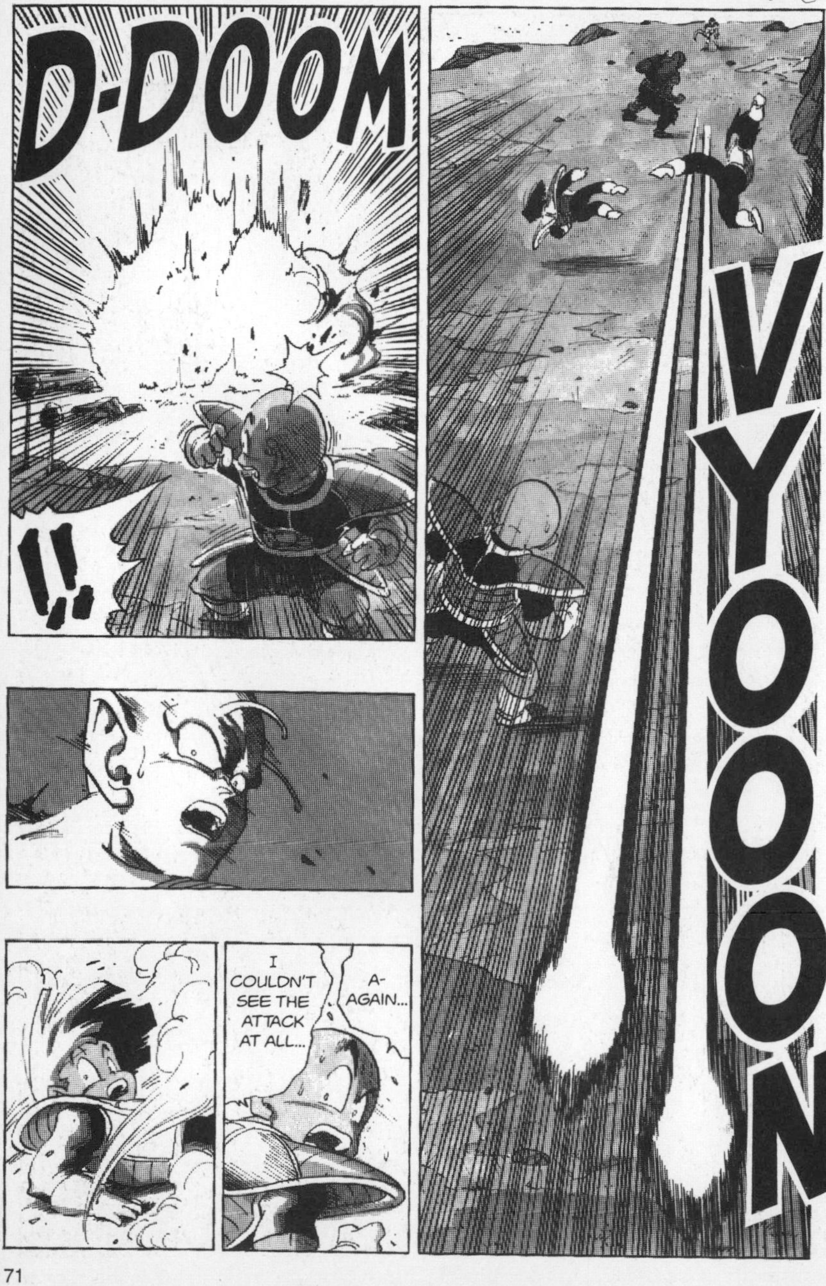
VYOOON
D-DOOM
!!
A-AGAIN...
I COULDN'T SEE THE ATTACK AT ALL...

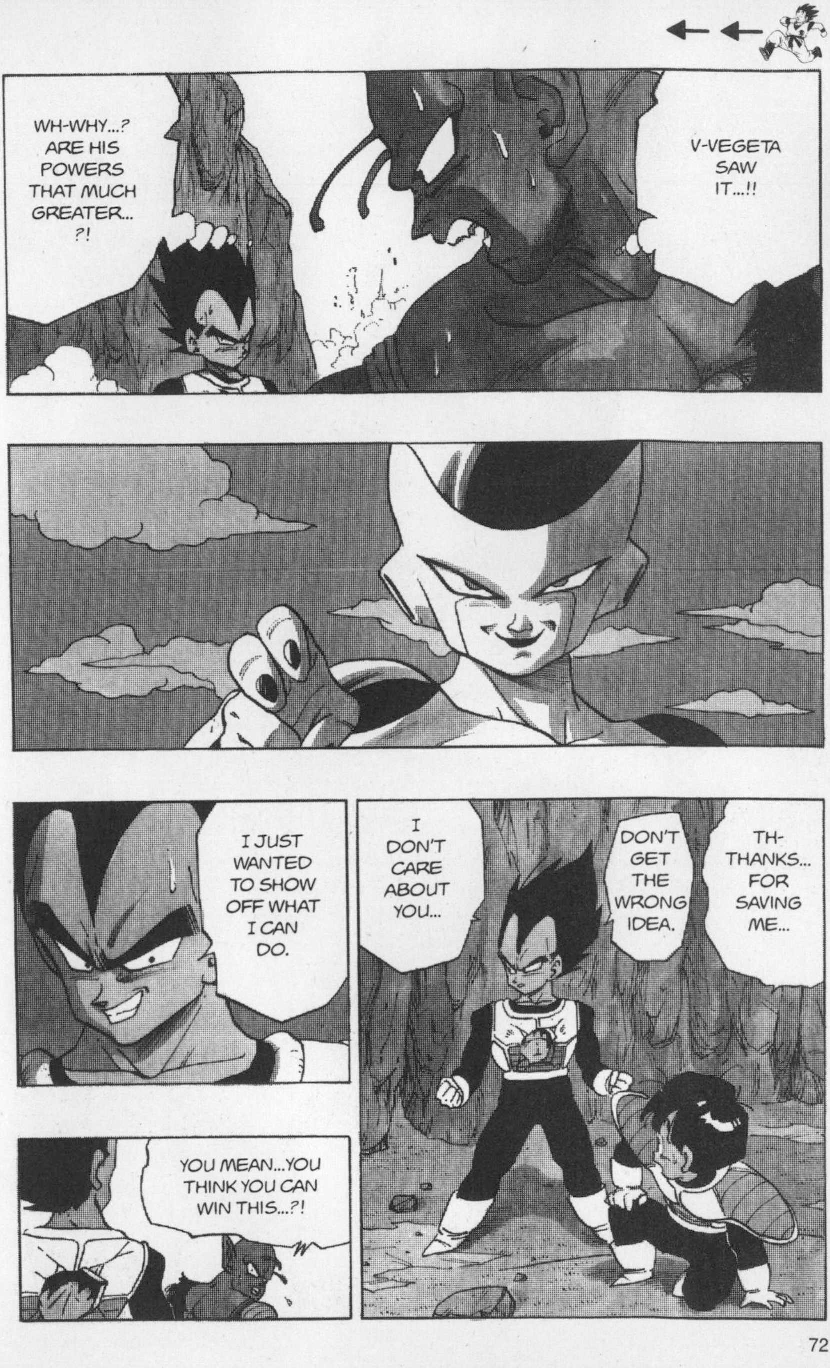
V-VEGETA SAW IT...!!
WH-WHY...? ARE HIS POWERS THAT MUCH GREATER... ?!
TH-THANKS... FOR SAVING ME...
DON'T GET THE WRONG IDEA.
I DON'T CARE ABOUT YOU...
I JUST WANTED TO SHOW OFF WHAT I CAN DO.
YOU MEAN...YOU THINK YOU CAN WIN THIS...?!

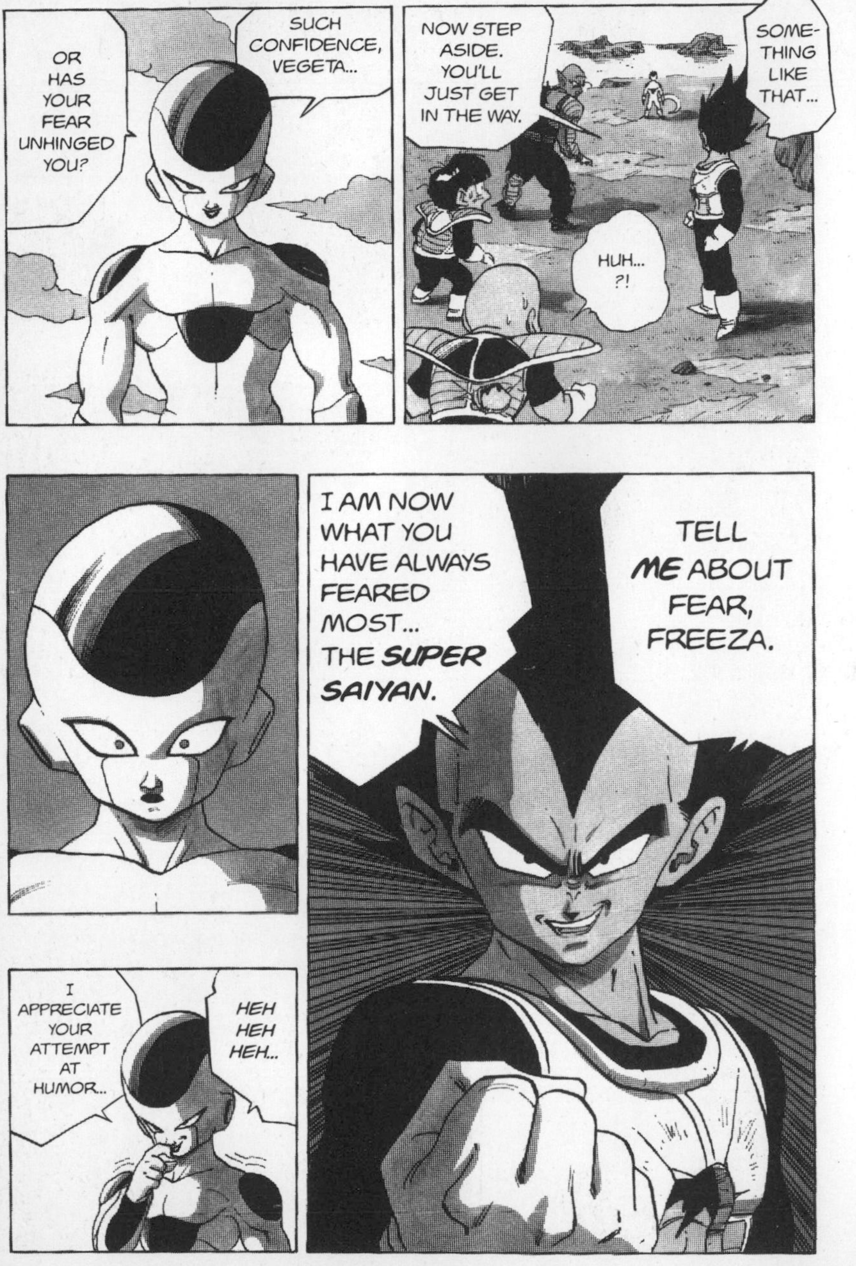
SOMETHING LIKE THAT...
NOW STEP ASIDE. YOU'LL JUST GET IN THE WAY.
HUH...?!
SUCH CONFIDENCE, VEGETA...
OR HAS YOUR FEAR UNHINGED YOU?
TELL ME ABOUT FEAR, FREEZA.
I AM NOW WHAT YOU HAVE ALWAYS FEARED MOST... THE SUPER SAIYAN.
HEH HEH HEH...
I APPRECIATE YOUR ATTEMPT AT HUMOR...

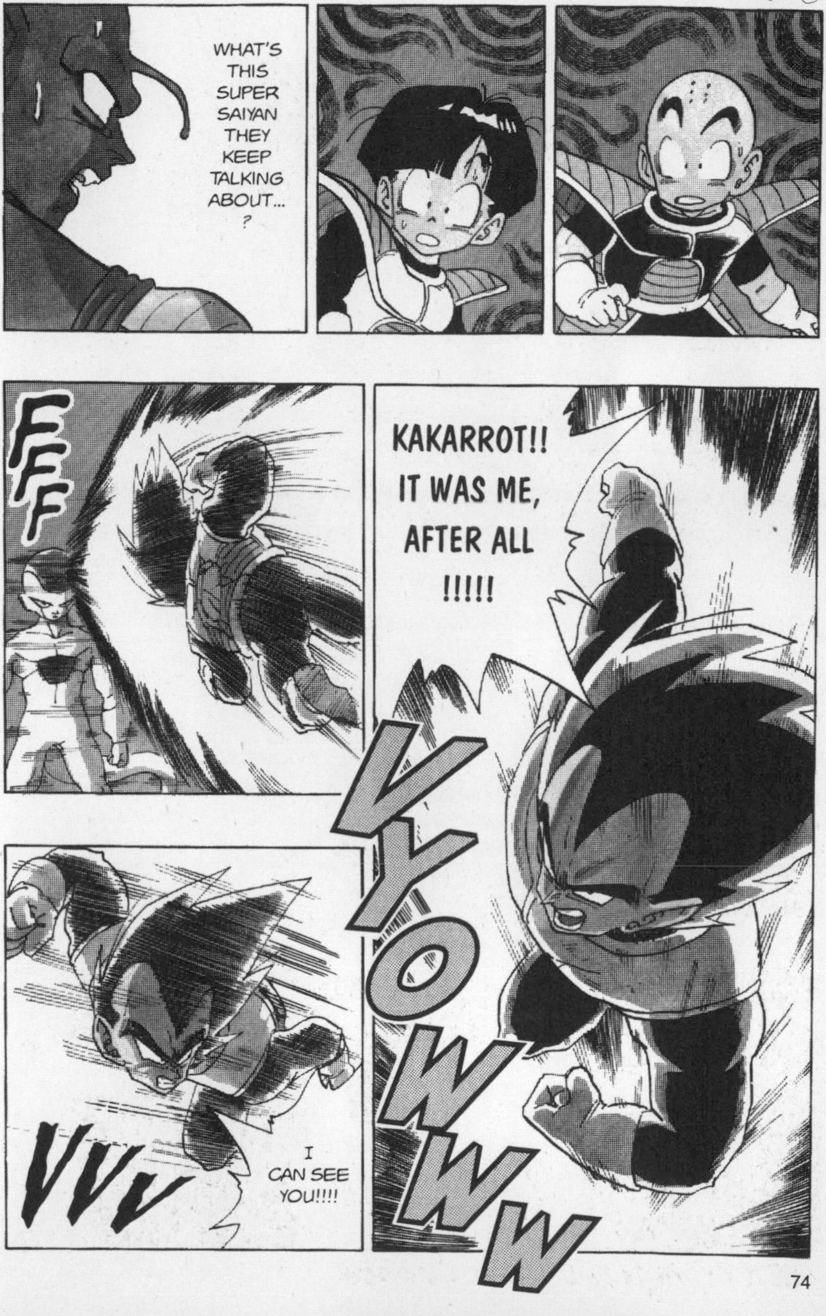
WHAT'S THIS SUPER SAIYAN THEY KEEP TALKING ABOUT... ?
KAKARROT!! IT WAS ME, AFTER ALL !!!!!
VYOWWWW
FFF
VVV
I CAN SEE YOU!!!!

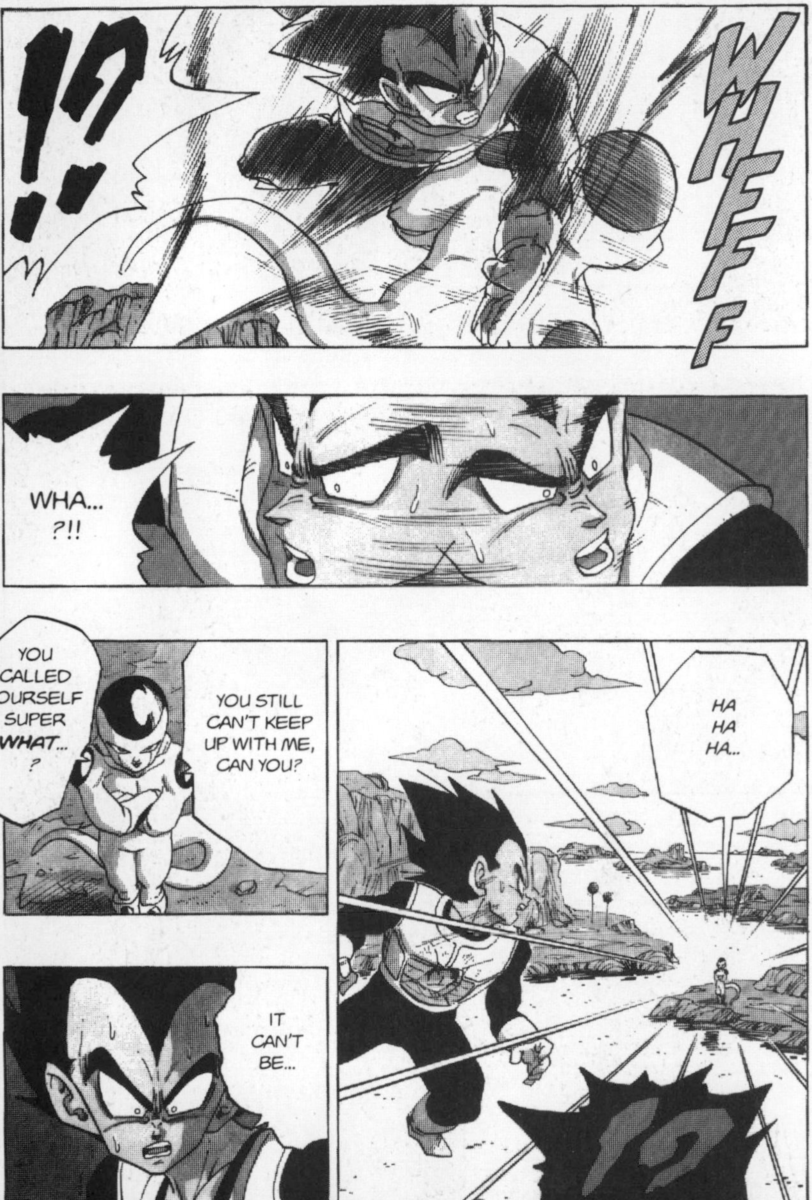
WHFFF
!?
WHA... ?!!
HA HA HA...
!?
YOU STILL CAN'T KEEP UP WITH ME, CAN YOU?
YOU CALLED YOURSELF SUPER **WHAT...**?
IT CAN'T BE...

NEXT: Vegeta's Last Chance

DBZ:112 • Son Goku... Resurrected!!

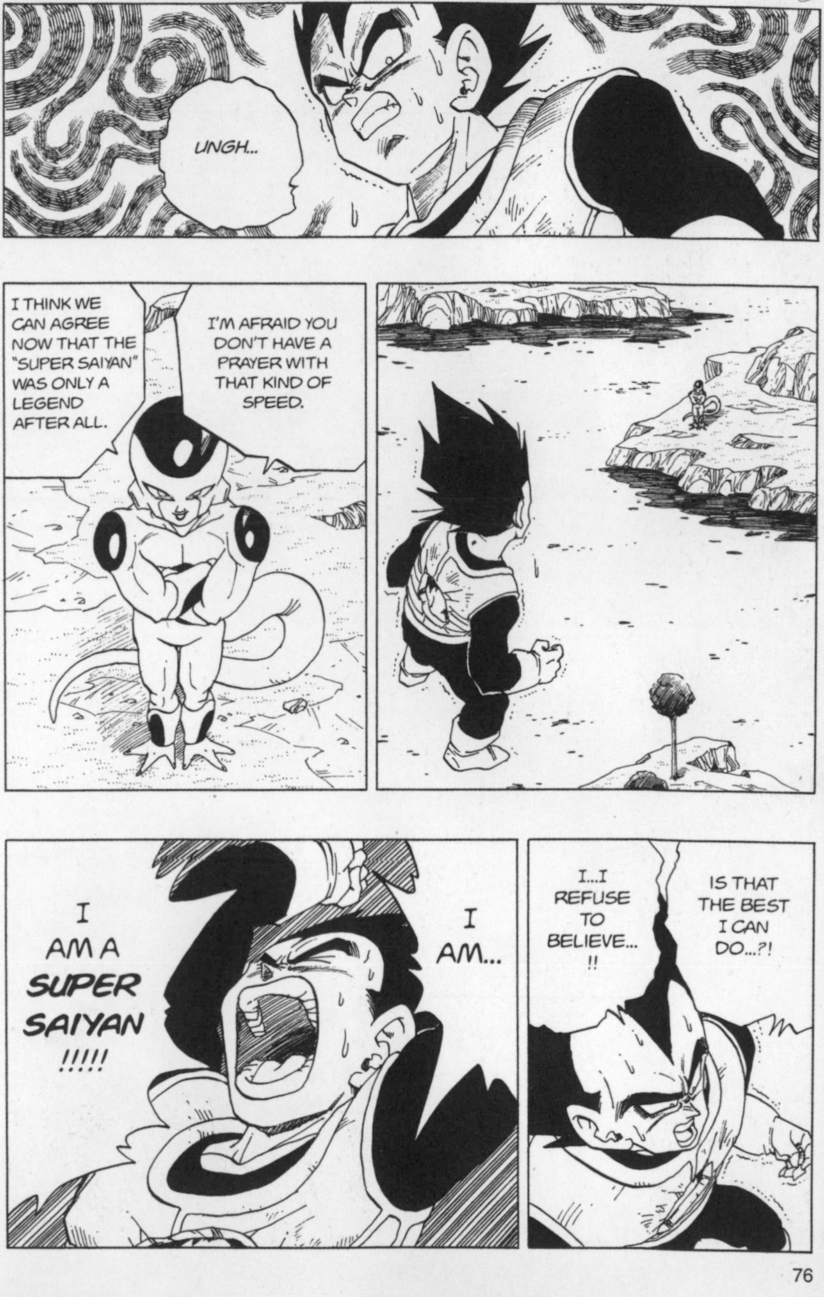
UNGH...
I'M AFRAID YOU DON'T HAVE A PRAYER WITH THAT KIND OF SPEED.
I THINK WE CAN AGREE NOW THAT THE "SUPER SAIYAN" WAS ONLY A LEGEND AFTER ALL.
IS THAT THE BEST I CAN DO...?!
I...I REFUSE TO BELIEVE... !!
I AM...
I AM A SUPER SAIYAN !!!!!

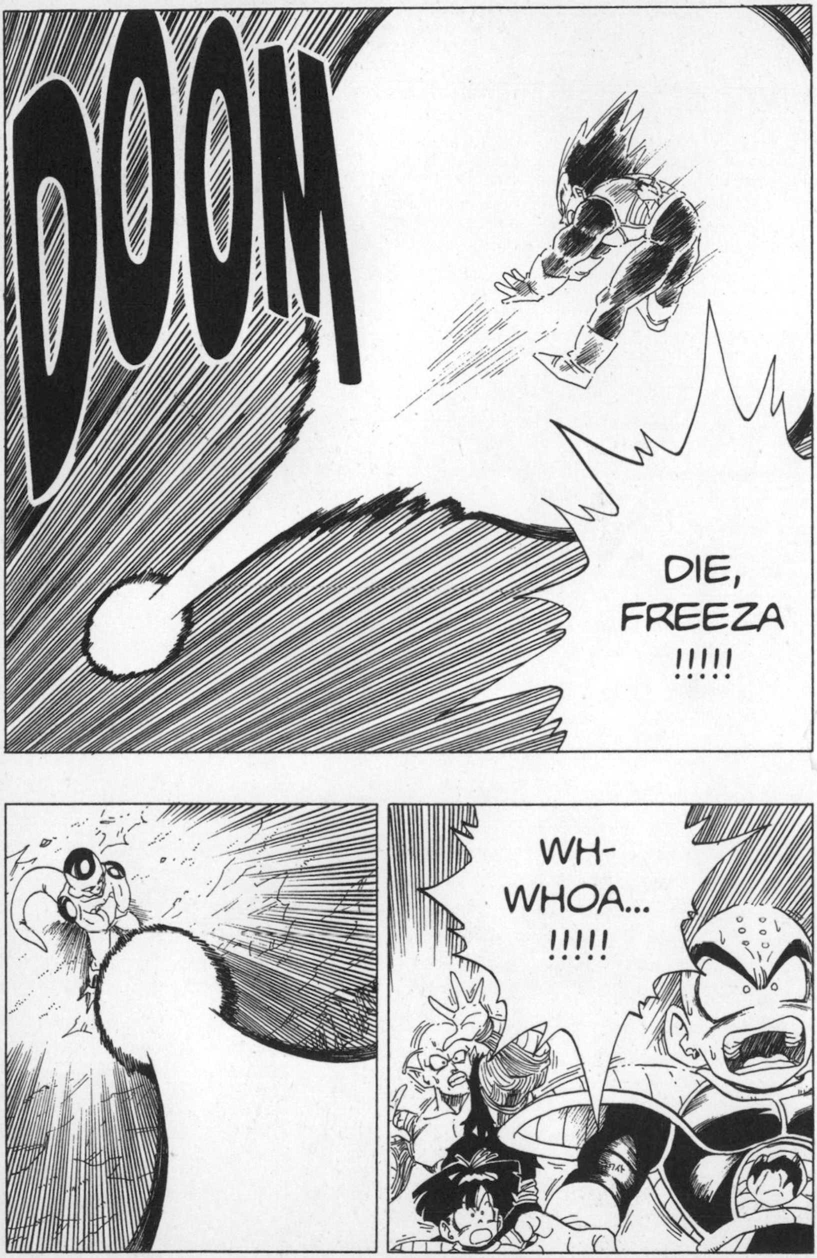
DOOM
DIE, FREEZA !!!!!
WH- WHOA... !!!!!

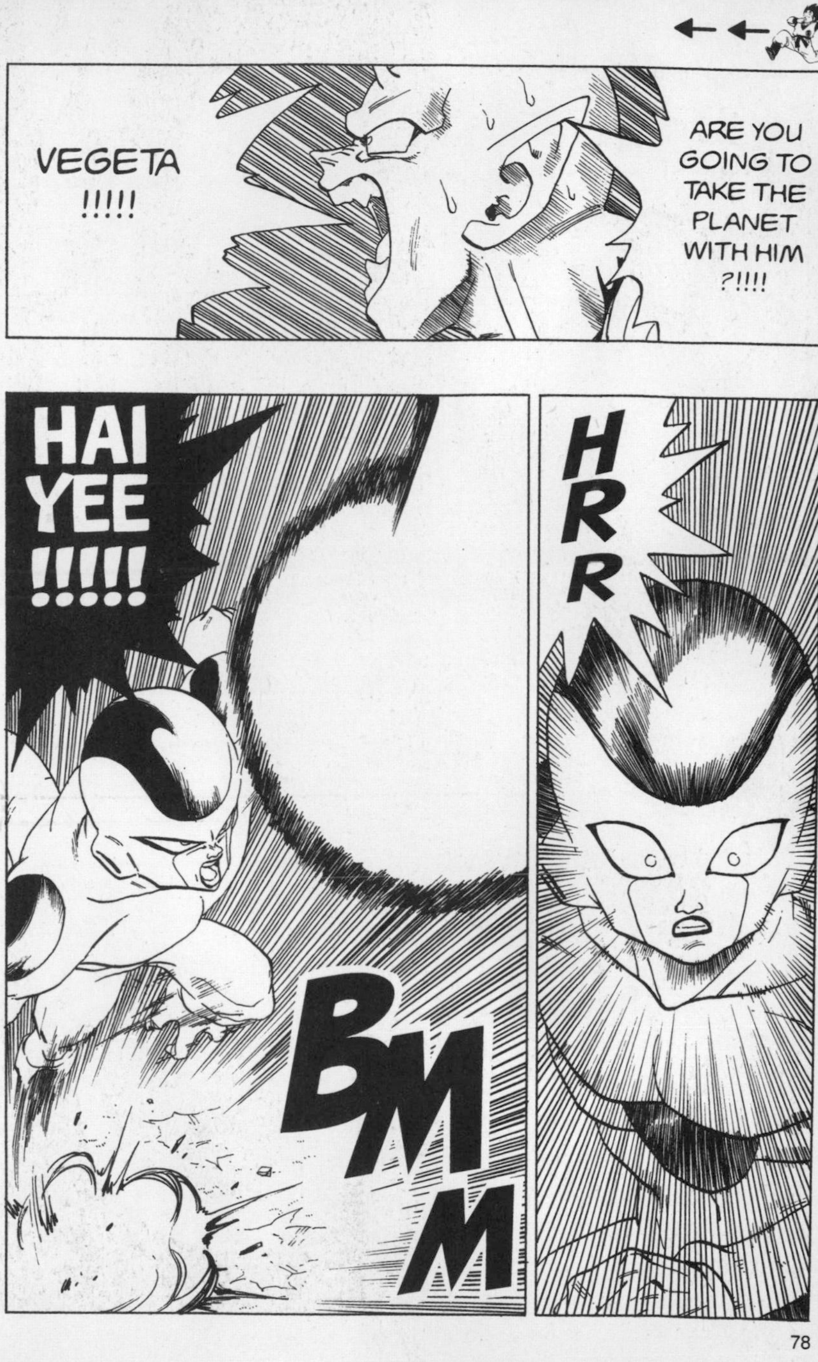
ARE YOU GOING TO TAKE THE PLANET WITH HIM ?!!!!
VEGETA !!!!!
HRR
HAI YEE !!!!!
BMM

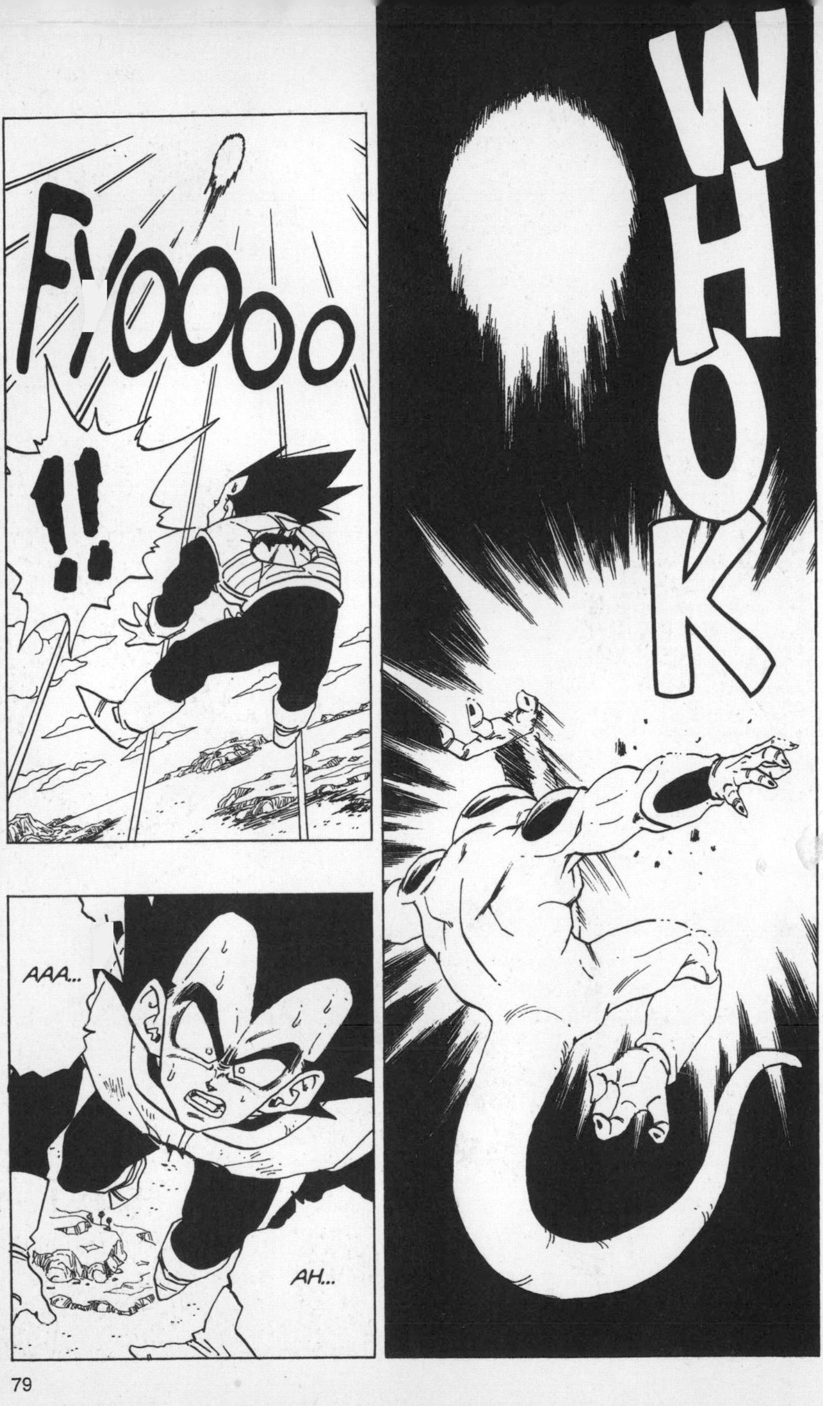
WHOK
FYOOOO
!!
AAA...
AH...

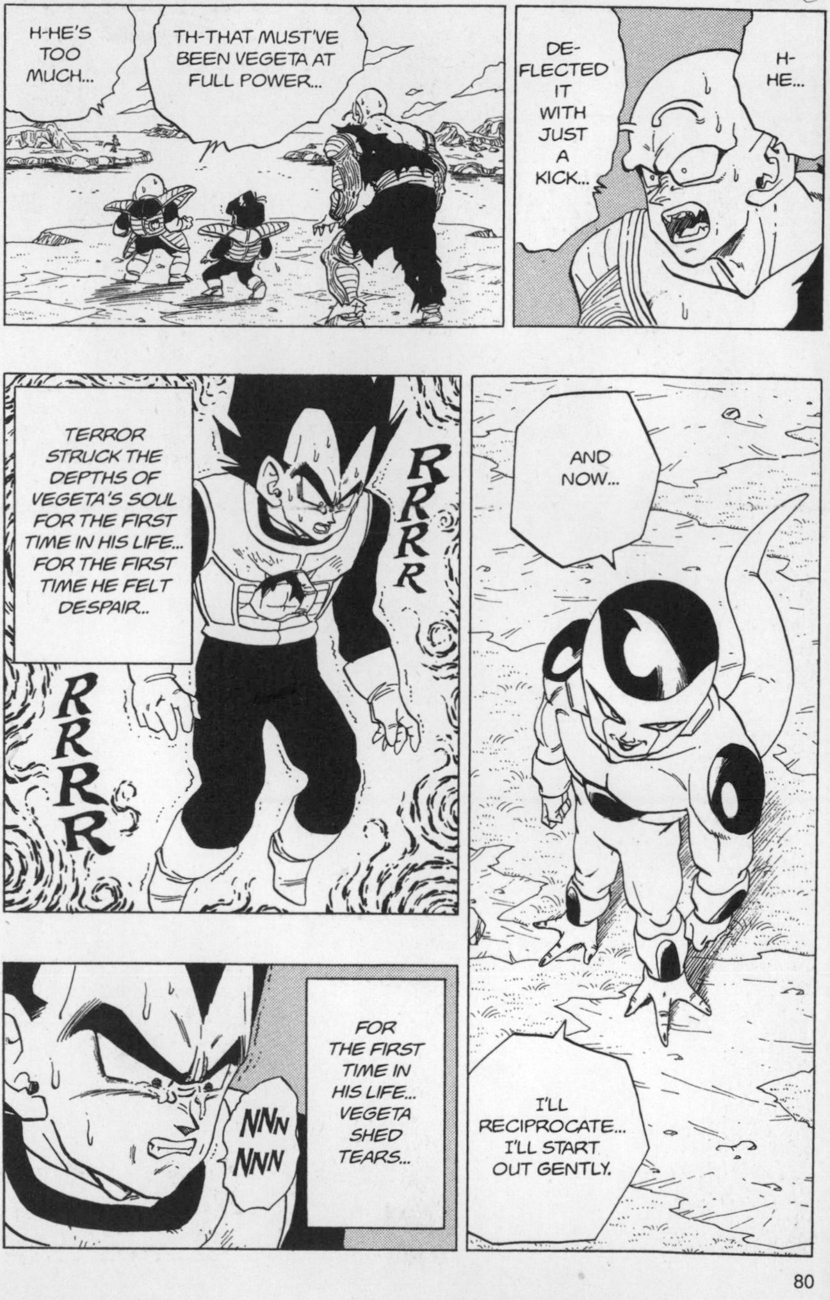
H- HE...
DE- FLECTED IT WITH JUST A KICK...
TH-THAT MUST'VE BEEN VEGETA AT FULL POWER...
H-HE'S TOO MUCH...
AND NOW...
I'LL RECIPROCATE... I'LL START OUT GENTLY.
TERROR STRUCK THE DEPTHS OF VEGETA'S SOUL FOR THE FIRST TIME IN HIS LIFE... FOR THE FIRST TIME HE FELT DESPAIR...
RRRR
RRRR
FOR THE FIRST TIME IN HIS LIFE... VEGETA SHED TEARS...
NNN NNN

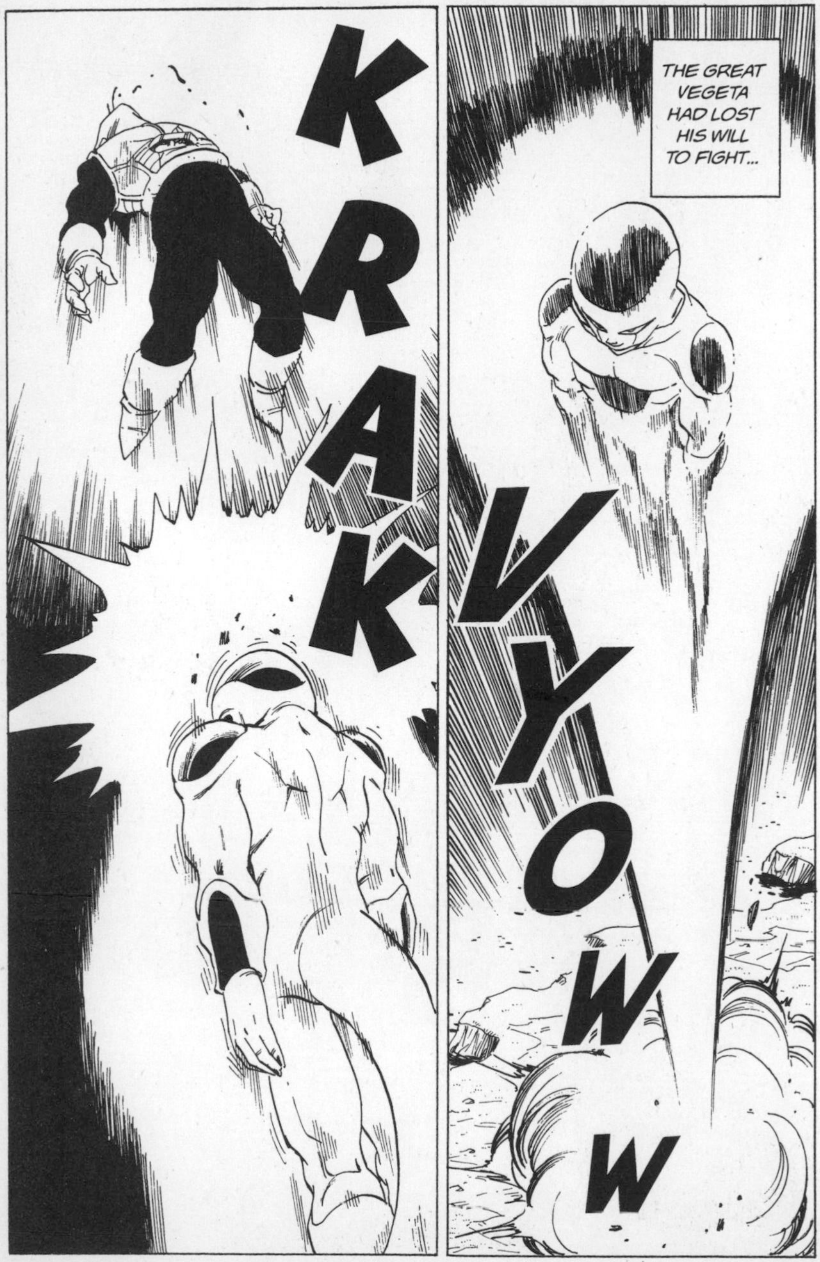
THE GREAT VEGETA HAD LOST HIS WILL TO FIGHT...
VYYOWW
KRAK

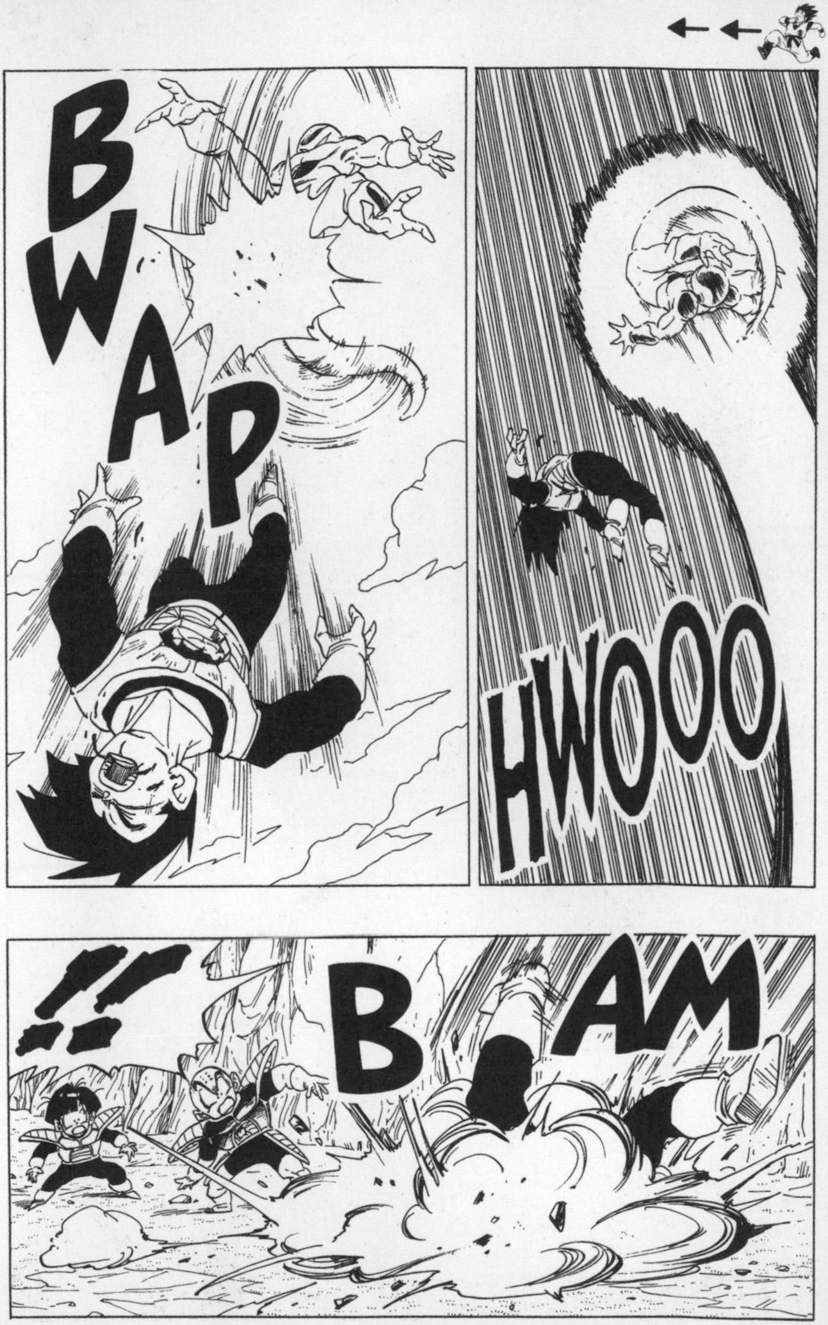
HWOOO
BWAP
BAM
!!

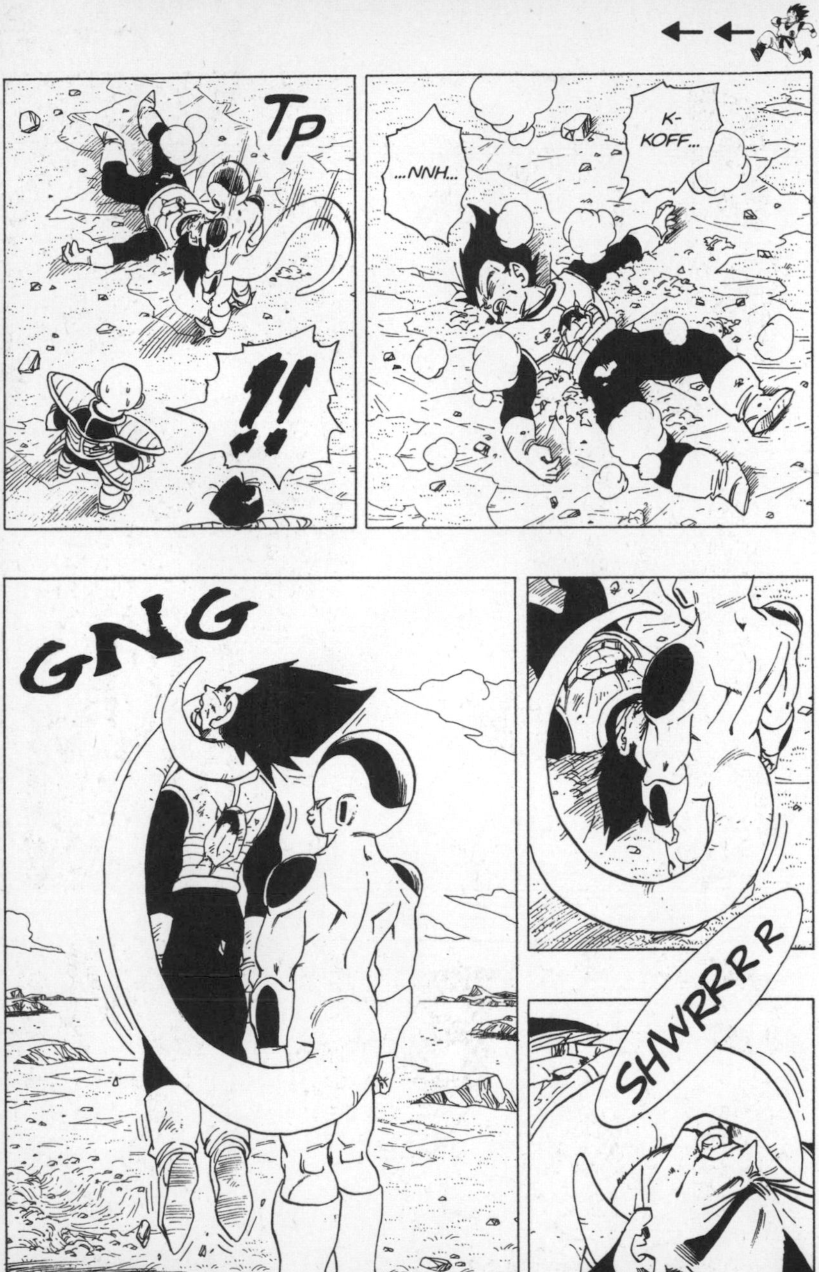
K-KOFF...
...NNH...
TP
!!
SHWRRR R
GNG

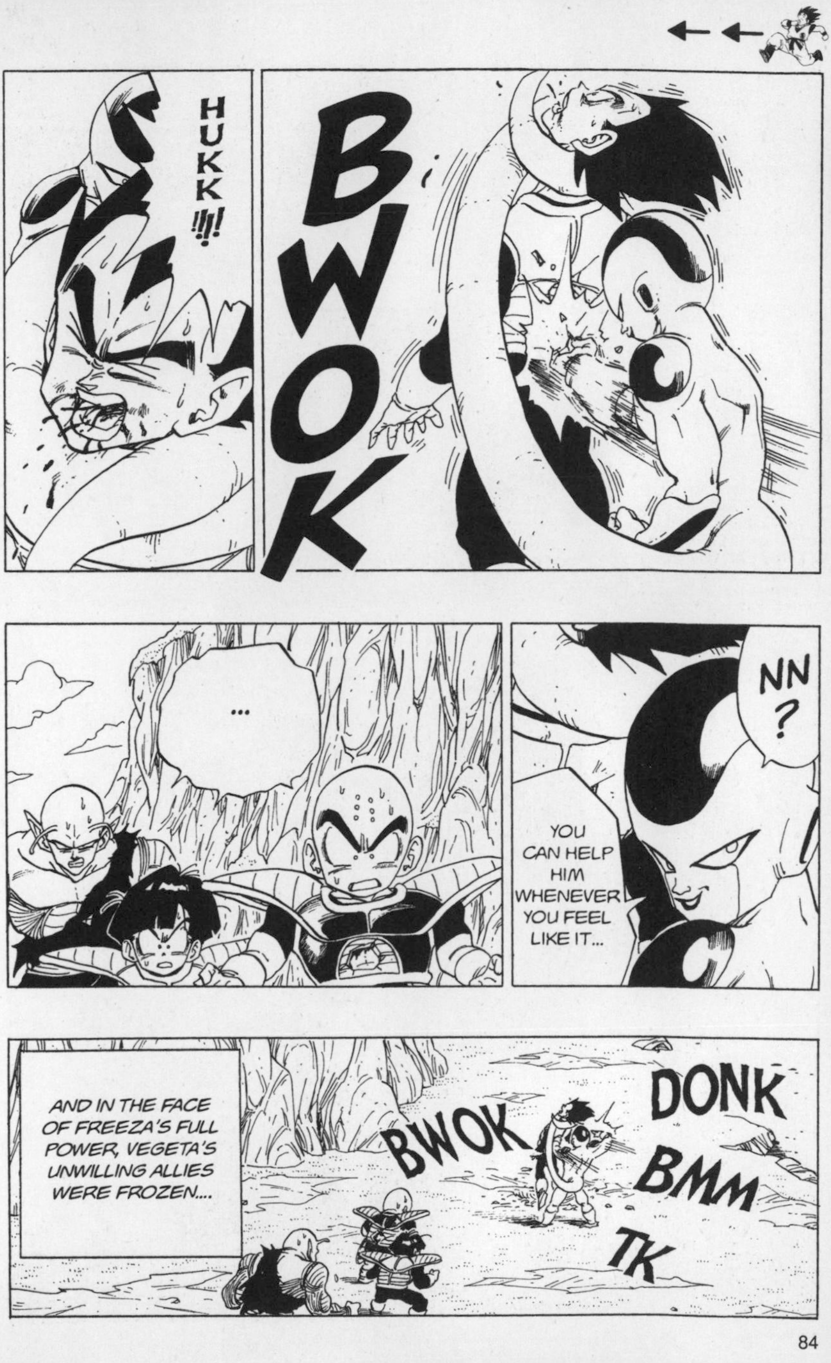
BWOK
HUKK!!!!
NN?
YOU CAN HELP HIM WHENEVER YOU FEEL LIKE IT...
...
DONK
BWOK
BMM
TK
AND IN THE FACE OF FREEZA'S FULL POWER, VEGETA'S UNWILLING ALLIES WERE FROZEN....

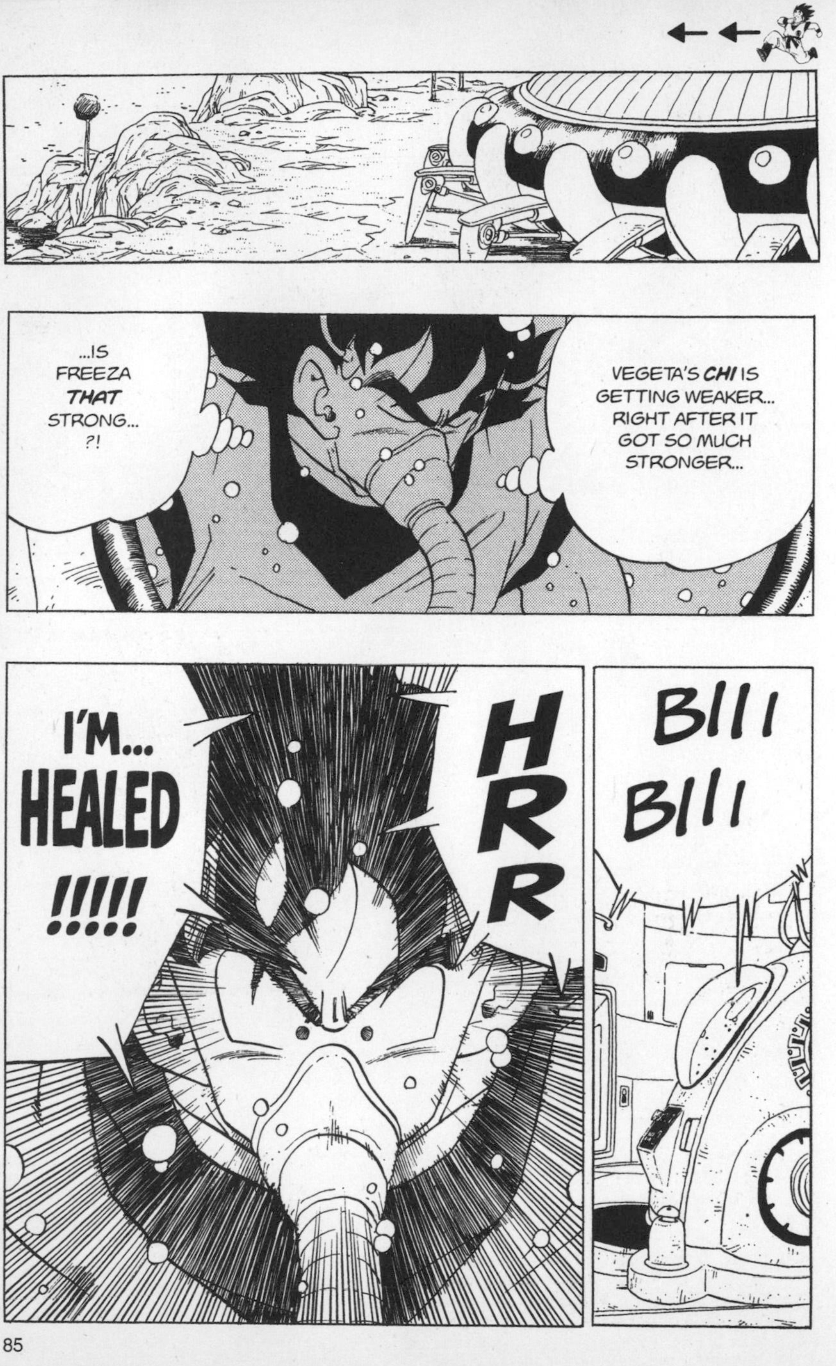

VEGETA'S **CHI** IS GETTING WEAKER... RIGHT AFTER IT GOT SO MUCH STRONGER...
...IS FREEZA **THAT** STRONG...?!
BIII BIII
HRR
I'M... HEALED!!!!!

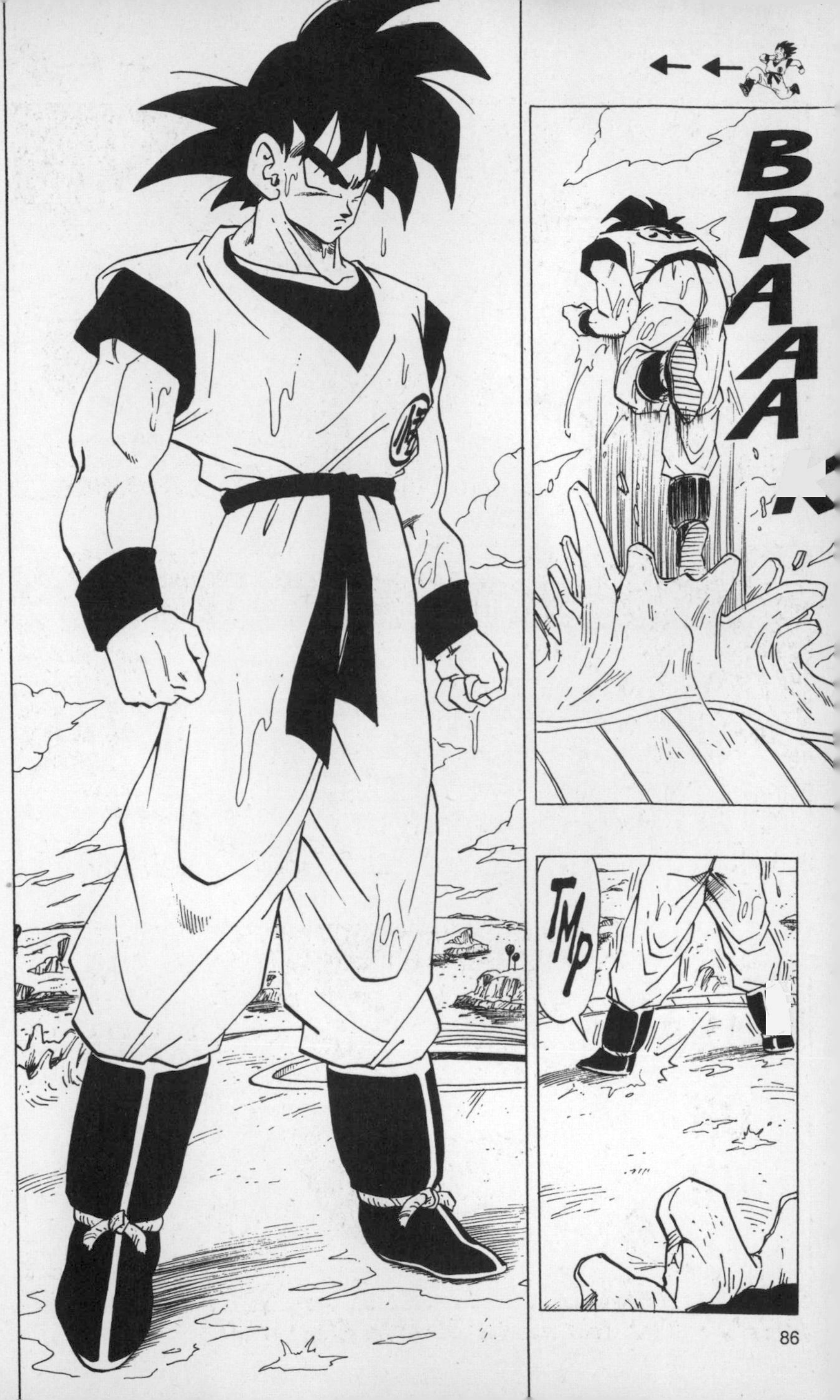
BRAAA
TMP

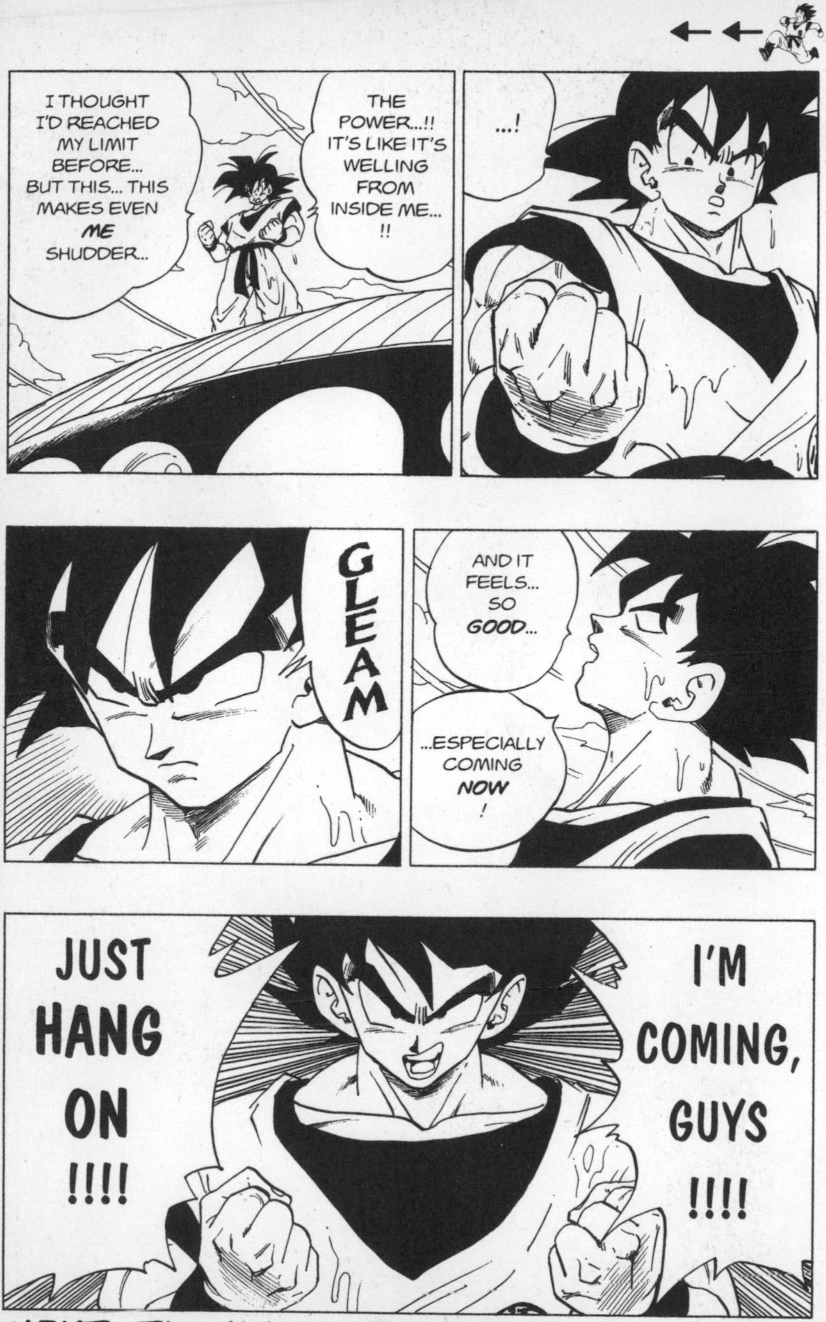
...!
THE POWER...!! IT'S LIKE IT'S WELLING FROM INSIDE ME... !!
I THOUGHT I'D REACHED MY LIMIT BEFORE... BUT THIS... THIS MAKES EVEN ME SHUDDER...
AND IT FEELS... SO GOOD...
...ESPECIALLY COMING NOW!
GLEAM
I'M COMING, GUYS !!!!
JUST HANG ON !!!!

NEXT: The Ultimate Battle Begins!!

DBZ:113 • The Ultimate Battle Begins!

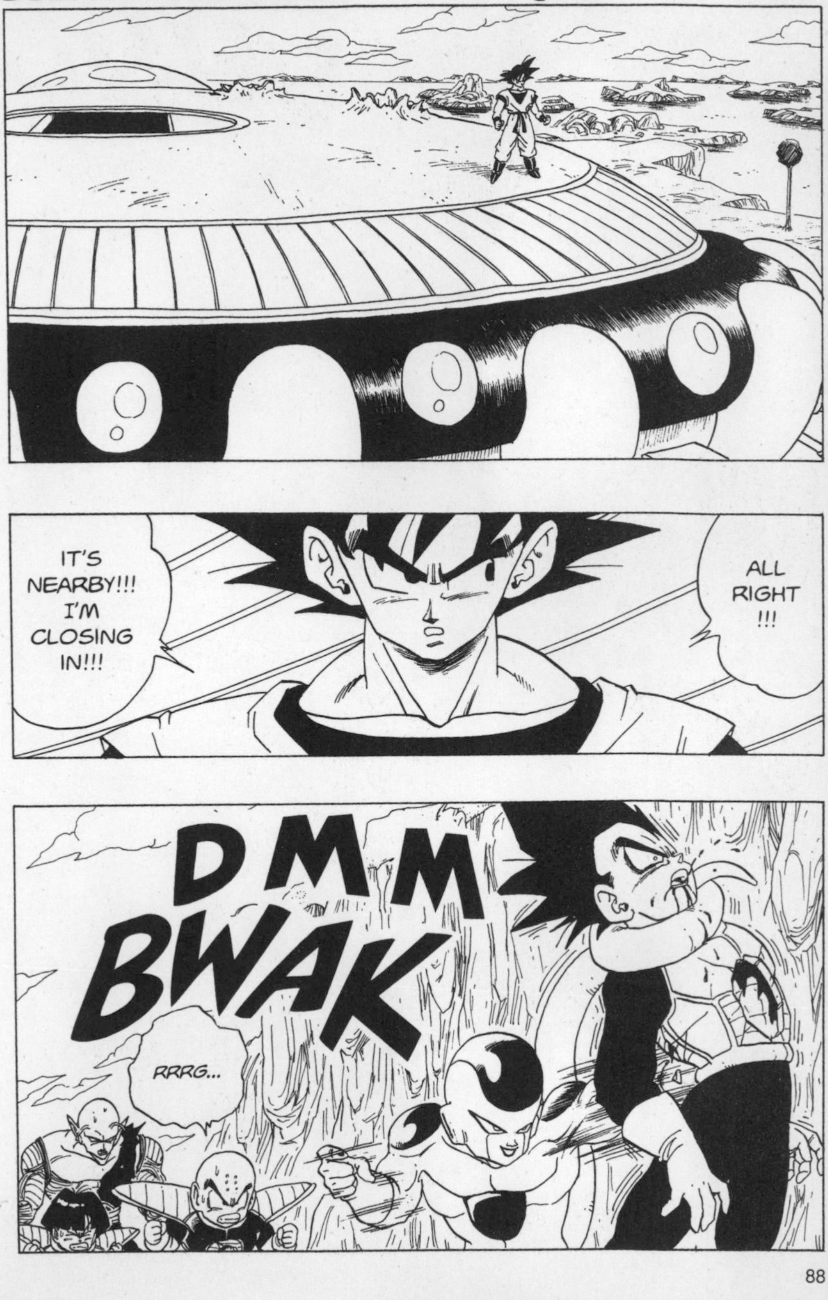
ALL RIGHT !!!
IT'S NEARBY!!! I'M CLOSING IN!!!
DMM
BWAK
RRRG...

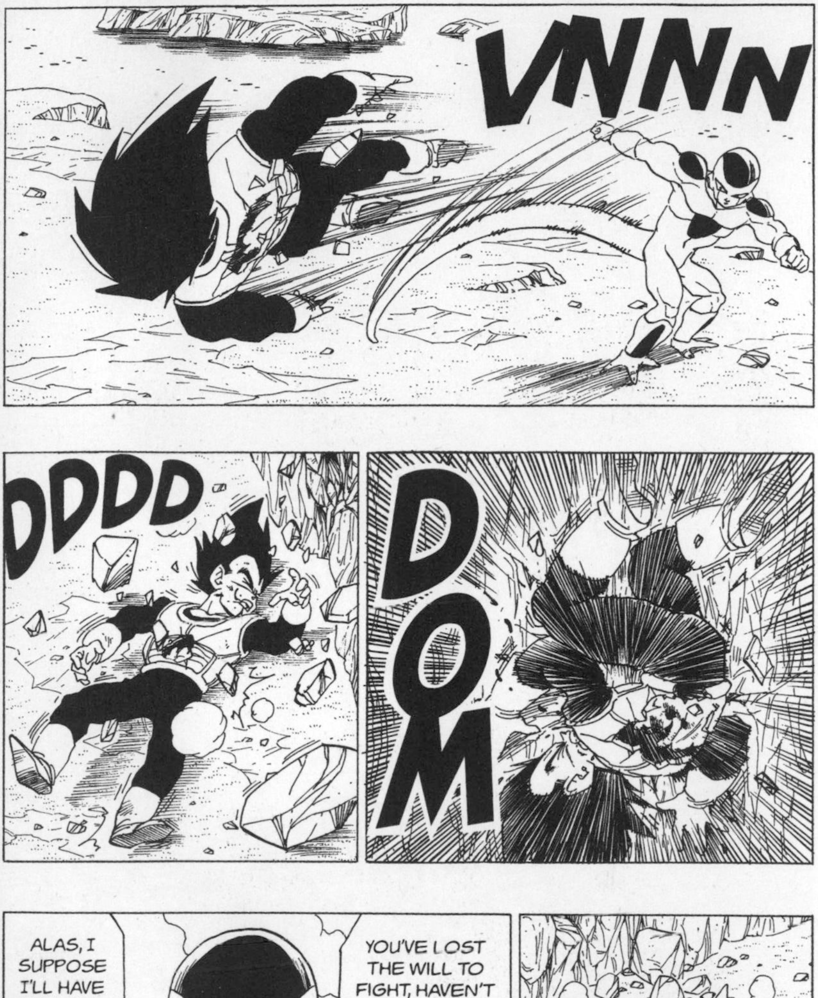
VNNN
DOM
DDDD
YOU'VE LOST THE WILL TO FIGHT, HAVEN'T YOU...? HOW BORING....
ALAS, I SUPPOSE I'LL HAVE TO FINISH YOU OFF EARLY...

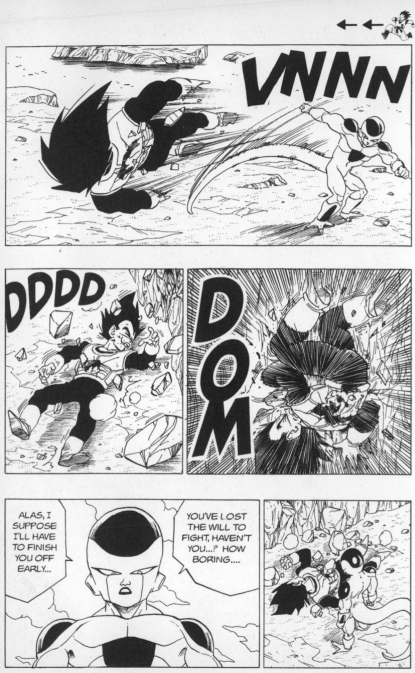

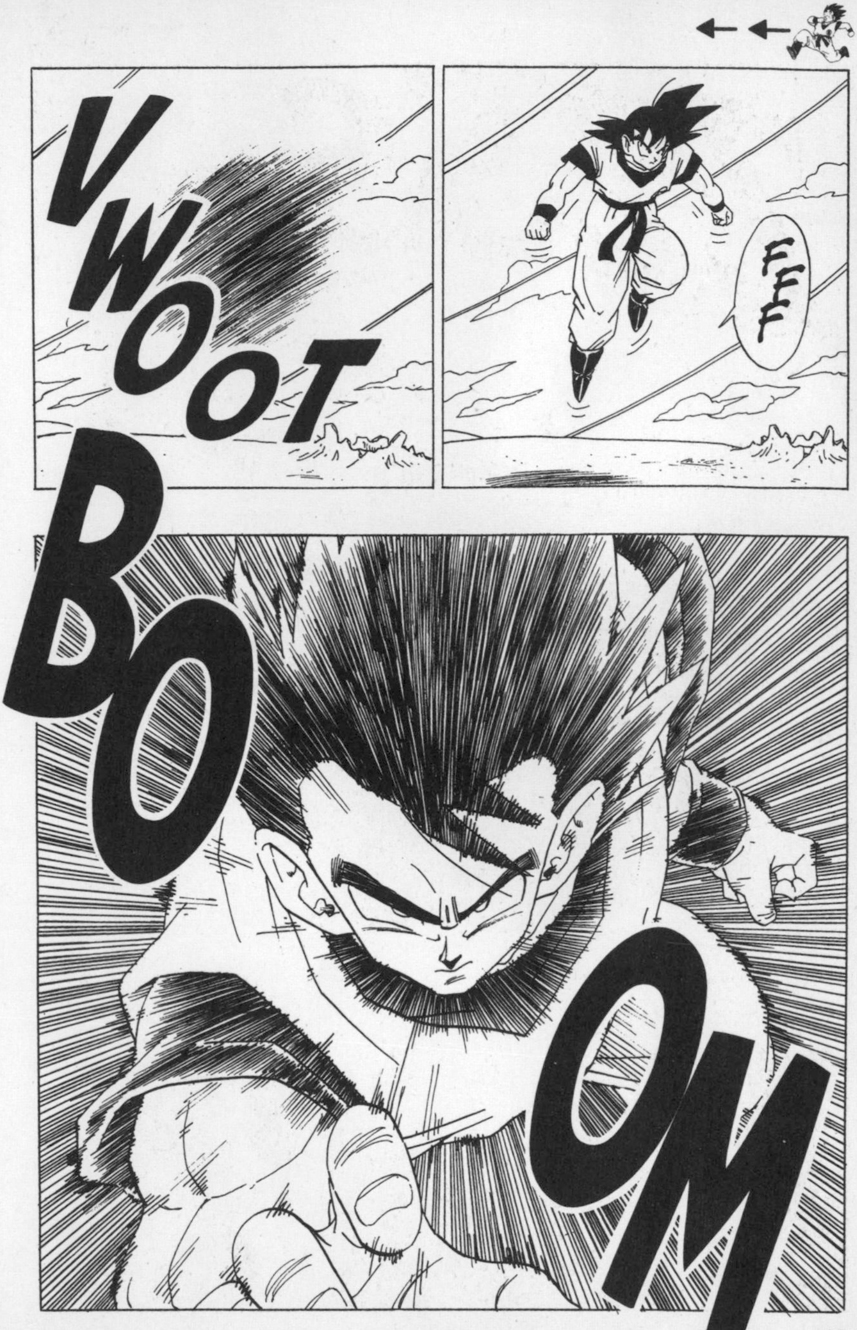
FFF
VWOOT
BOOM

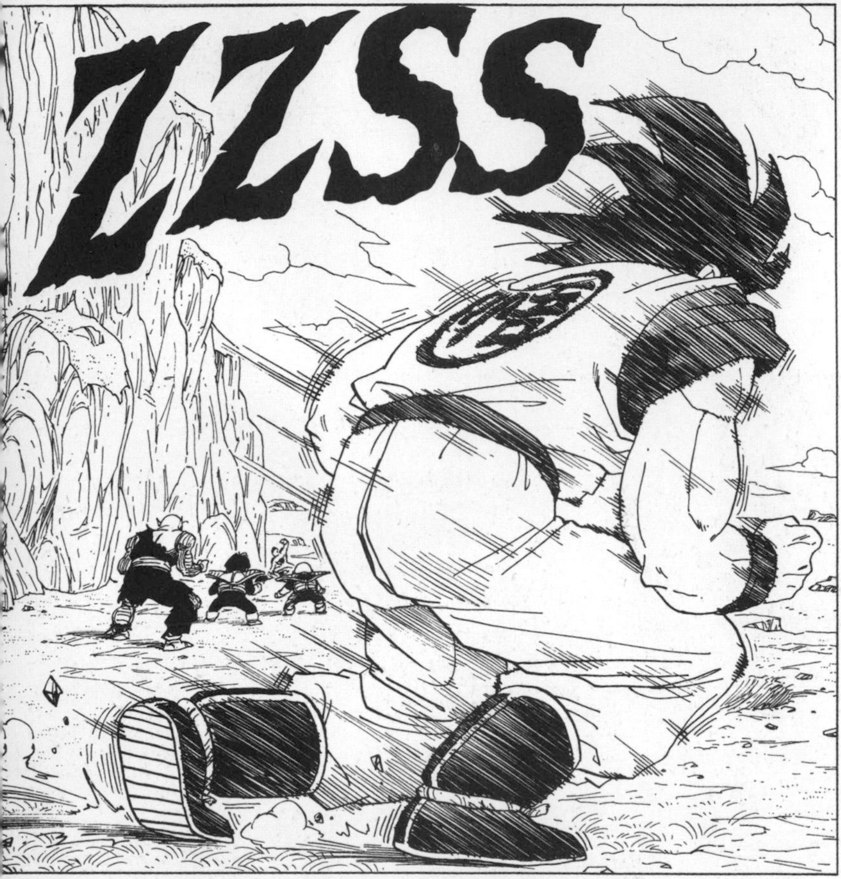
ZZSS
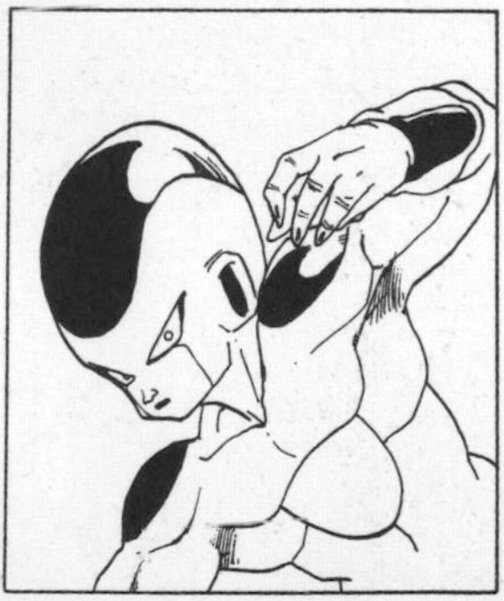
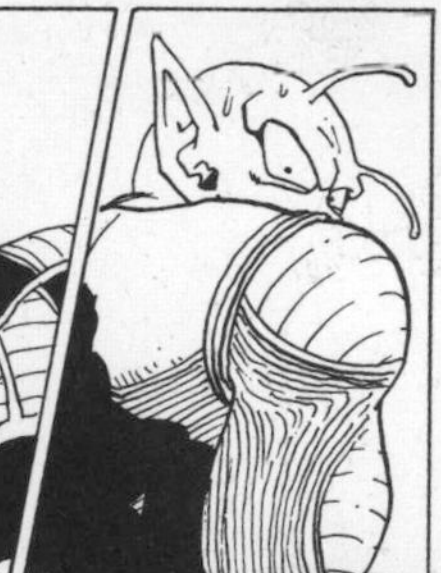
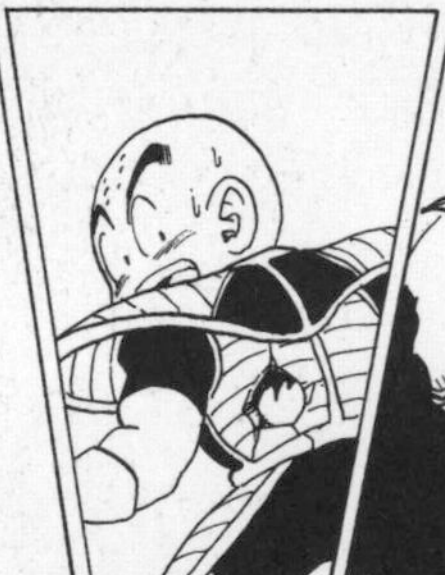
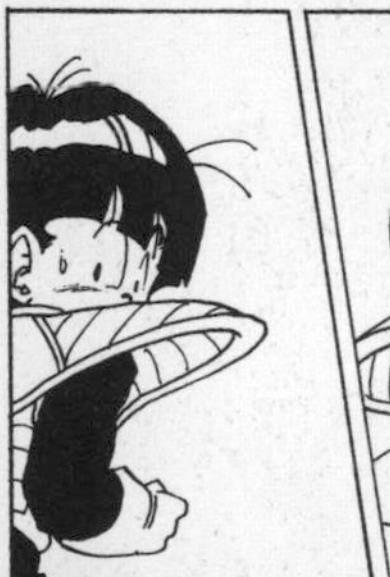

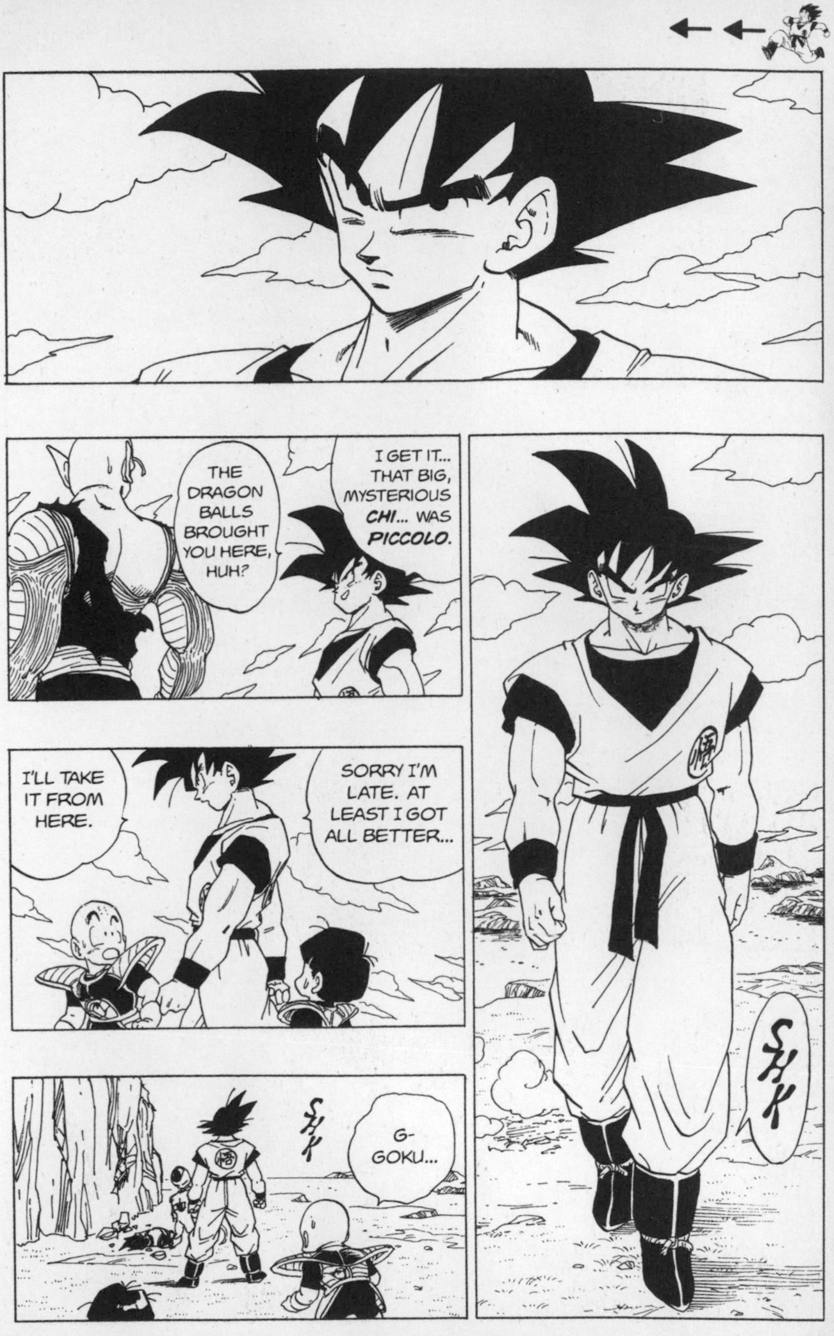
SHK
I GET IT... THAT BIG, MYSTERIOUS CHI... WAS PICCOLO.
THE DRAGON BALLS BROUGHT YOU HERE, HUH?
SORRY I'M LATE. AT LEAST I GOT ALL BETTER...
I'LL TAKE IT FROM HERE.
G-GOKU...
SHK

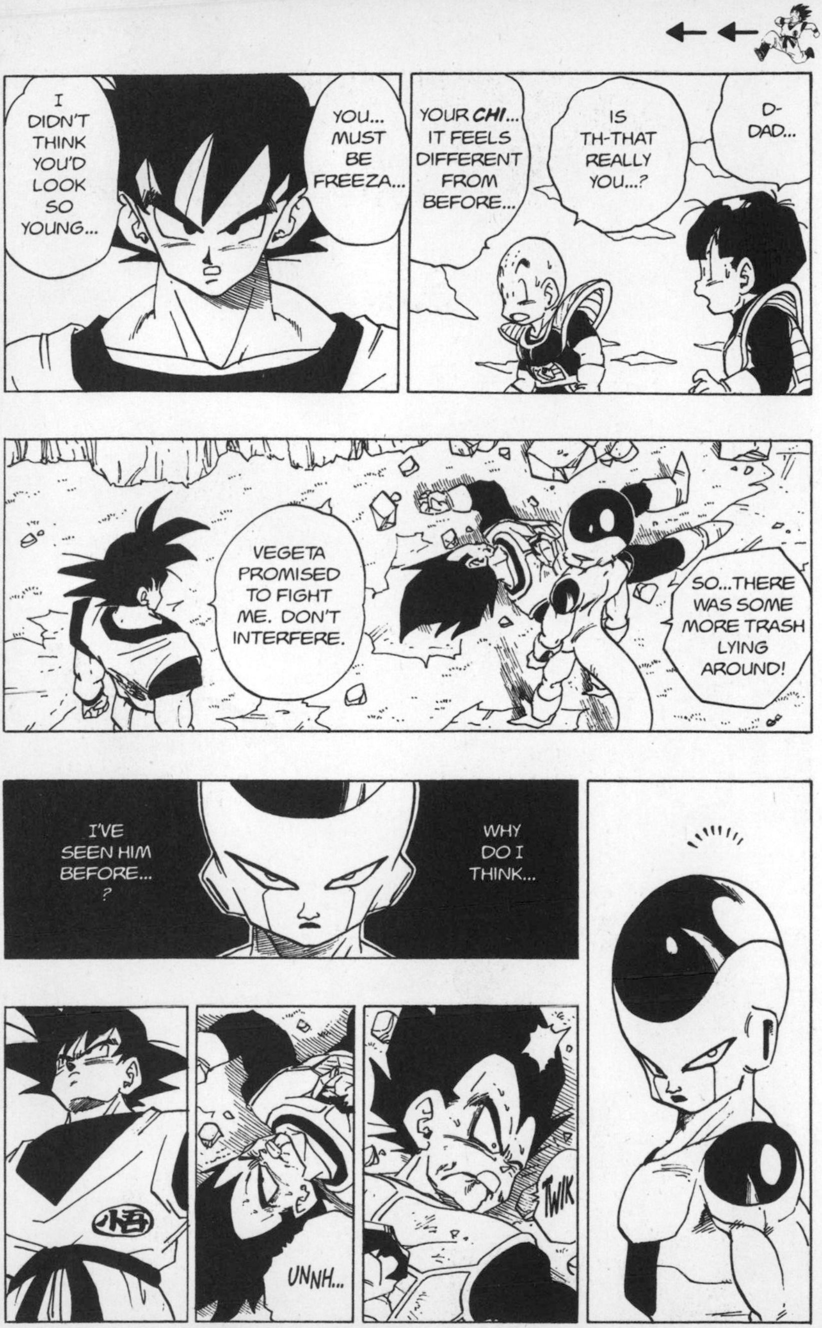
D-DAD...
IS TH-THAT REALLY YOU...?
YOUR CHI... IT FEELS DIFFERENT FROM BEFORE...
YOU... MUST BE FREEZA...
I DIDN'T THINK YOU'D LOOK SO YOUNG...
SO...THERE WAS SOME MORE TRASH LYING AROUND!
VEGETA PROMISED TO FIGHT ME. DON'T INTERFERE.
WHY DO I THINK...
I'VE SEEN HIM BEFORE... ?
TWIK
UNNH...

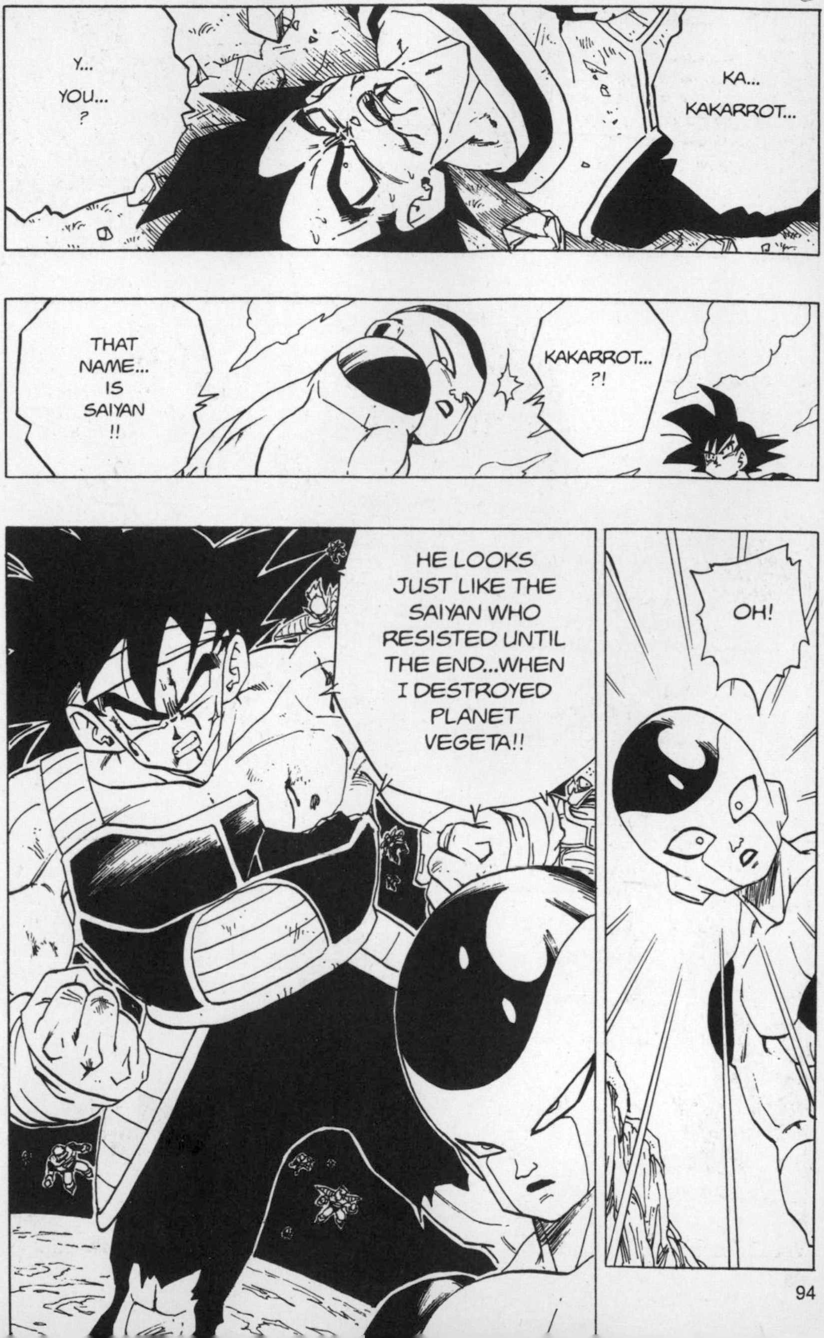
KA... KAKARROT...
Y... YOU... ?
KAKARROT... ?!
THAT NAME... IS SAIYAN !!
OH!
HE LOOKS JUST LIKE THE SAIYAN WHO RESISTED UNTIL THE END...WHEN I DESTROYED PLANET VEGETA!!

NEITHER FREEZA NOR GOKU KNEW THAT THE SAIYAN FREEZA KILLED THAT DAY WAS BURDOCK... GOKU'S FATHER

COULD HE... REALLY BE... ?!

HE'S OVERCOME... THE LIMITS OF HIS POWERS...

HE'S... NOT THE SAME KAKARROT HE WAS BEFORE...

I'VE SWORN THAT I WILL ALLOW NO SAIYAN TO LIVE!

YOU SHOULD HAVE STAYED IN HIDING!

OH YEAH ?!

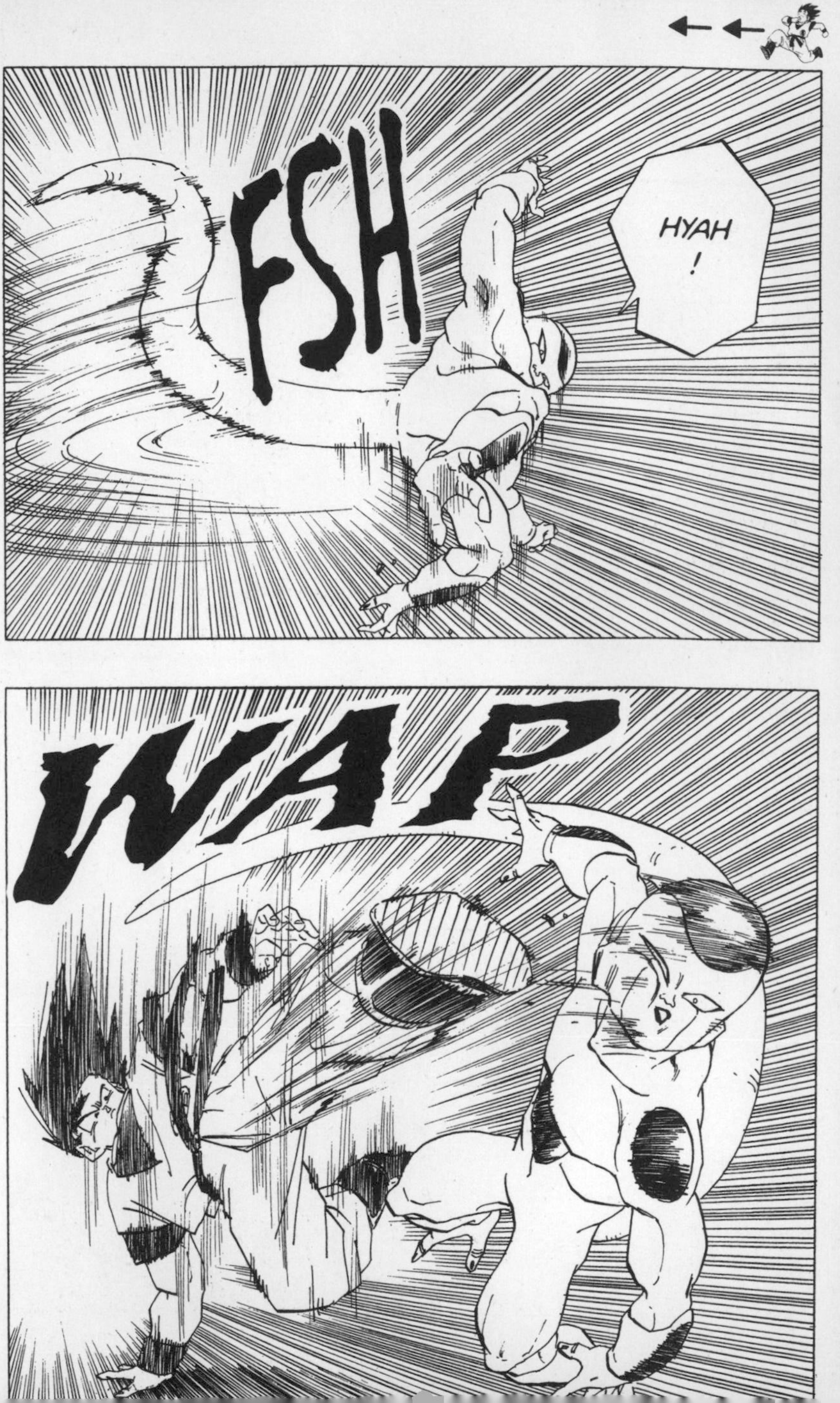
HYAH!
FSH
WAP

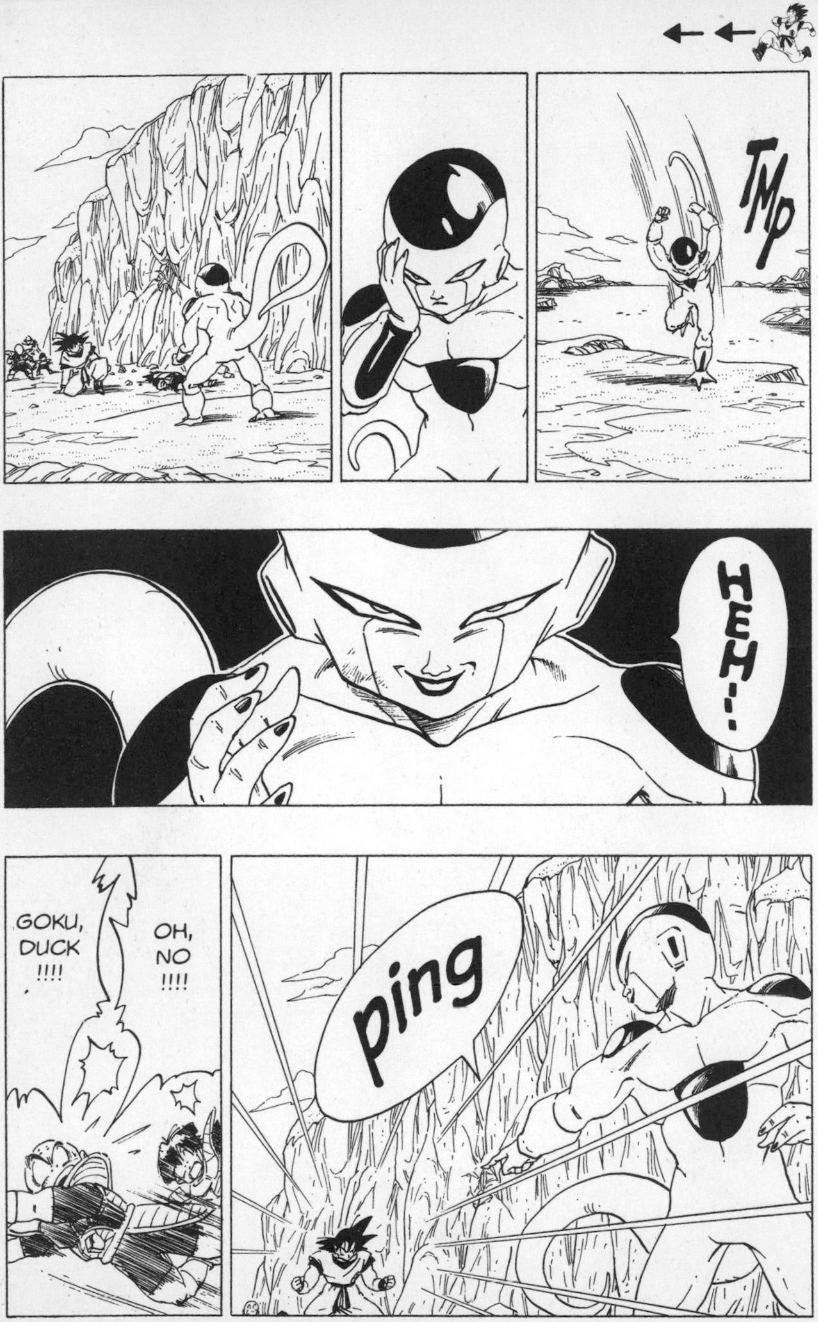
TMP
HEH...
ping
OH, NO !!!!
GOKU, DUCK !!!!

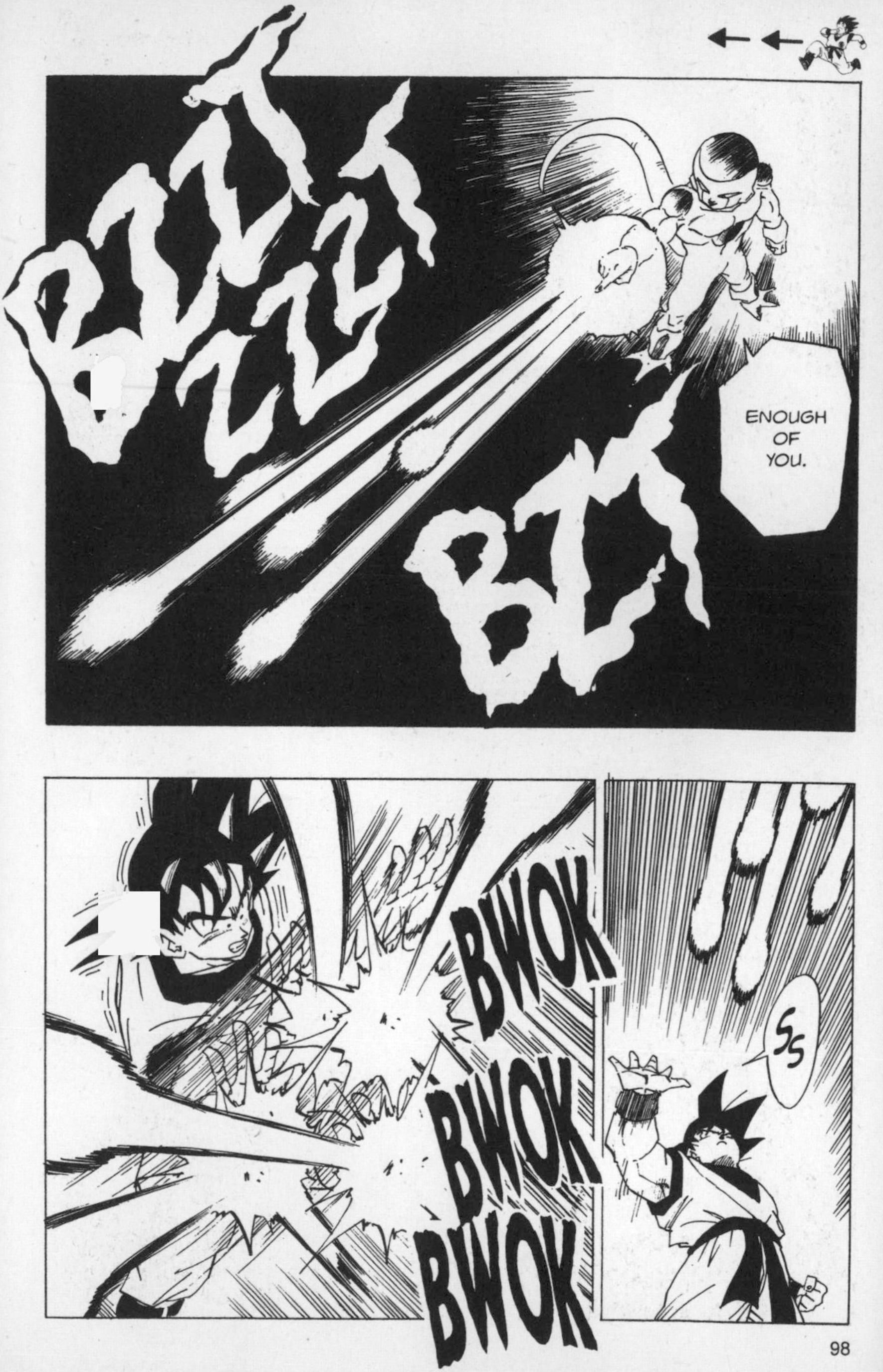
ENOUGH OF YOU.
BZZT
BZZZT
BZT
SS
BWOK
BWOK
BWOK

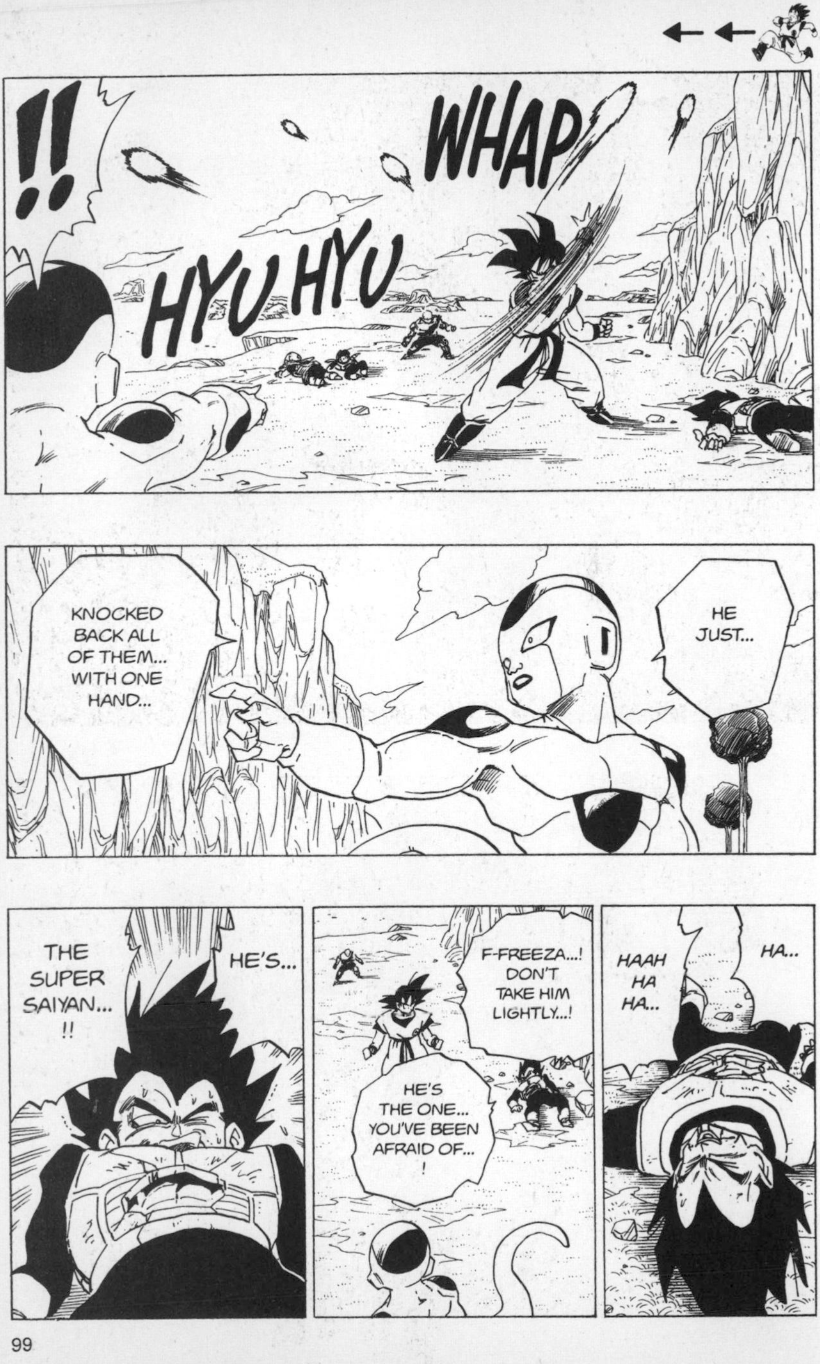
WHAP
!!
HYU HYU
HE JUST...
KNOCKED BACK ALL OF THEM... WITH ONE HAND...
HA...
HAAH HA HA...
F-FREEZA...! DON'T TAKE HIM LIGHTLY...!
HE'S THE ONE... YOU'VE BEEN AFRAID OF... !
HE'S...
THE SUPER SAIYAN... !!

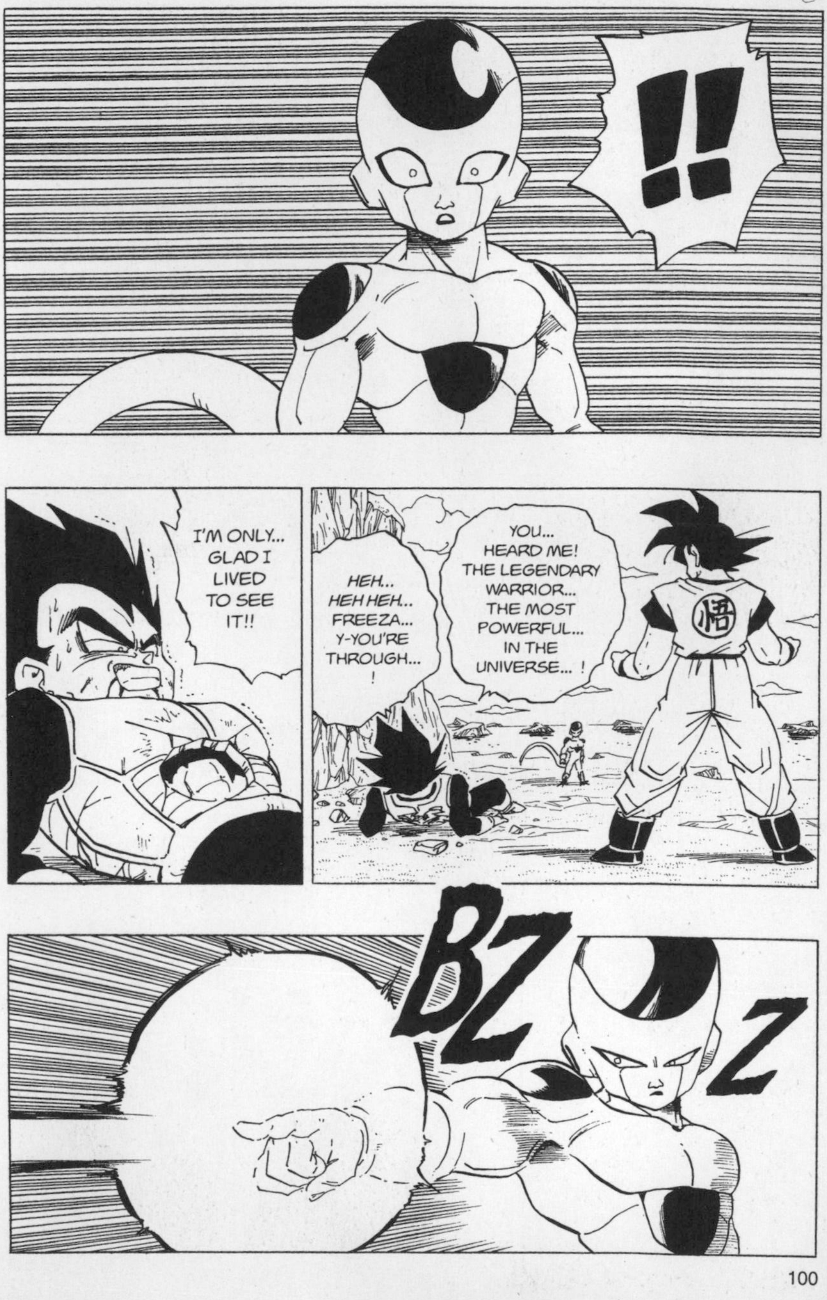
!!
YOU... HEARD ME! THE LEGENDARY WARRIOR... THE MOST POWERFUL... IN THE UNIVERSE... !
HEH... HEH HEH... FREEZA... Y-YOU'RE THROUGH... !
I'M ONLY... GLAD I LIVED TO SEE IT!!
BZZ

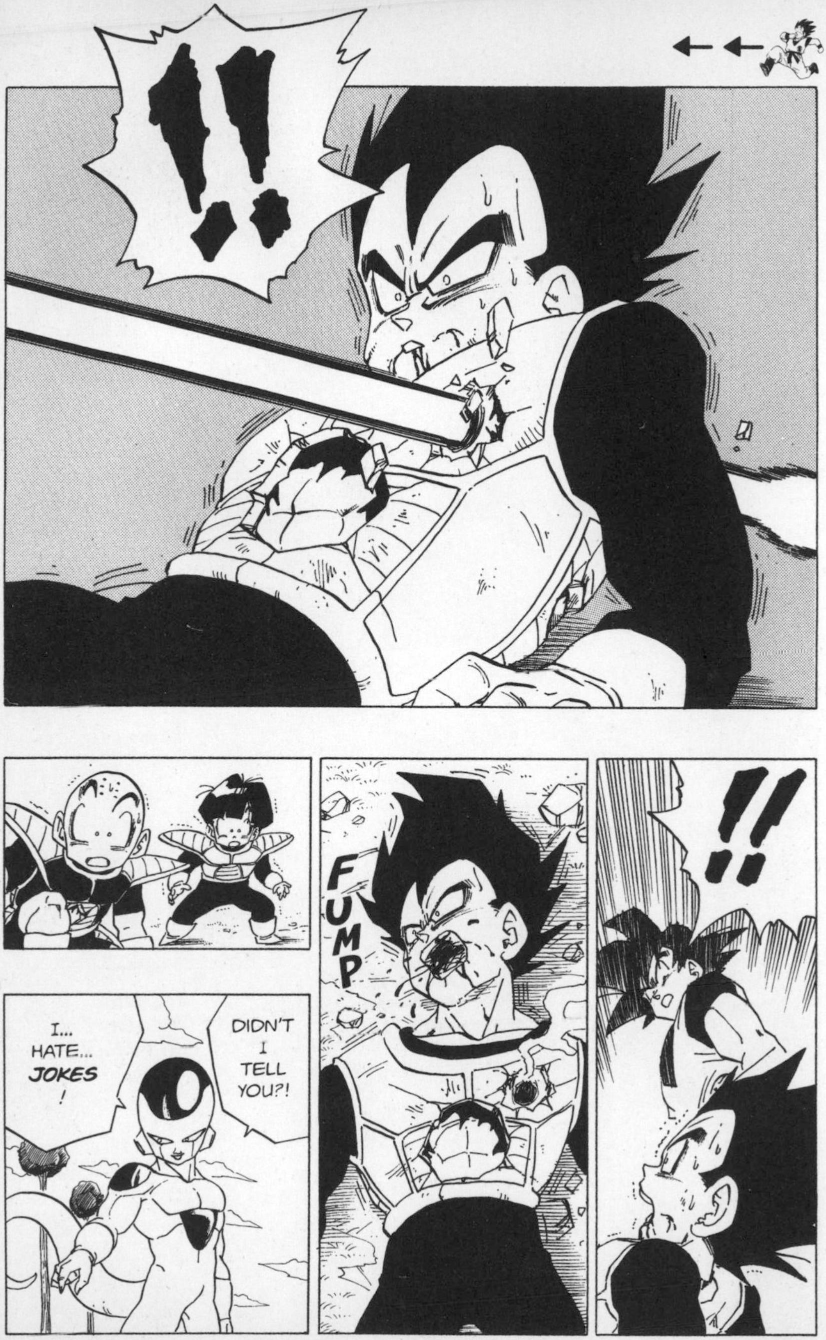
!!
!!
FUMP
DIDN'T I TELL YOU?!
I... HATE... JOKES!

NEXT: Vegeta Dies!!

DBZ:114 • The Death of Vegeta

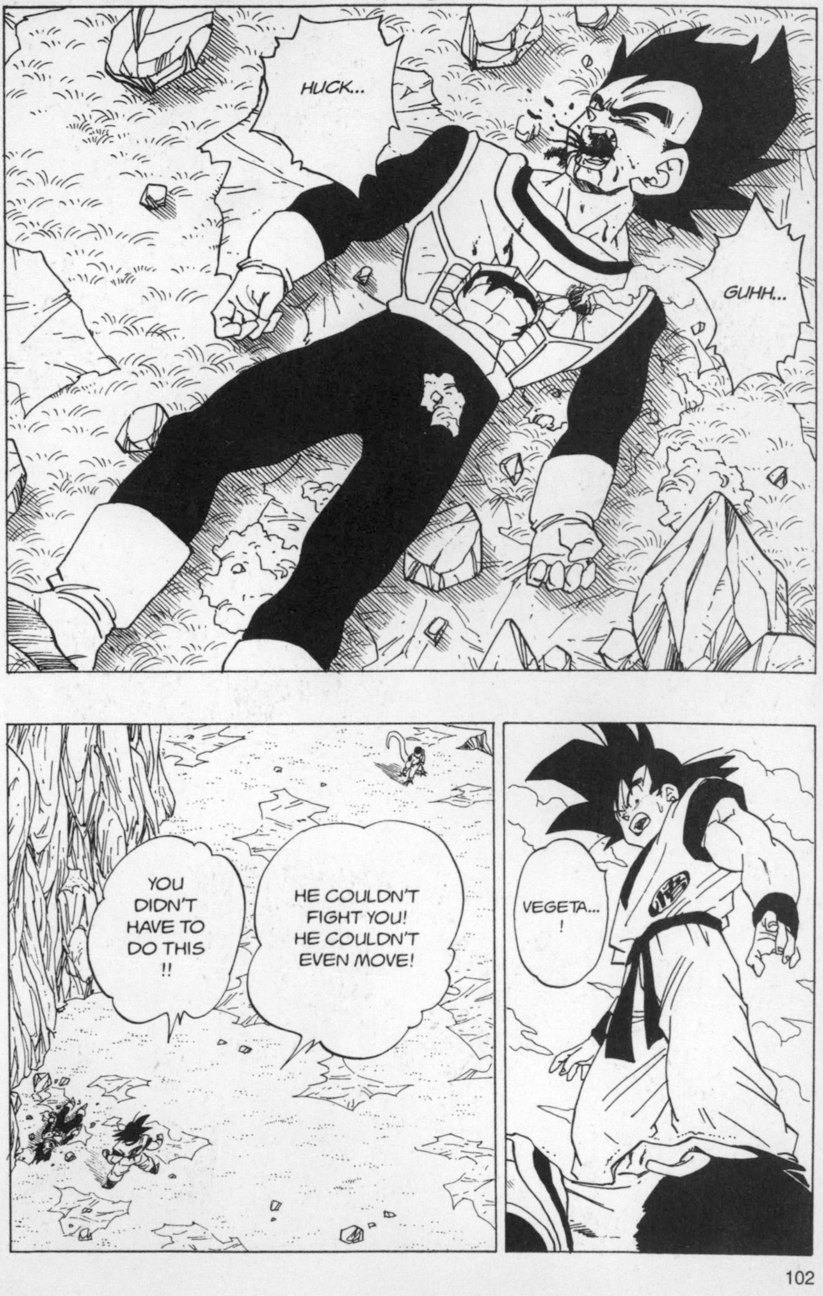
HUCK...
GUHH...
VEGETA... !
HE COULDN'T FIGHT YOU! HE COULDN'T EVEN MOVE!
YOU DIDN'T HAVE TO DO THIS !!

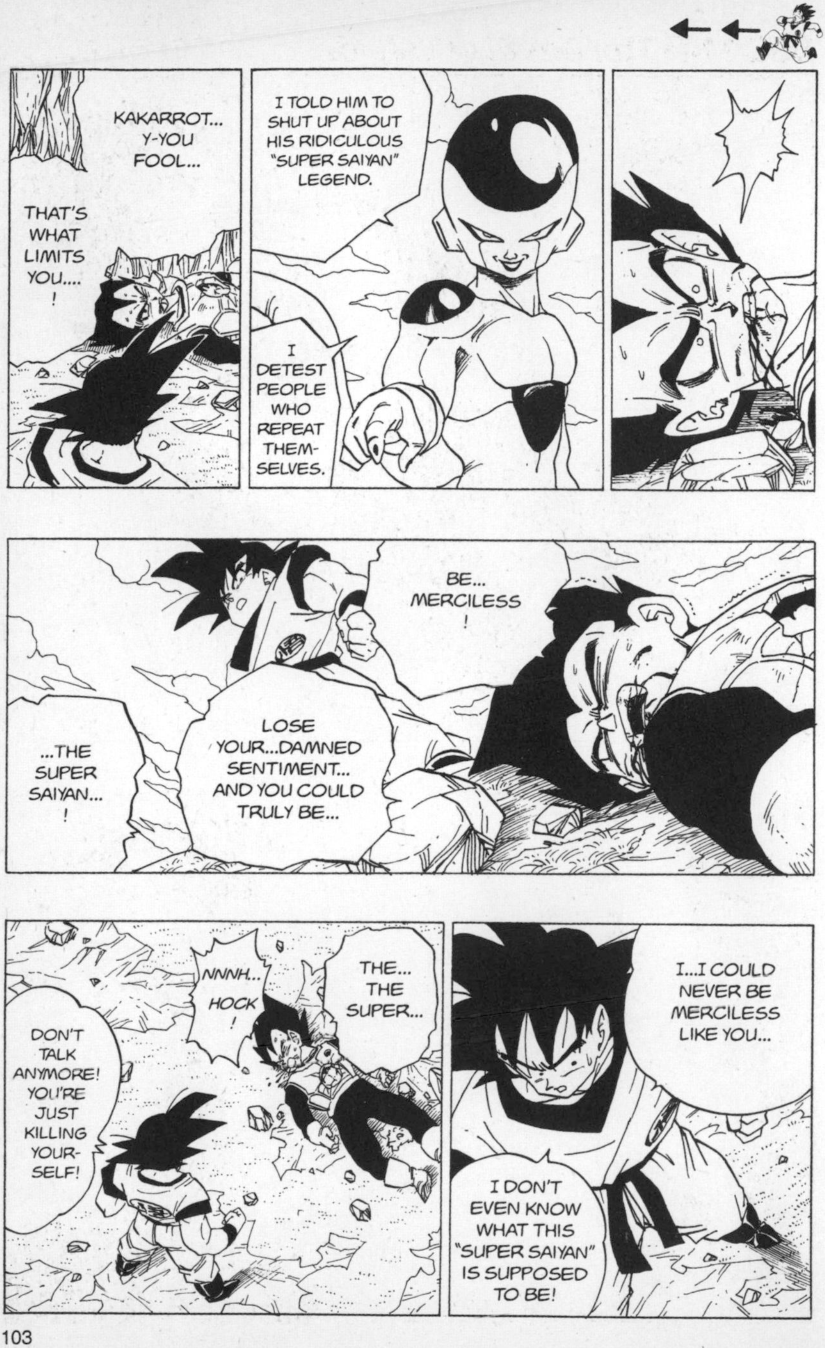
I TOLD HIM TO SHUT UP ABOUT HIS RIDICULOUS "SUPER SAIYAN" LEGEND.
I DETEST PEOPLE WHO REPEAT THEM-SELVES.
KAKARROT... Y-YOU FOOL...
THAT'S WHAT LIMITS YOU....!
BE... MERCILESS!
LOSE YOUR...DAMNED SENTIMENT... AND YOU COULD TRULY BE...
...THE SUPER SAIYAN...!
I...I COULD NEVER BE MERCILESS LIKE YOU...
I DON'T EVEN KNOW WHAT THIS "SUPER SAIYAN" IS SUPPOSED TO BE!
THE... THE SUPER...
NNNH... HOCK!
DON'T TALK ANYMORE! YOU'RE JUST KILLING YOUR-SELF!

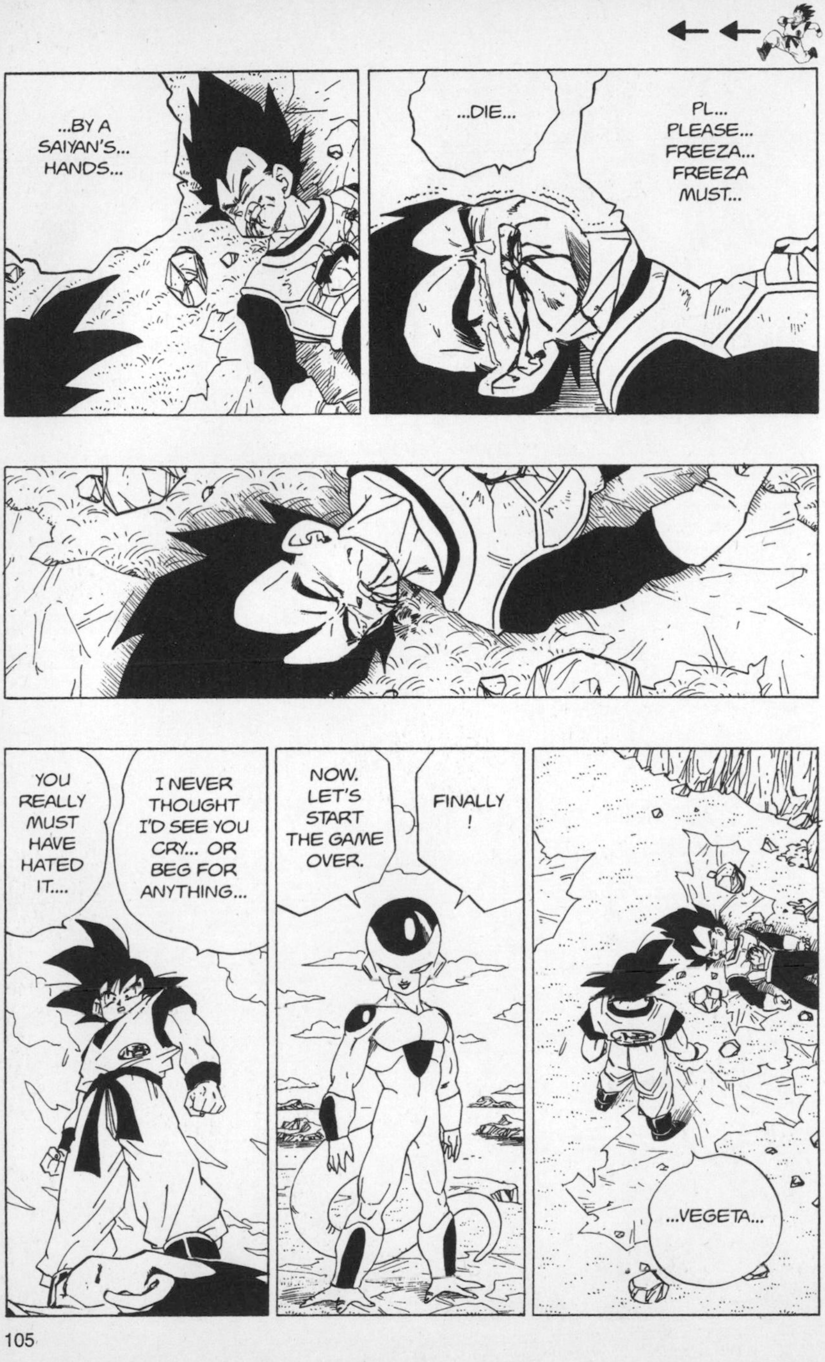

PL... PLEASE... FREEZA... FREEZA MUST...
...DIE...
...BY A SAIYAN'S... HANDS...
...VEGETA...
FINALLY!
NOW. LET'S START THE GAME OVER.
I NEVER THOUGHT I'D SEE YOU CRY... OR BEG FOR ANYTHING...
YOU REALLY MUST HAVE HATED IT....

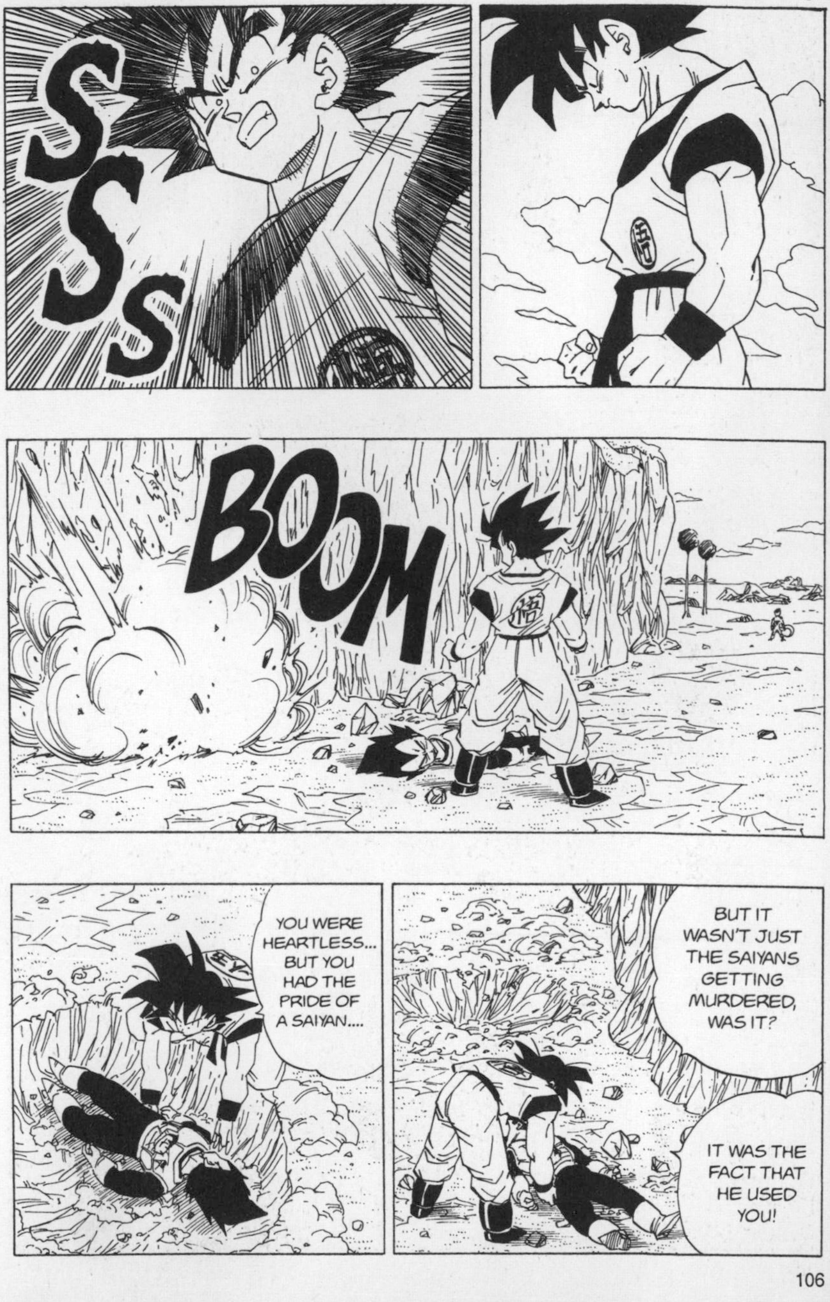
SSS
BOOM
BUT IT WASN'T JUST THE SAIYANS GETTING MURDERED, WAS IT?
IT WAS THE FACT THAT HE USED YOU!
YOU WERE HEARTLESS... BUT YOU HAD THE PRIDE OF A SAIYAN....

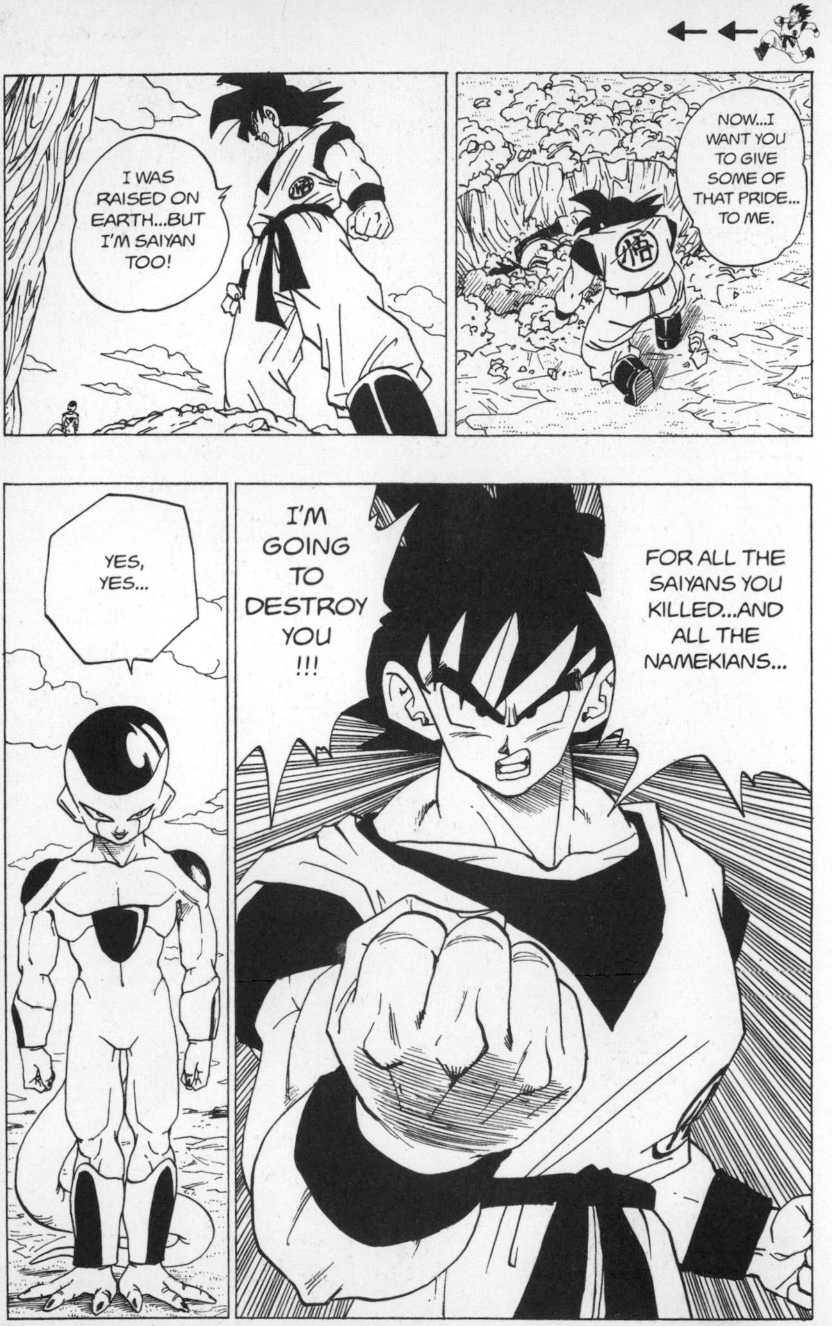
NOW...I WANT YOU TO GIVE SOME OF THAT PRIDE... TO ME.
I WAS RAISED ON EARTH...BUT I'M SAIYAN TOO!
FOR ALL THE SAIYANS YOU KILLED...AND ALL THE NAMEKIANS...
I'M GOING TO DESTROY YOU !!!
YES, YES...

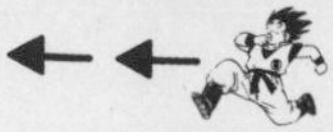

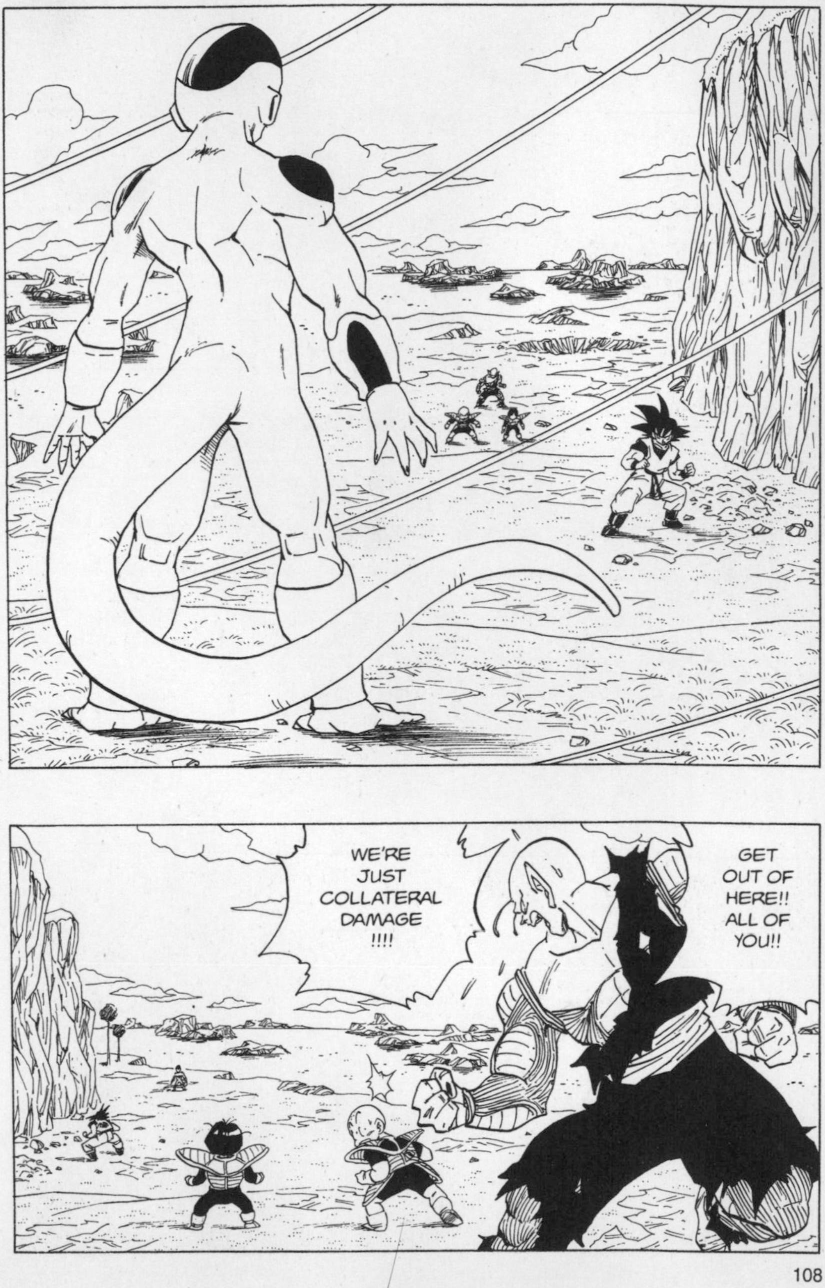
GET OUT OF HERE!! ALL OF YOU!!
WE'RE JUST COLLATERAL DAMAGE !!!!

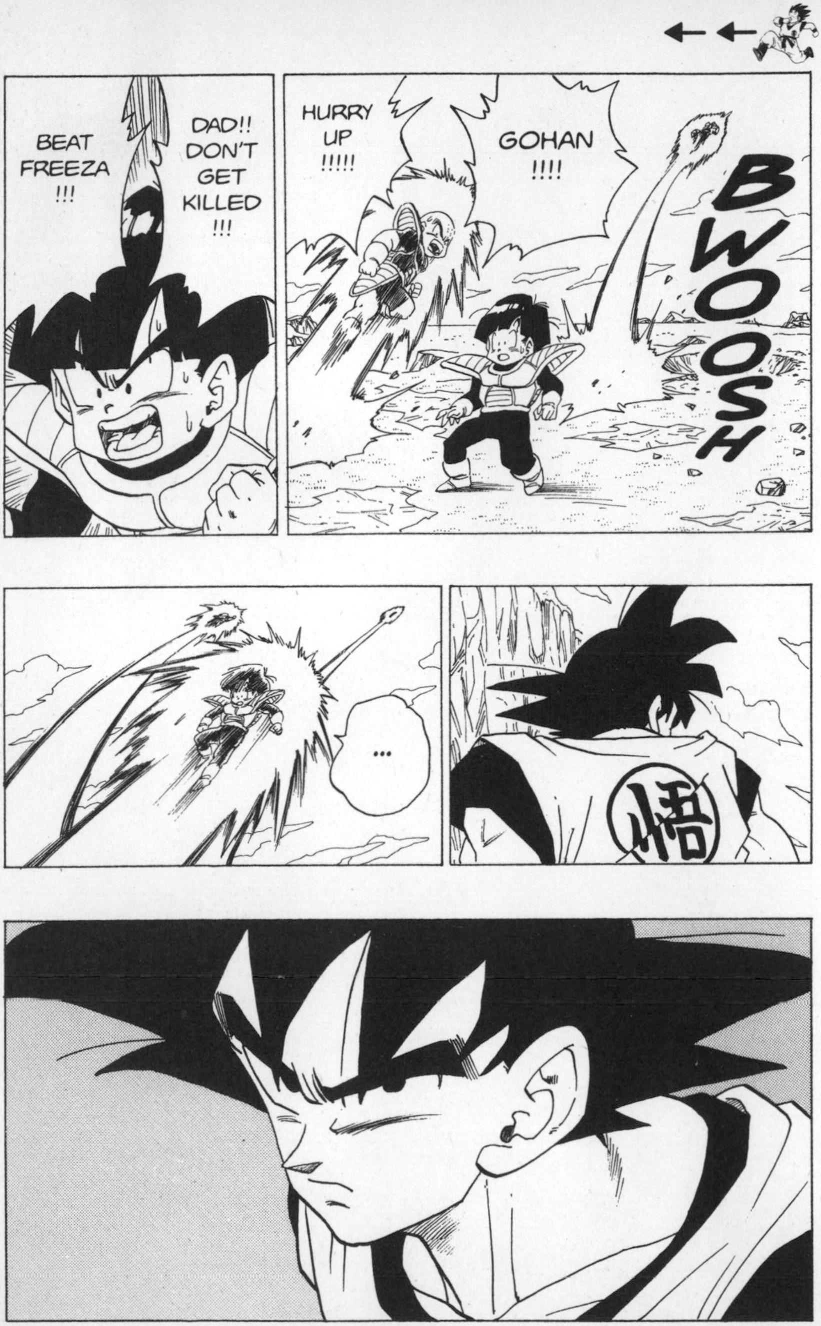
BWOOSH
GOHAN!!!!
HURRY UP!!!!!
DAD!! DON'T GET KILLED!!!
BEAT FREEZA!!!
...

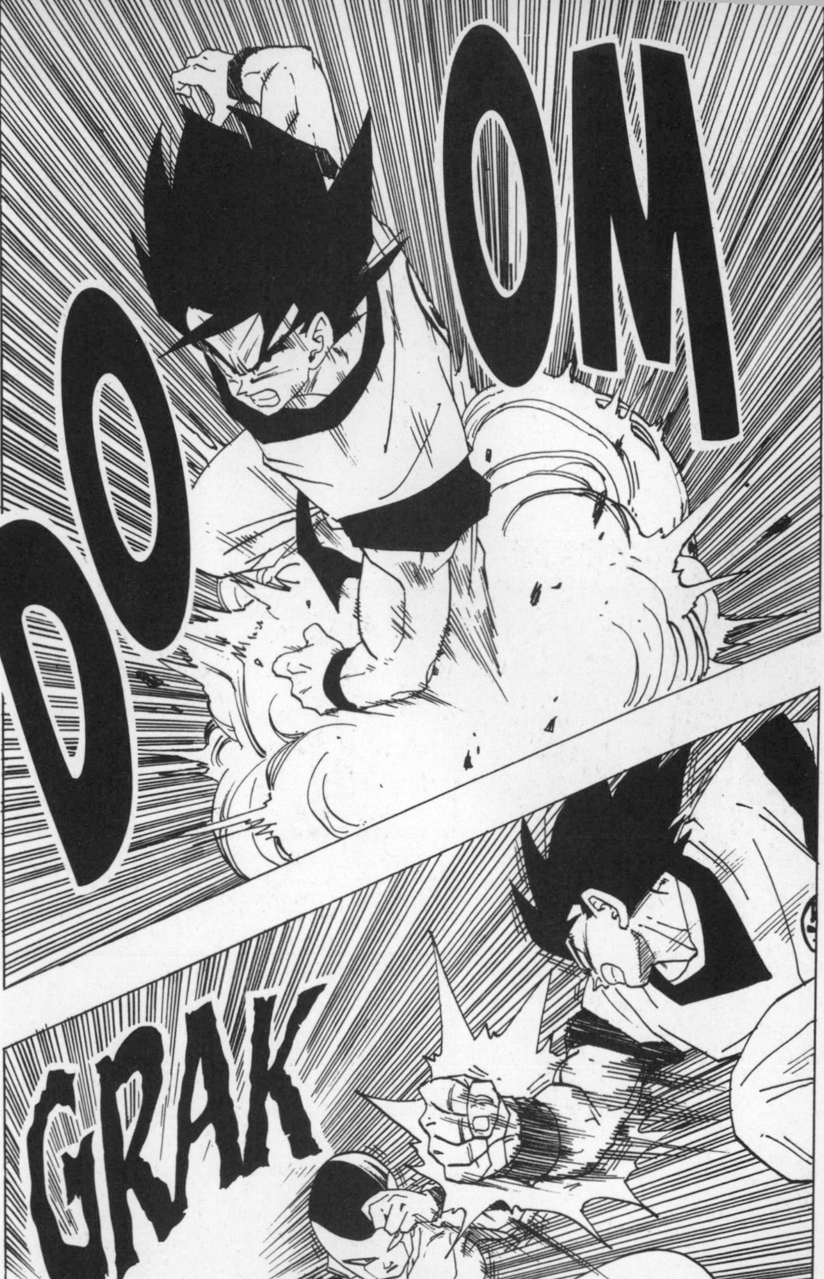
DOOM
GRAK

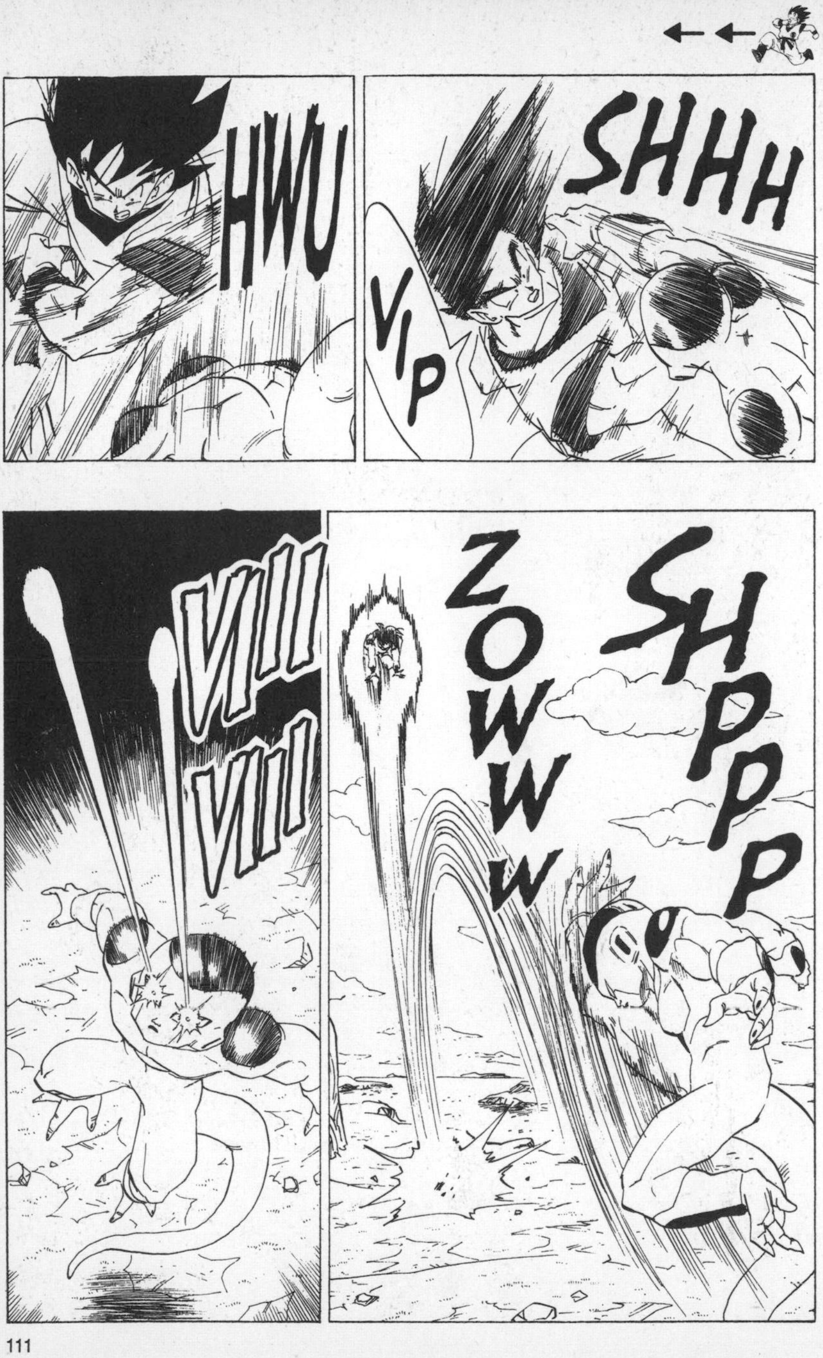
SHHH
VIP
HWU
SHPPP
ZOWWW
VIII
VIII

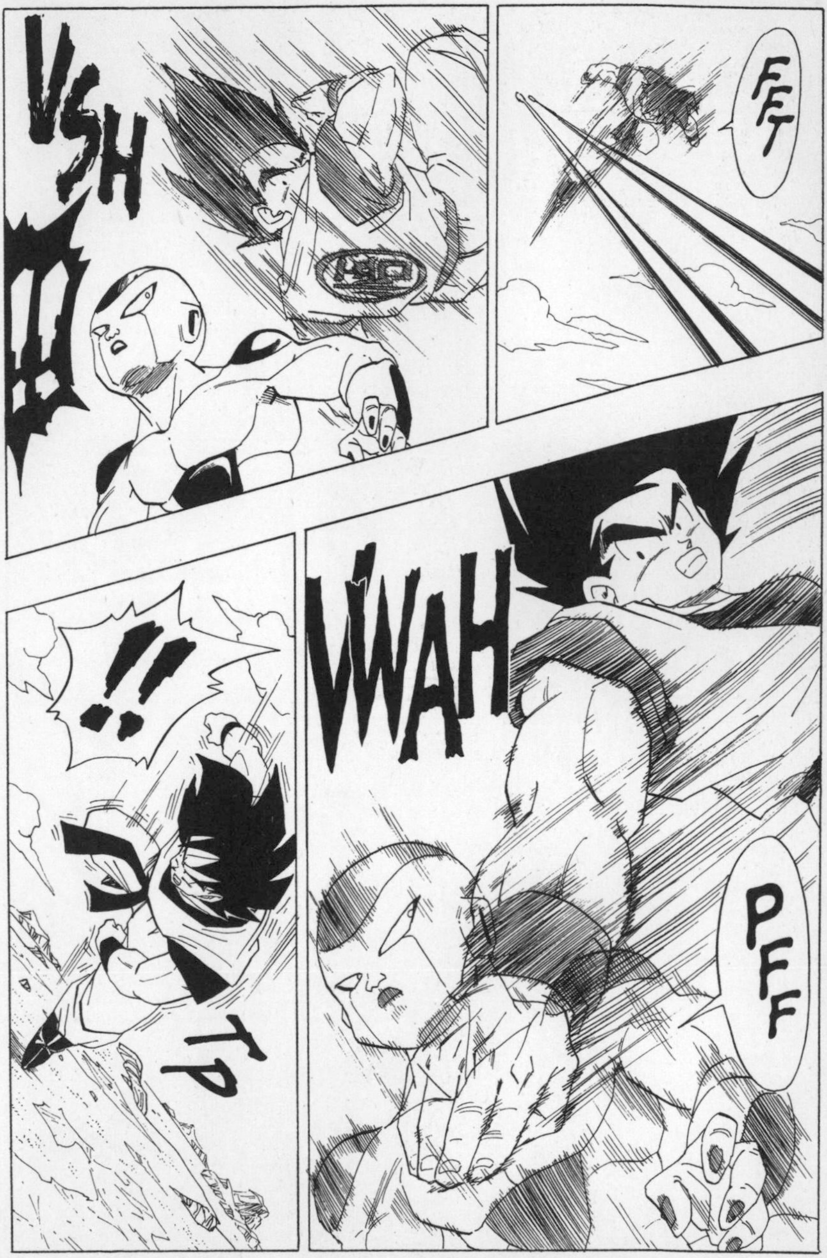
FFT
VSH
VWAH
PFF
!!
TP

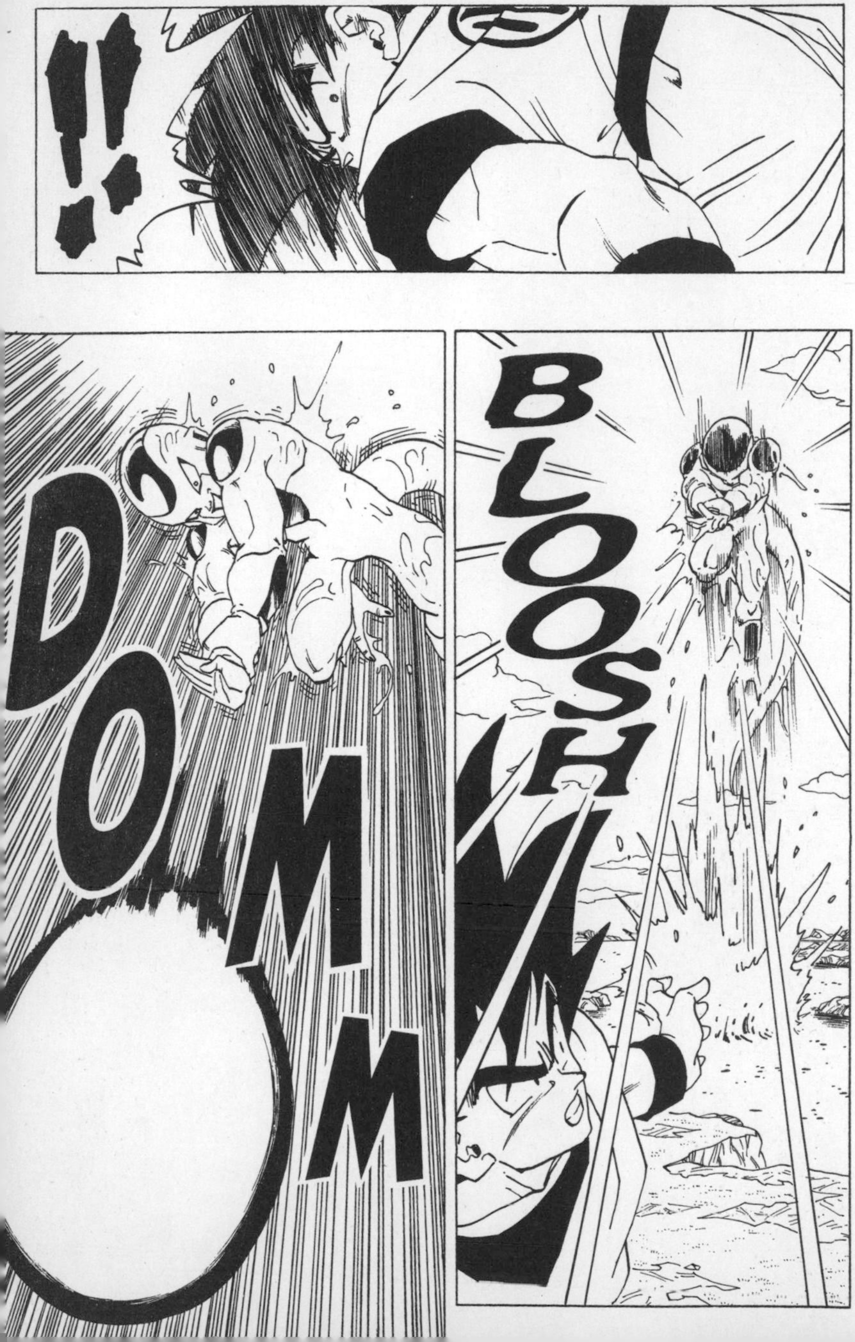
!!
BLOOSH
DOOMMM

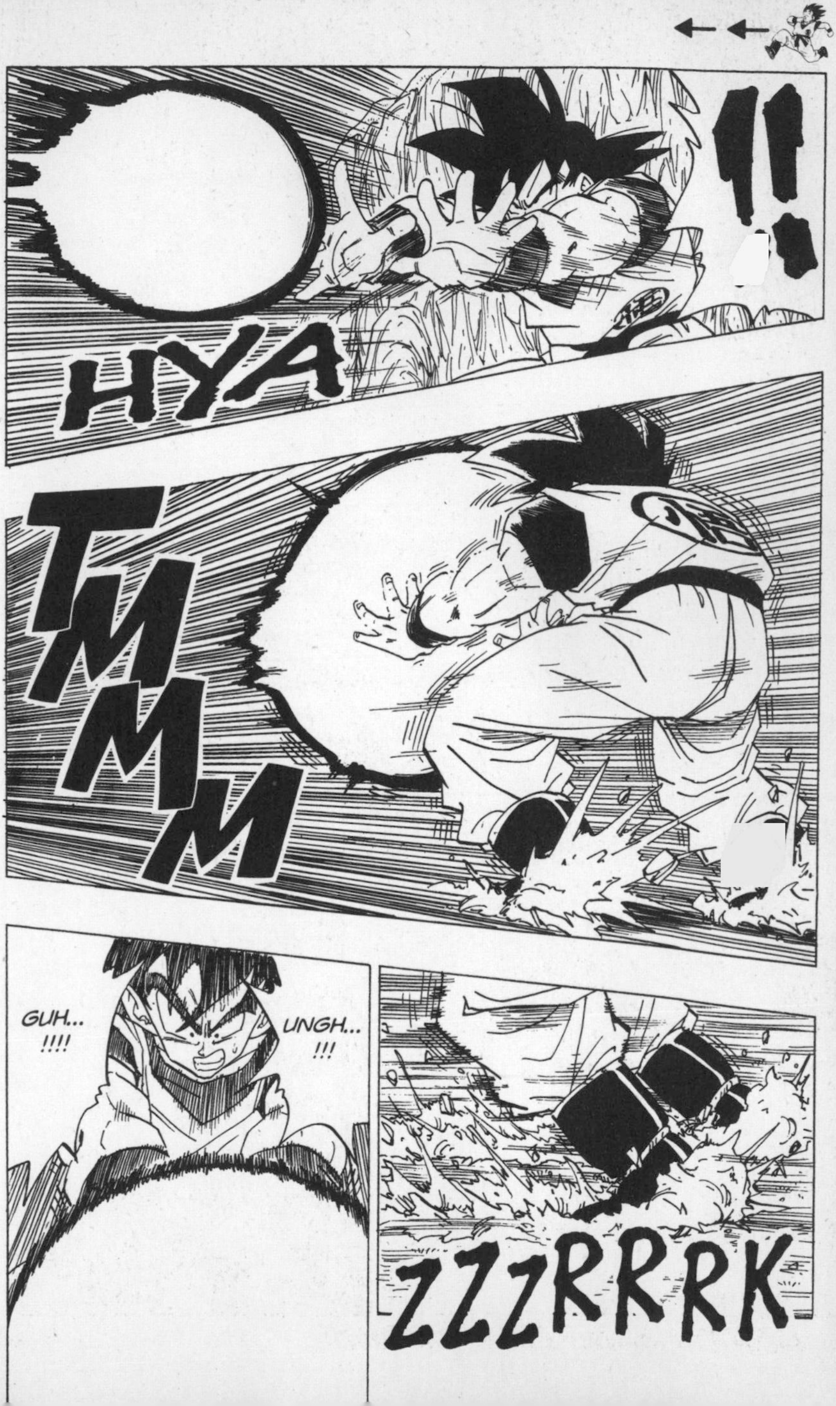
!!
HYA
TMMM
UNGH... !!!
GUH... !!!!
ZZZRRRK

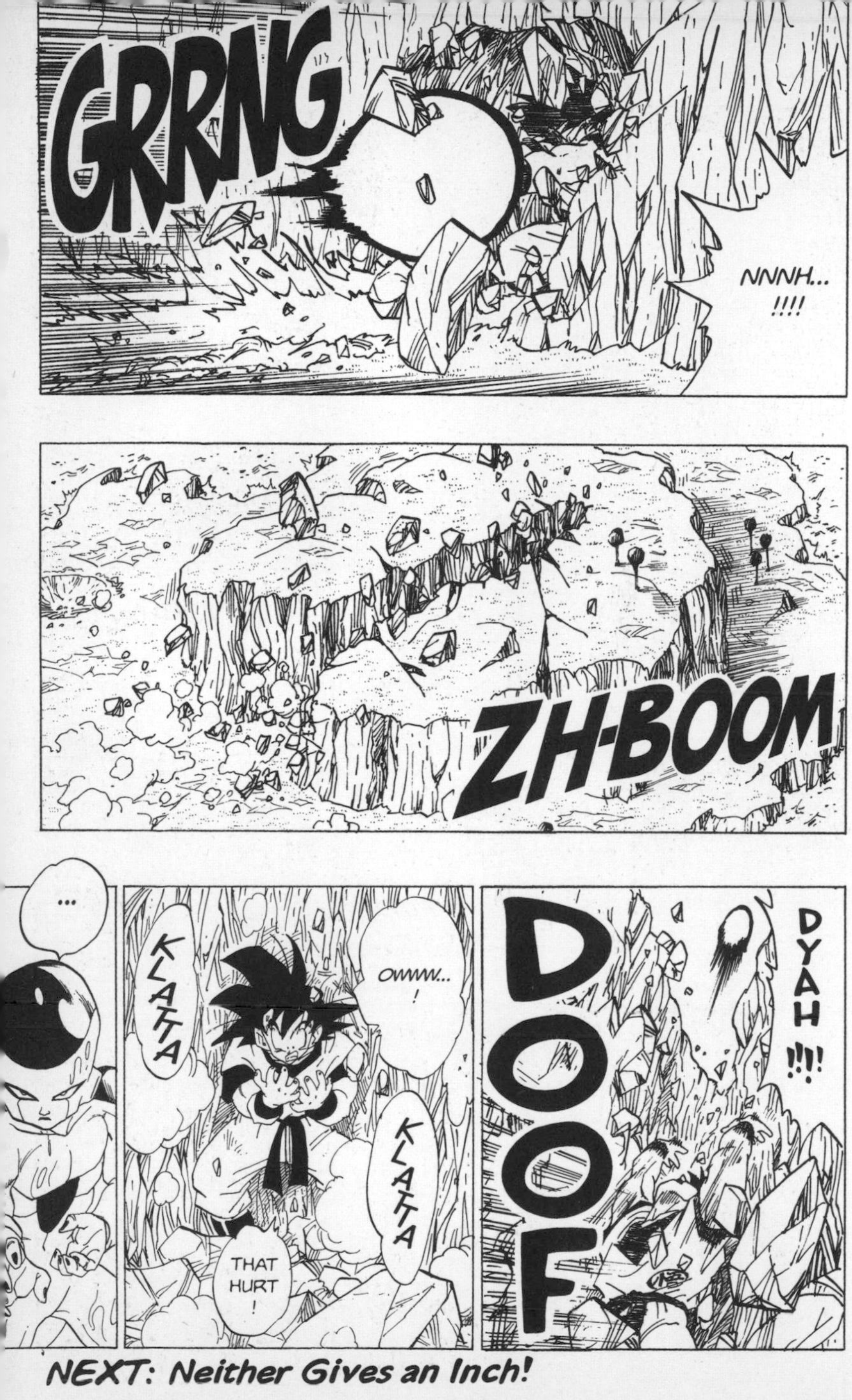
NNNH... !!!!
GRRNG
ZH-BOOM
DYAH !!!!
DOOF
OWWW... !
KLATTA
KLATTA
THAT HURT !
...

NEXT: Neither Gives an Inch!

DBZ:115 • Underwater Battle

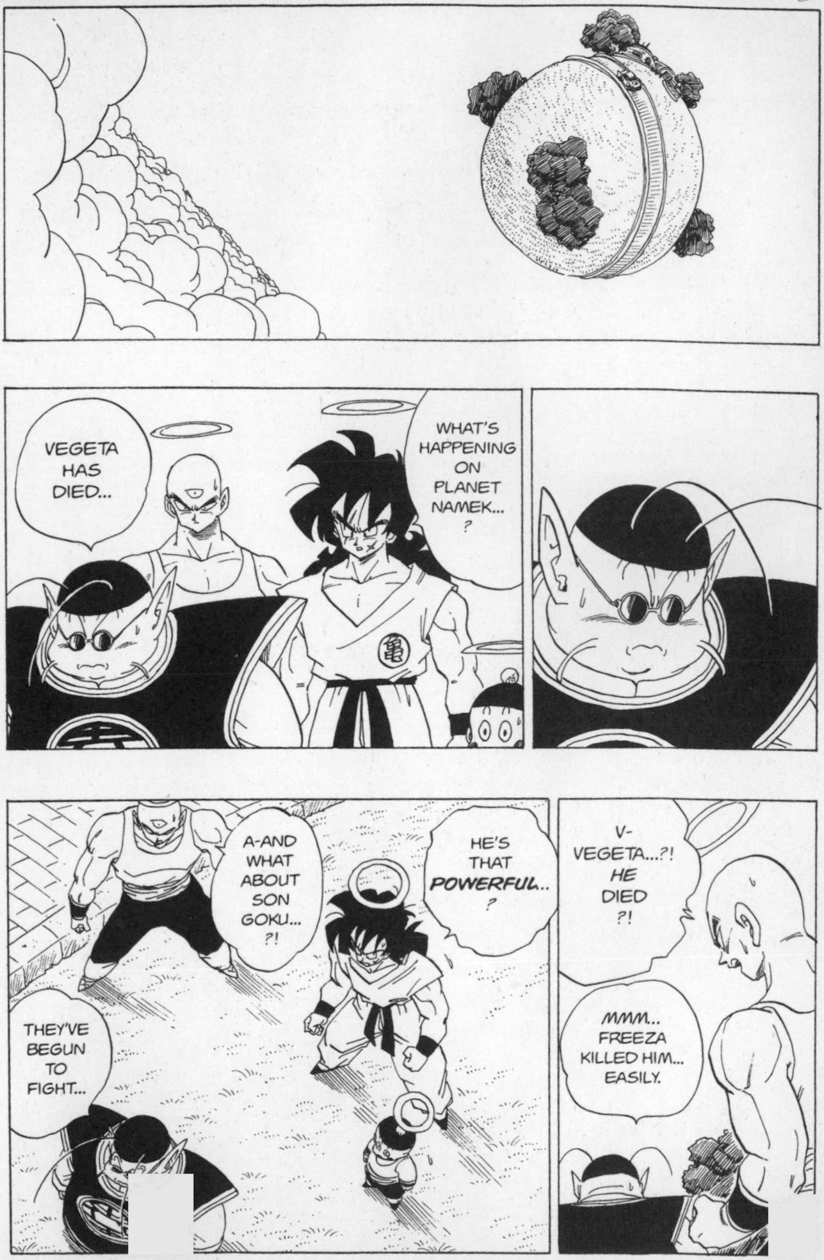
WHAT'S HAPPENING ON PLANET NAMEK...?
VEGETA HAS DIED...
V-VEGETA...?! HE DIED ?!
MMM... FREEZA KILLED HIM... EASILY.
HE'S THAT **POWERFUL**...?
A-AND WHAT ABOUT SON GOKU...?!
THEY'VE BEGUN TO FIGHT...

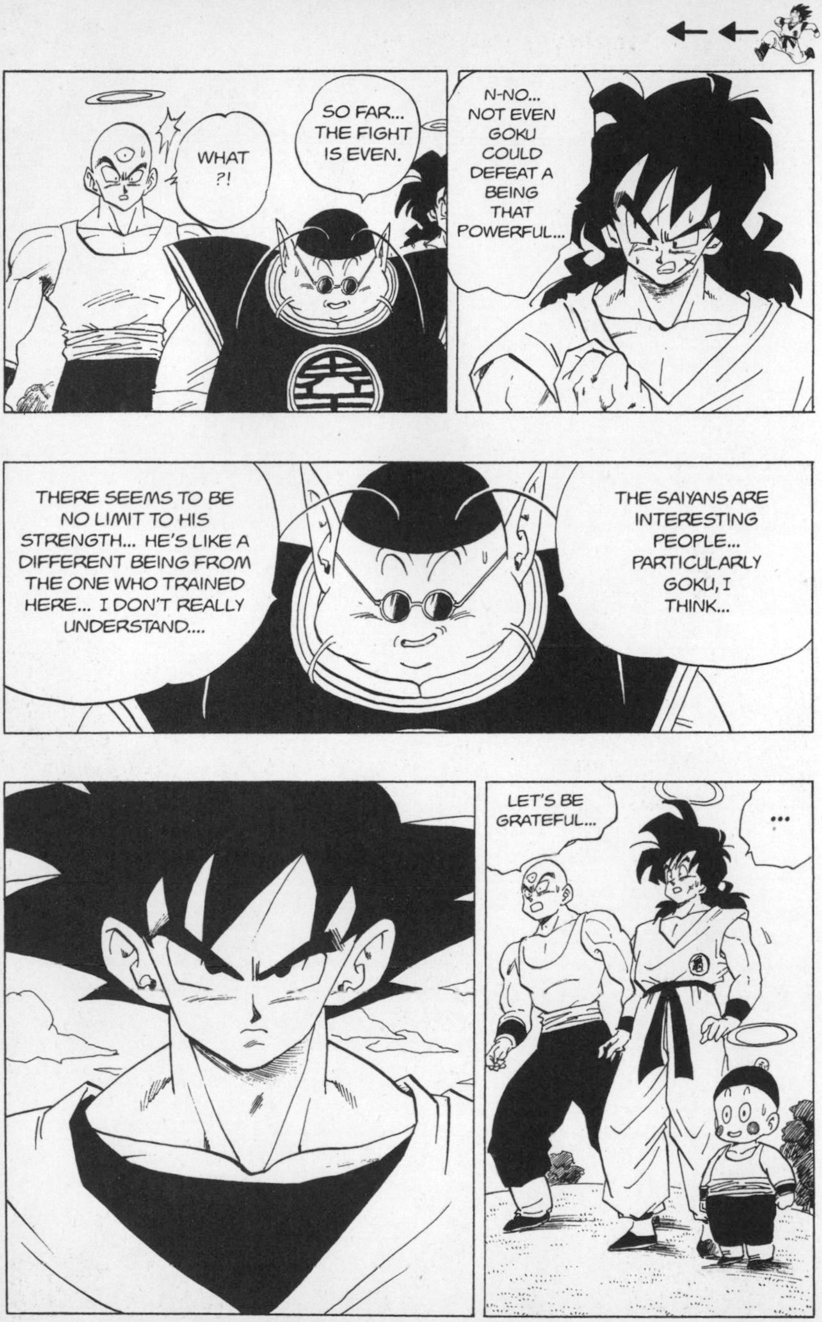
N-NO... NOT EVEN GOKU COULD DEFEAT A BEING THAT POWERFUL...
SO FAR... THE FIGHT IS EVEN.
WHAT ?!
THE SAIYANS ARE INTERESTING PEOPLE... PARTICULARLY GOKU, I THINK...
THERE SEEMS TO BE NO LIMIT TO HIS STRENGTH... HE'S LIKE A DIFFERENT BEING FROM THE ONE WHO TRAINED HERE... I DON'T REALLY UNDERSTAND....
...
LET'S BE GRATEFUL...

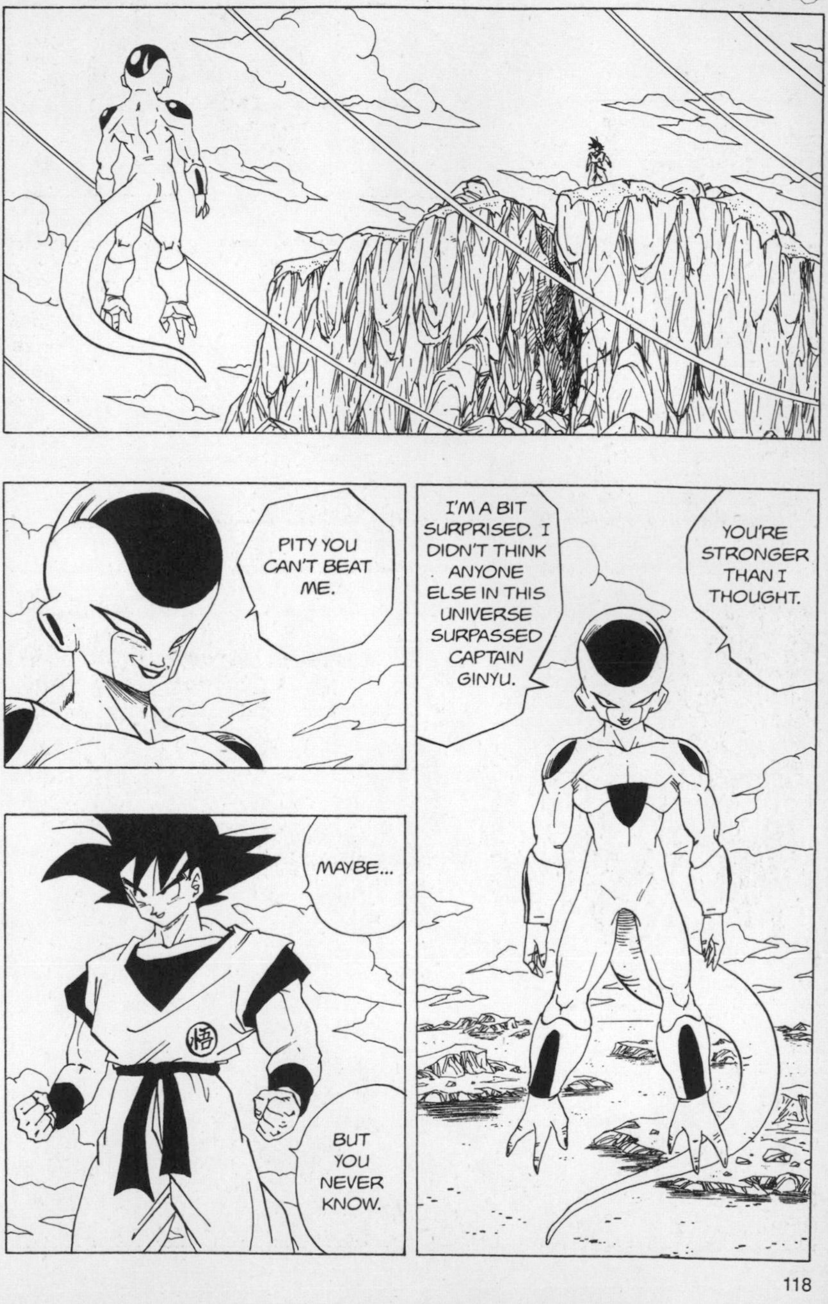
YOU'RE STRONGER THAN I THOUGHT.
I'M A BIT SURPRISED. I DIDN'T THINK ANYONE ELSE IN THIS UNIVERSE SURPASSED CAPTAIN GINYU.
PITY YOU CAN'T BEAT ME.
MAYBE...
BUT YOU NEVER KNOW.

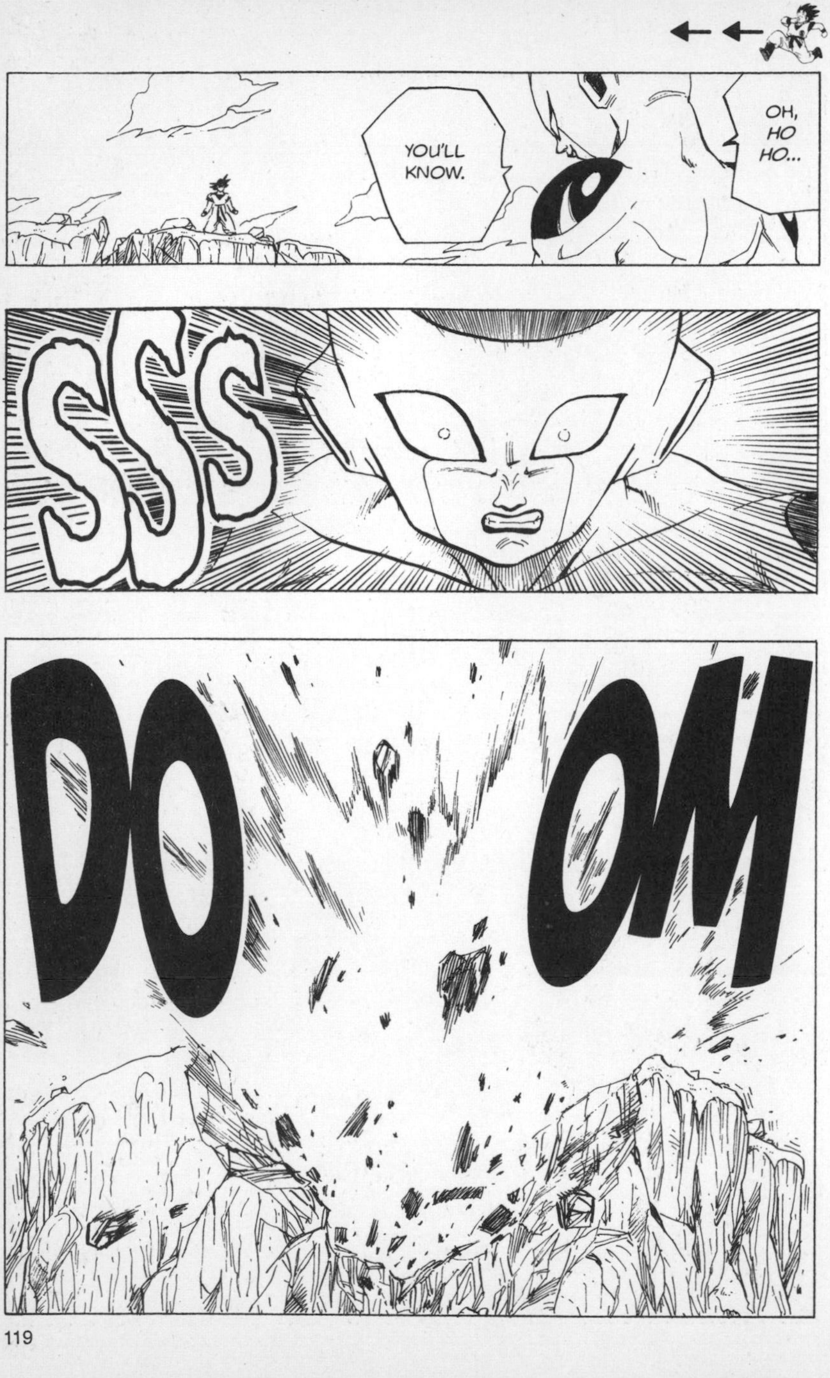
OH, HO HO...
YOU'LL KNOW.
SSS
DOOM

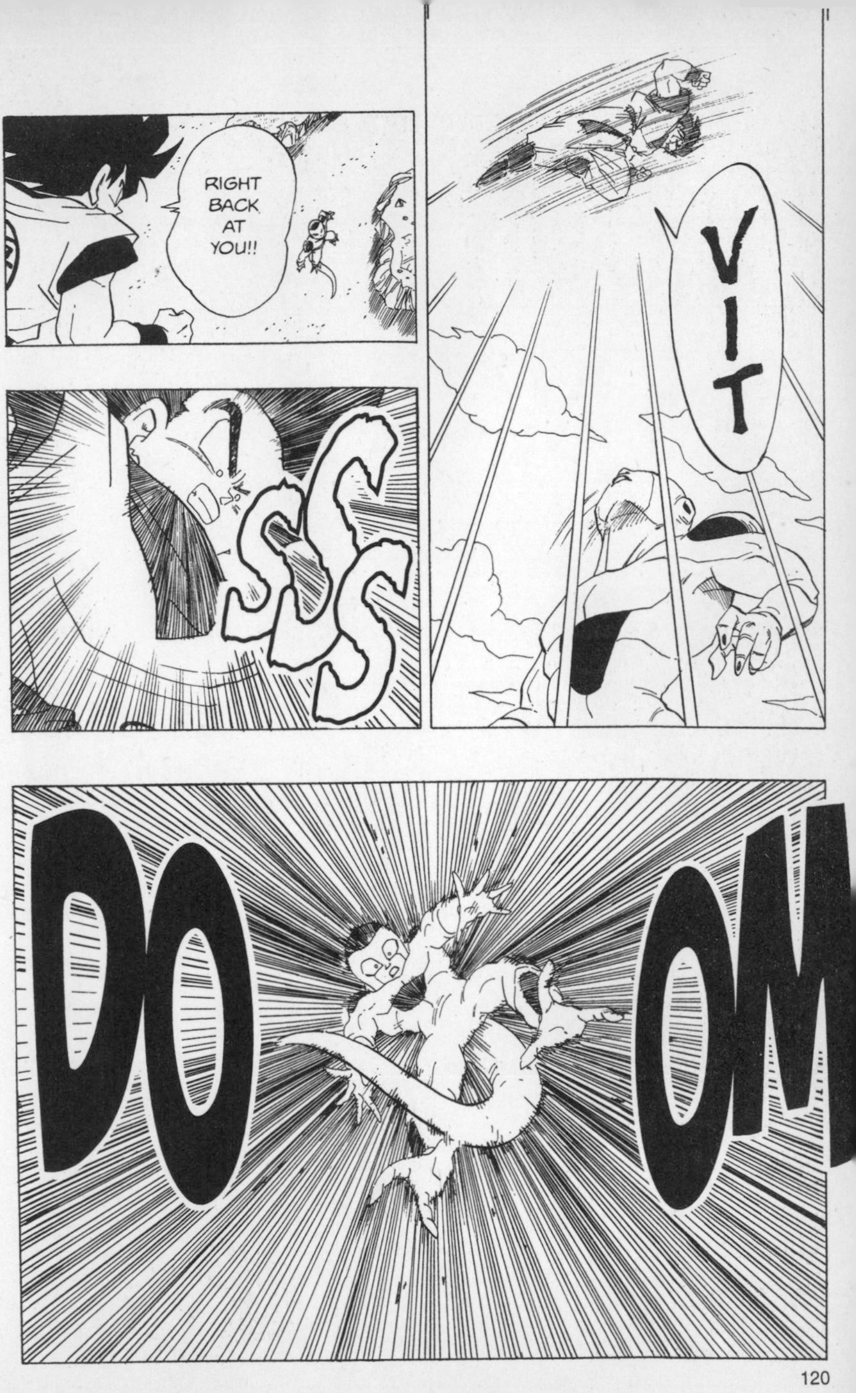
VIT
RIGHT BACK AT YOU!!
SSS
DOOM

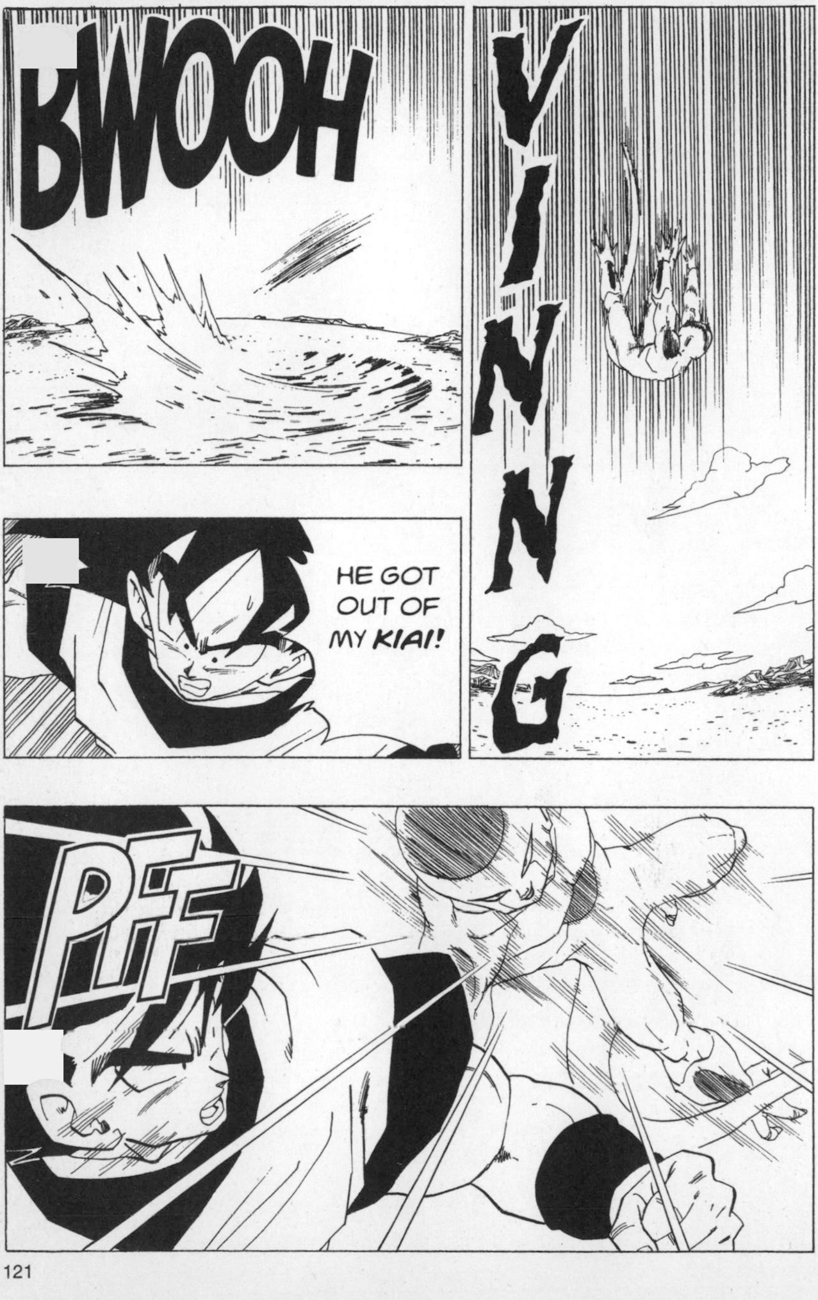
VIINNG
BWOOH
HE GOT OUT OF MY KIAI!
PIF

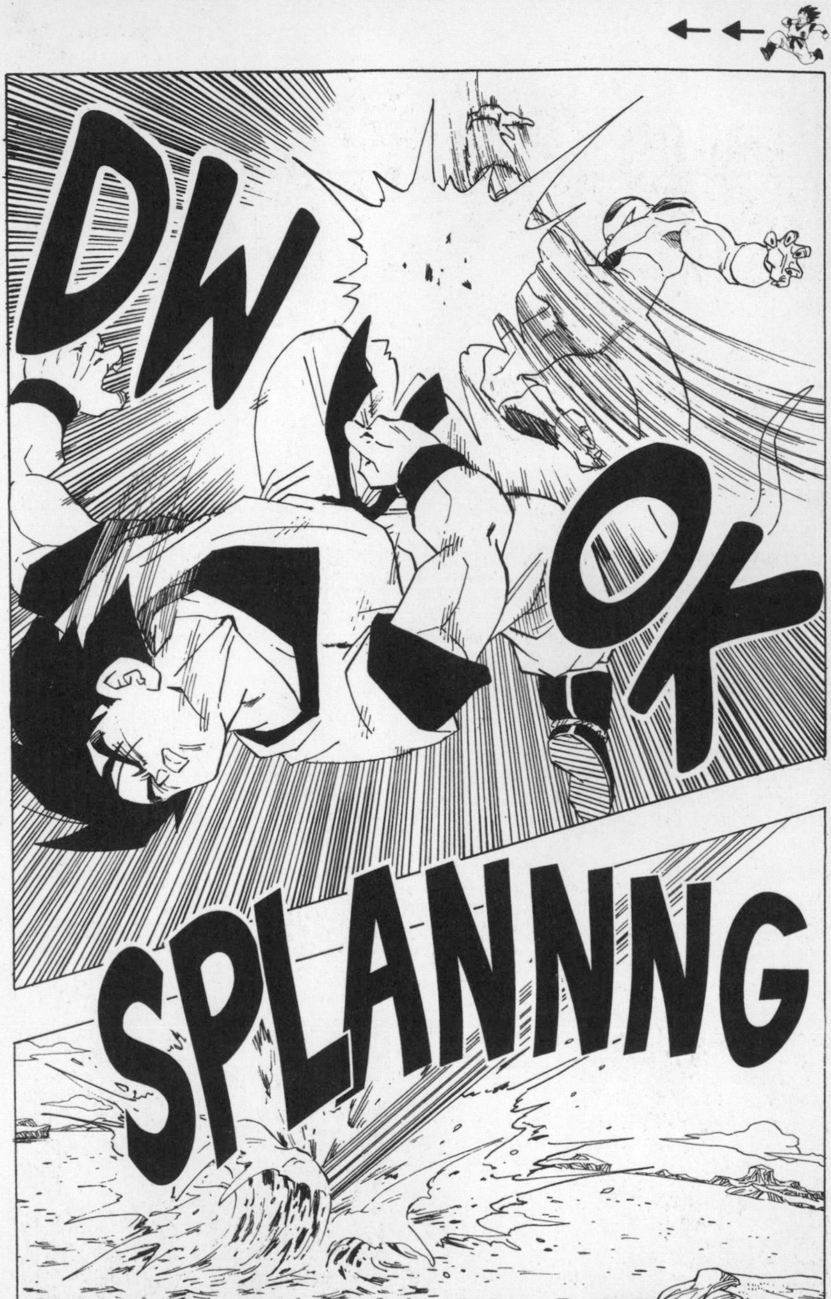
DWOK
SPLANNNG

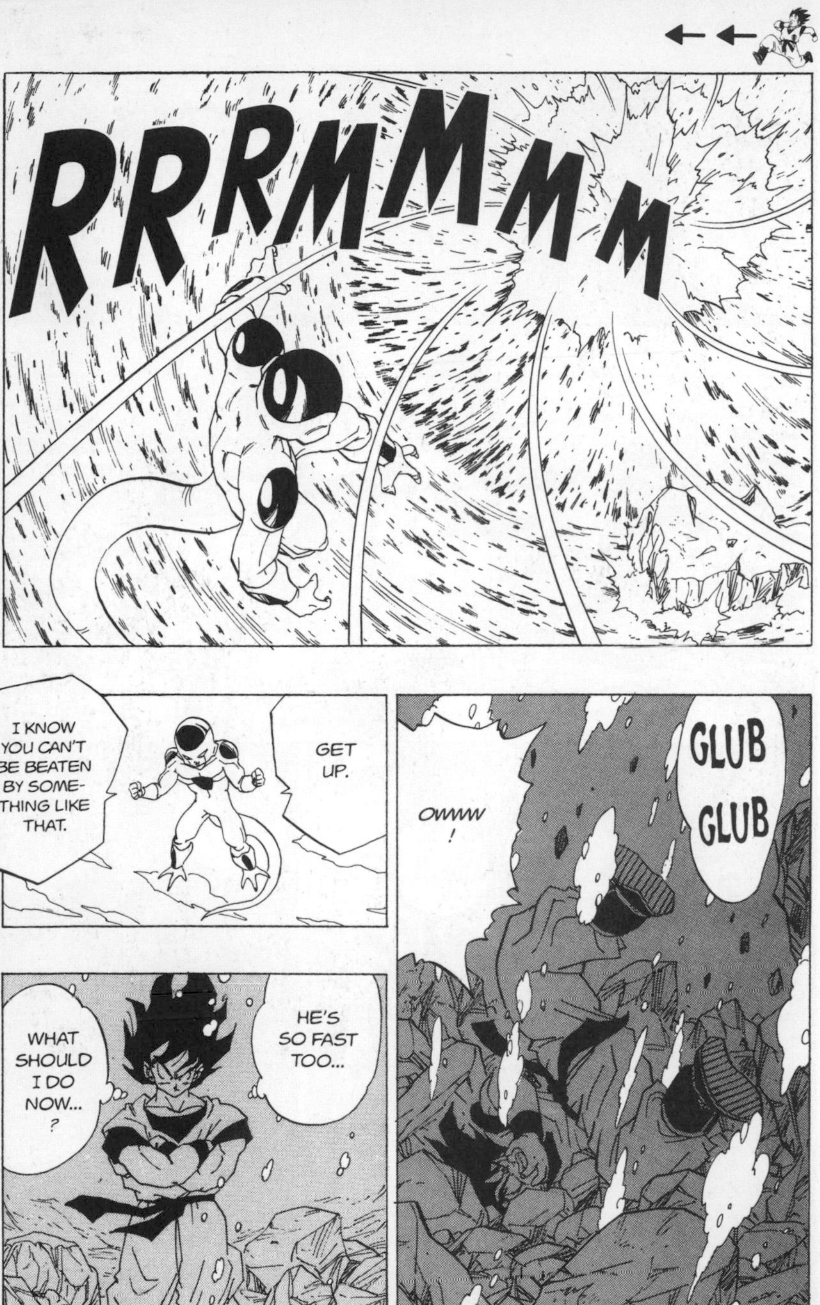
RRRMMMMM
GLUB GLUB
OWWW !
GET UP.
I KNOW YOU CAN'T BE BEATEN BY SOMETHING LIKE THAT.
HE'S SO FAST TOO...
WHAT SHOULD I DO NOW... ?

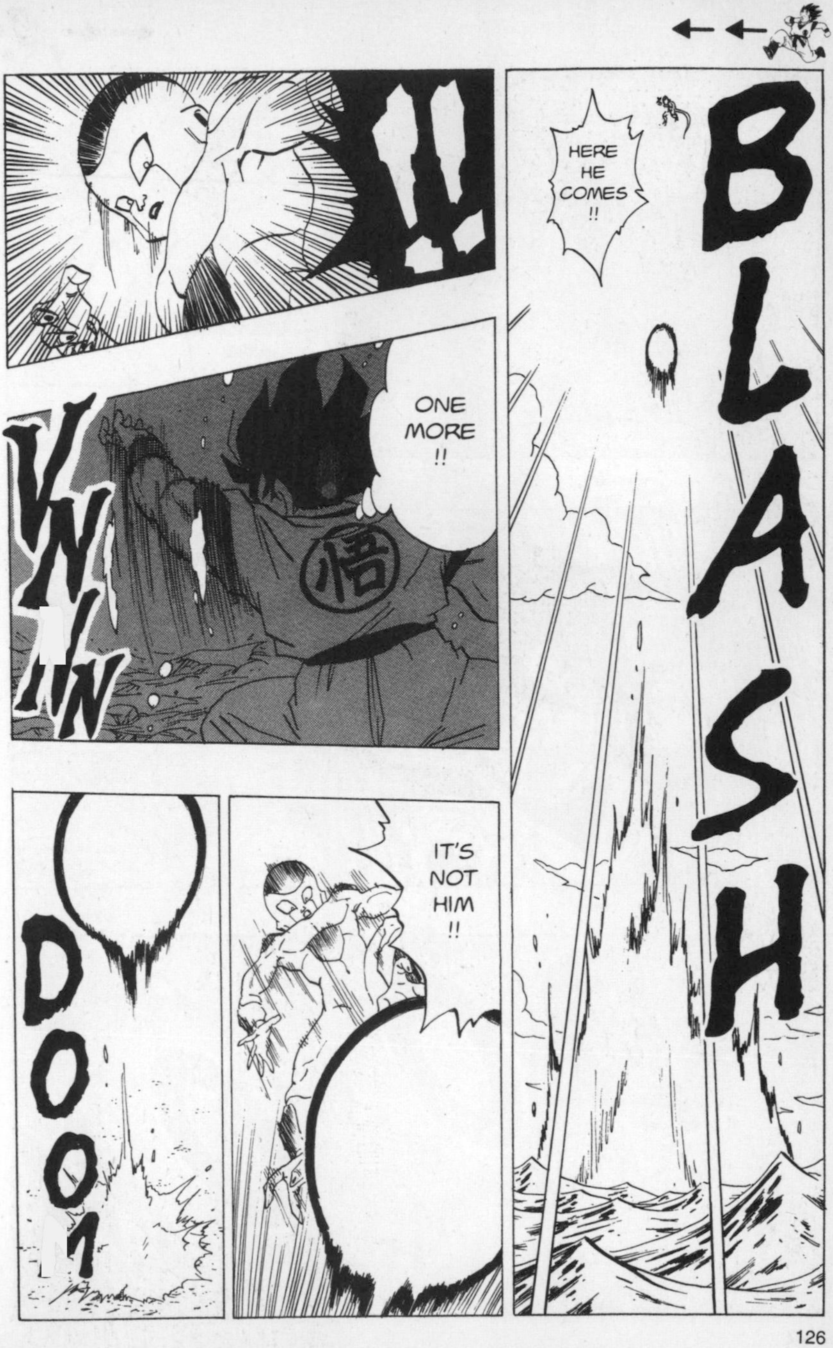
HERE HE COMES !!
BLASH
!!
VNNN
ONE MORE !!
IT'S NOT HIM !!
DOOM

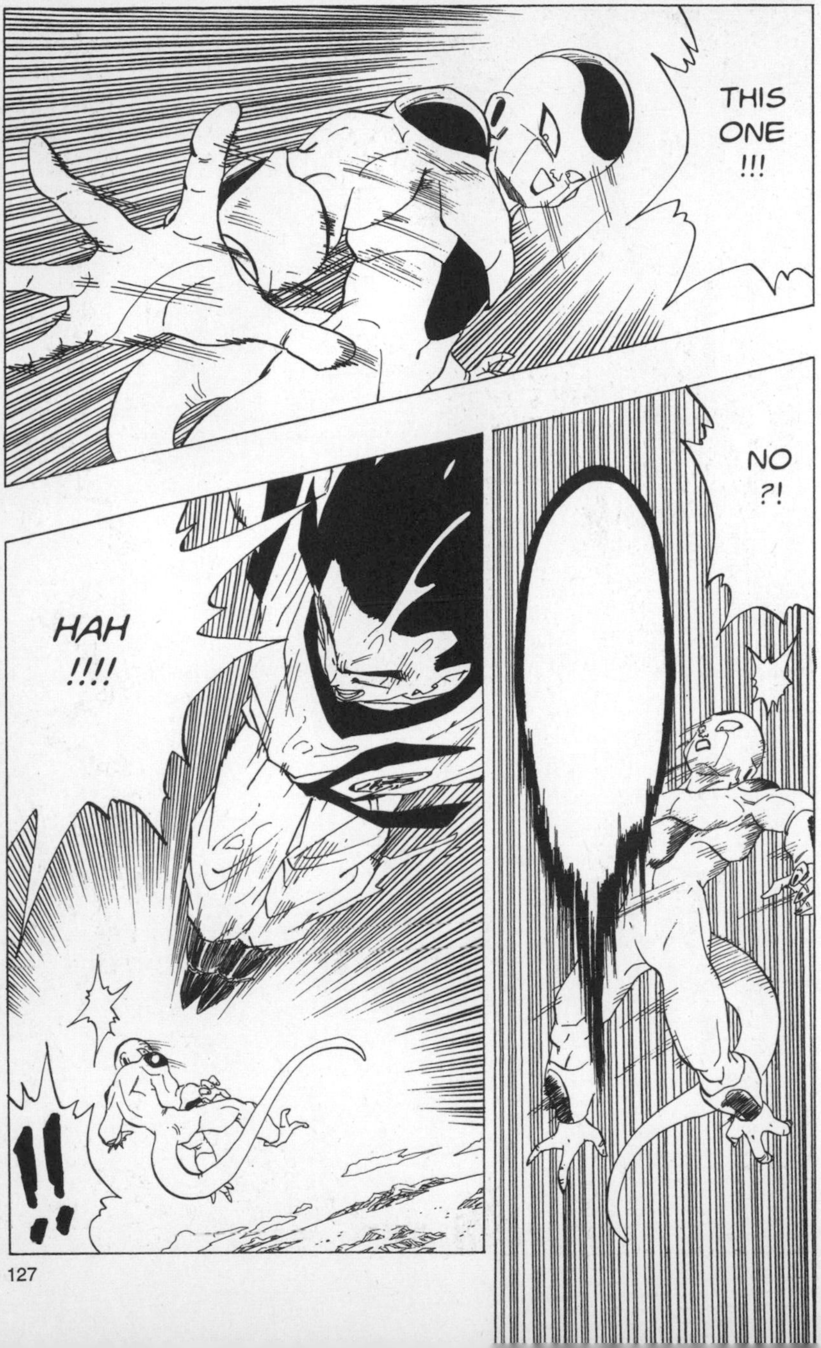
THIS ONE !!!
NO ?!
HAH !!!!
!!

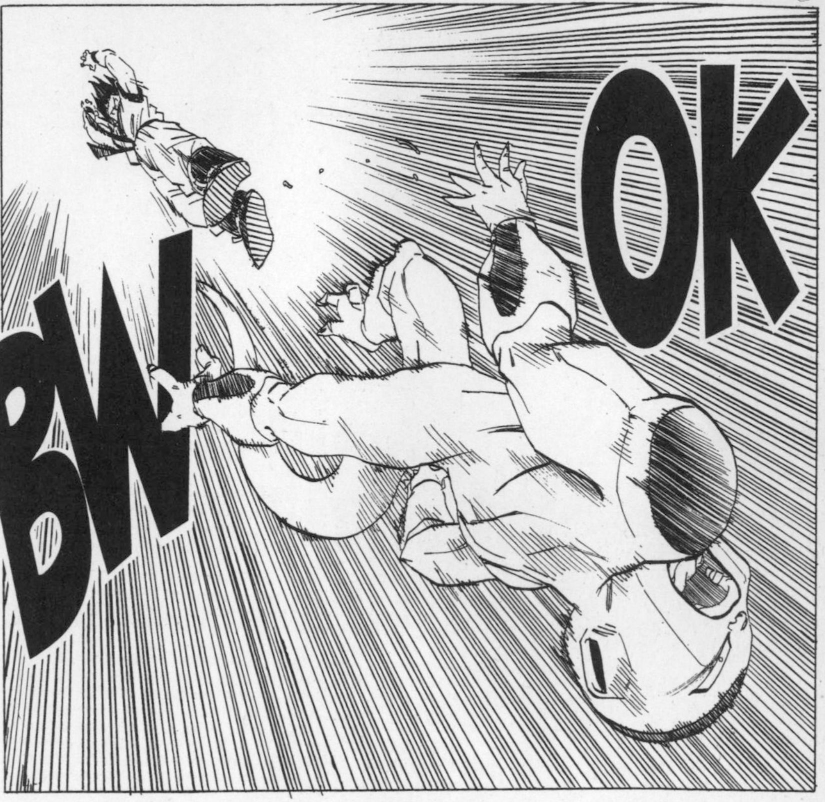
BWOK

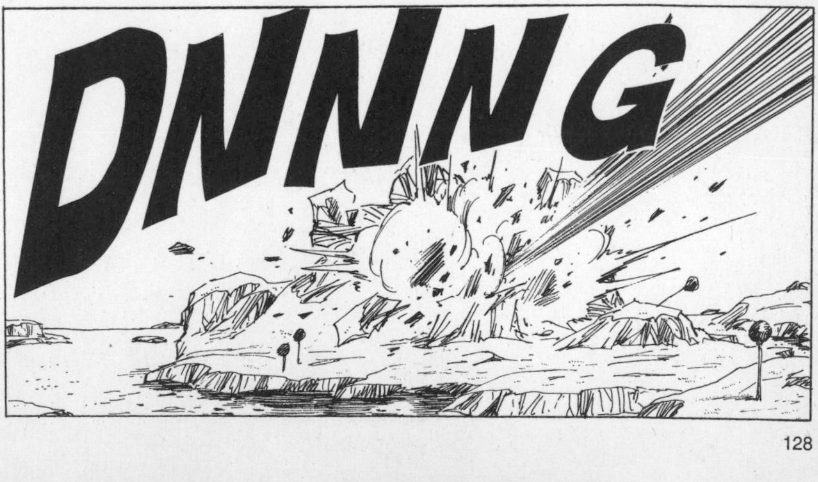
DNNNG

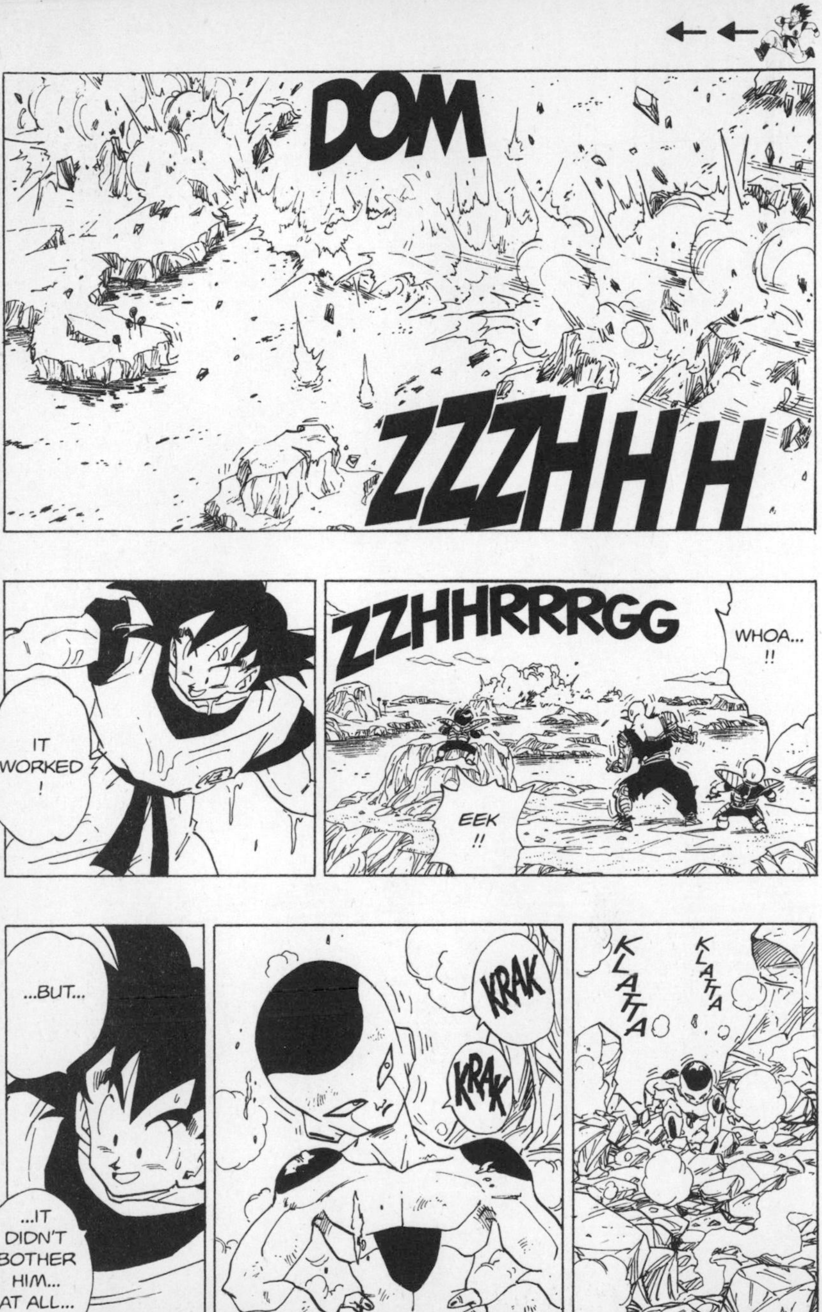
DOM
ZZZHHH
ZZHHRRRGG
WHOA... !!
EEK !!
IT WORKED !
KLATTA
KLATTA
KRAK
KRAK
...BUT...
...IT DIDN'T BOTHER HIM... AT ALL...

NEXT: Who Is Stronger?

DBZ:116 • Aerial Battle

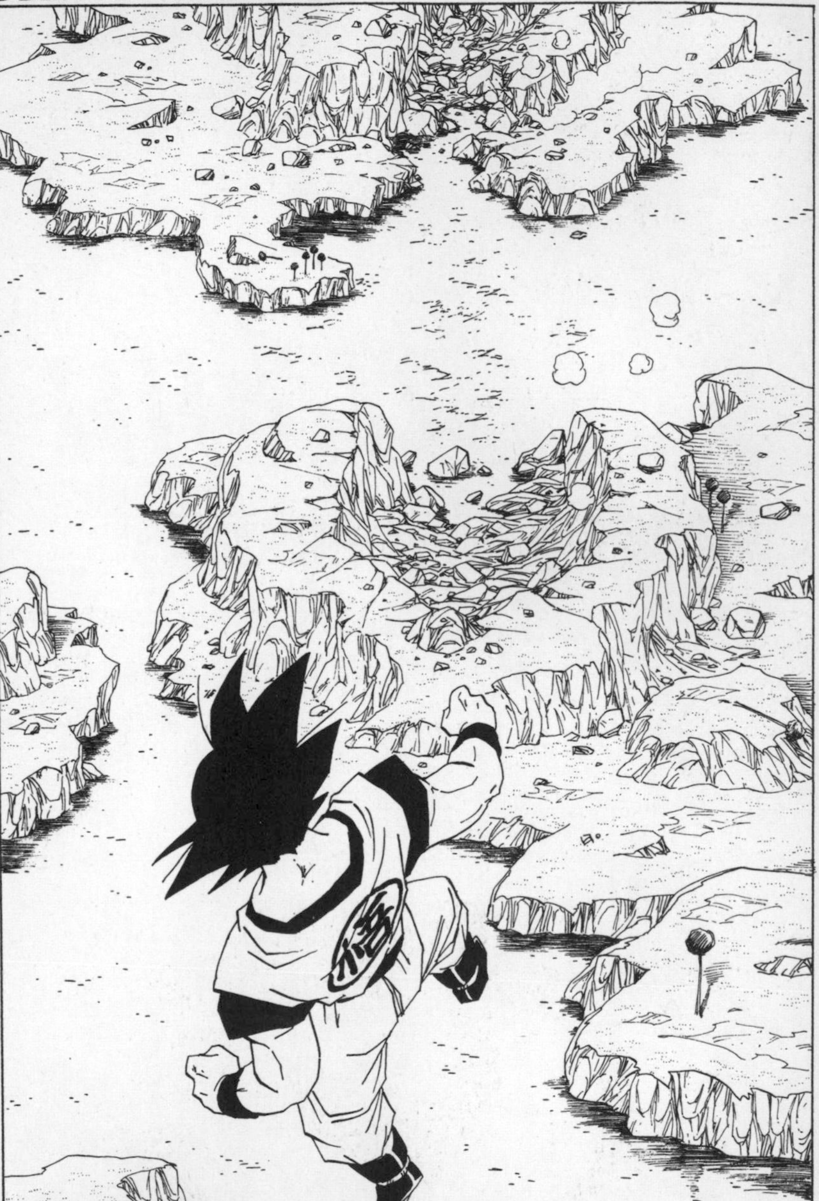

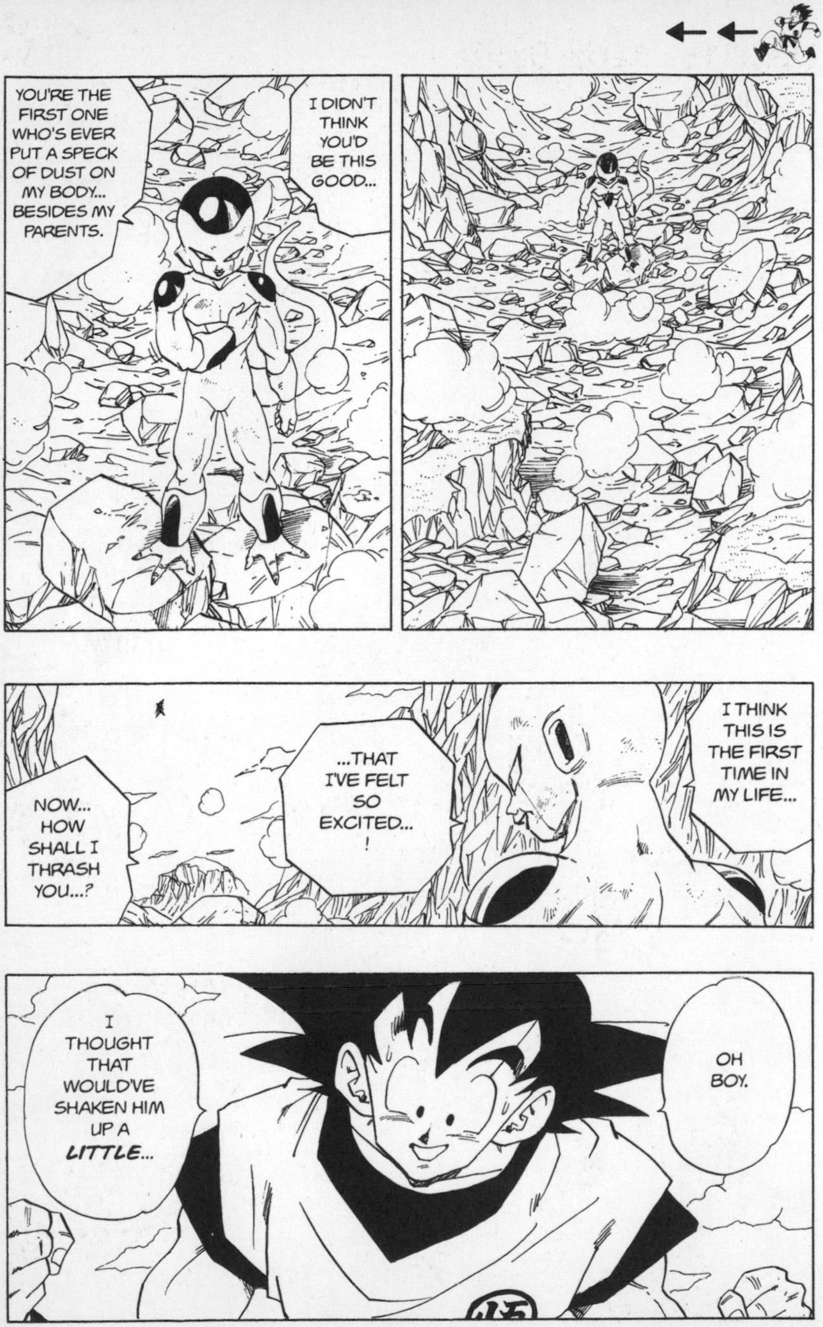
I DIDN'T THINK YOU'D BE THIS GOOD...
YOU'RE THE FIRST ONE WHO'S EVER PUT A SPECK OF DUST ON MY BODY... BESIDES MY PARENTS.
I THINK THIS IS THE FIRST TIME IN MY LIFE...
...THAT I'VE FELT SO EXCITED...!
NOW... HOW SHALL I THRASH YOU...?
OH BOY.
I THOUGHT THAT WOULD'VE SHAKEN HIM UP A *LITTLE*...

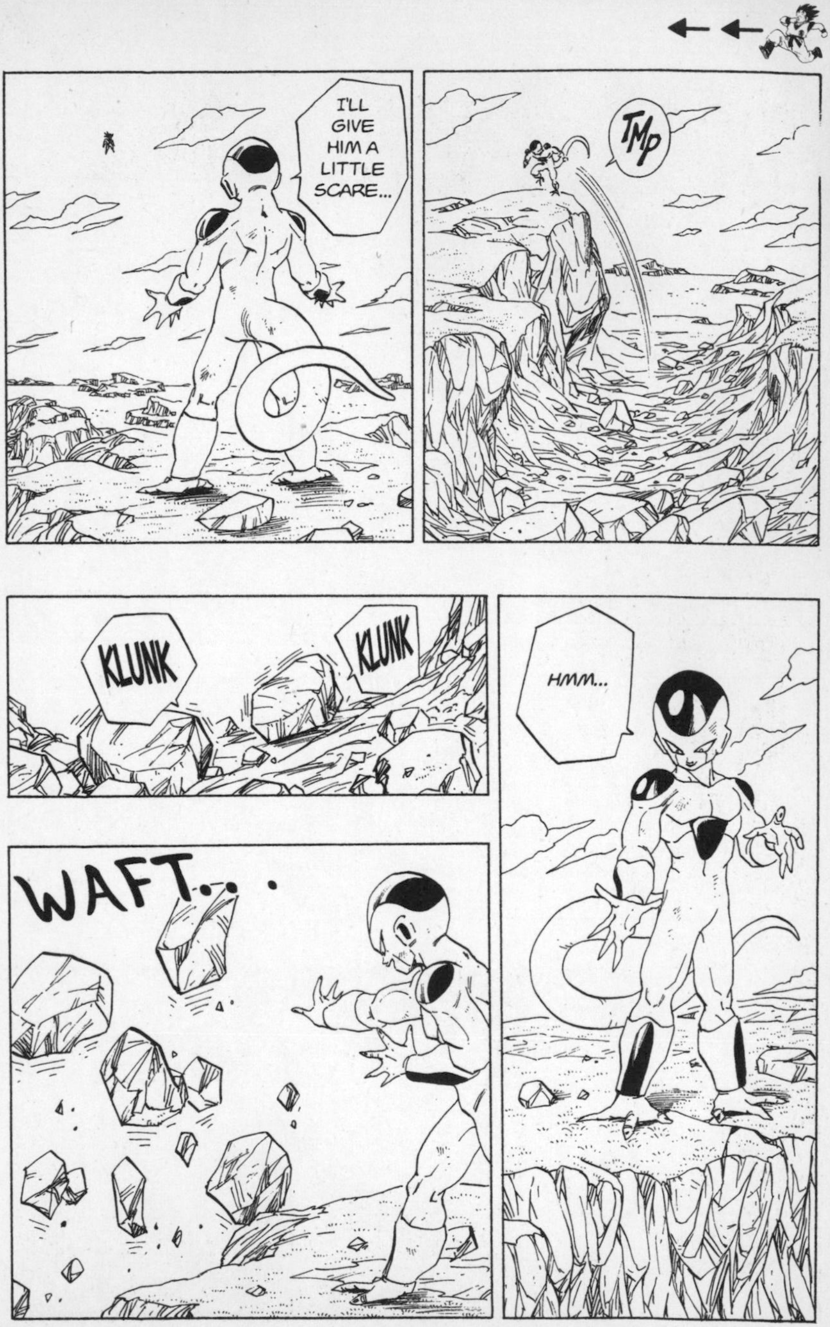
TMP
I'LL GIVE HIM A LITTLE SCARE...
HMM...
KLUNK
KLUNK
WAFT...

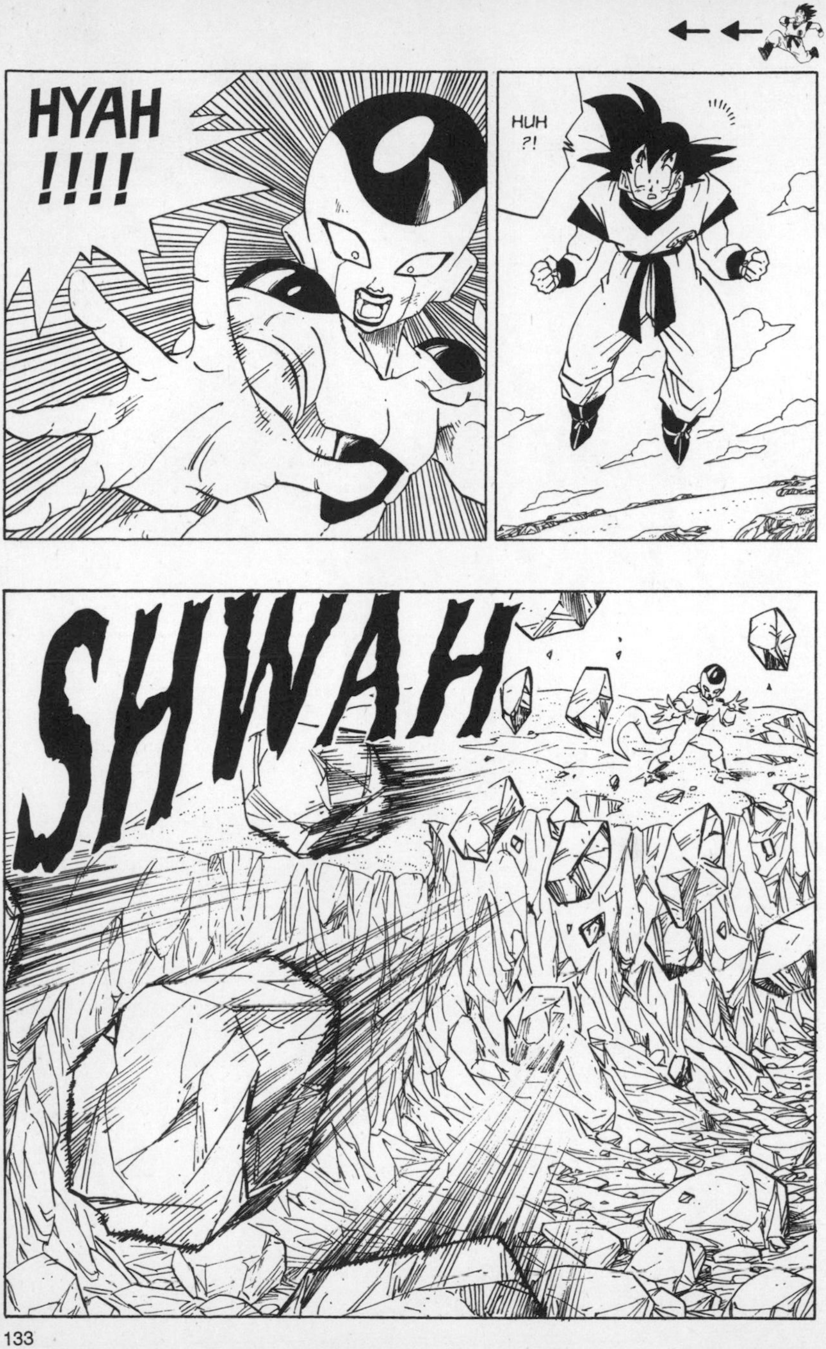
HUH ?!
HYAH !!!!
SHWAH

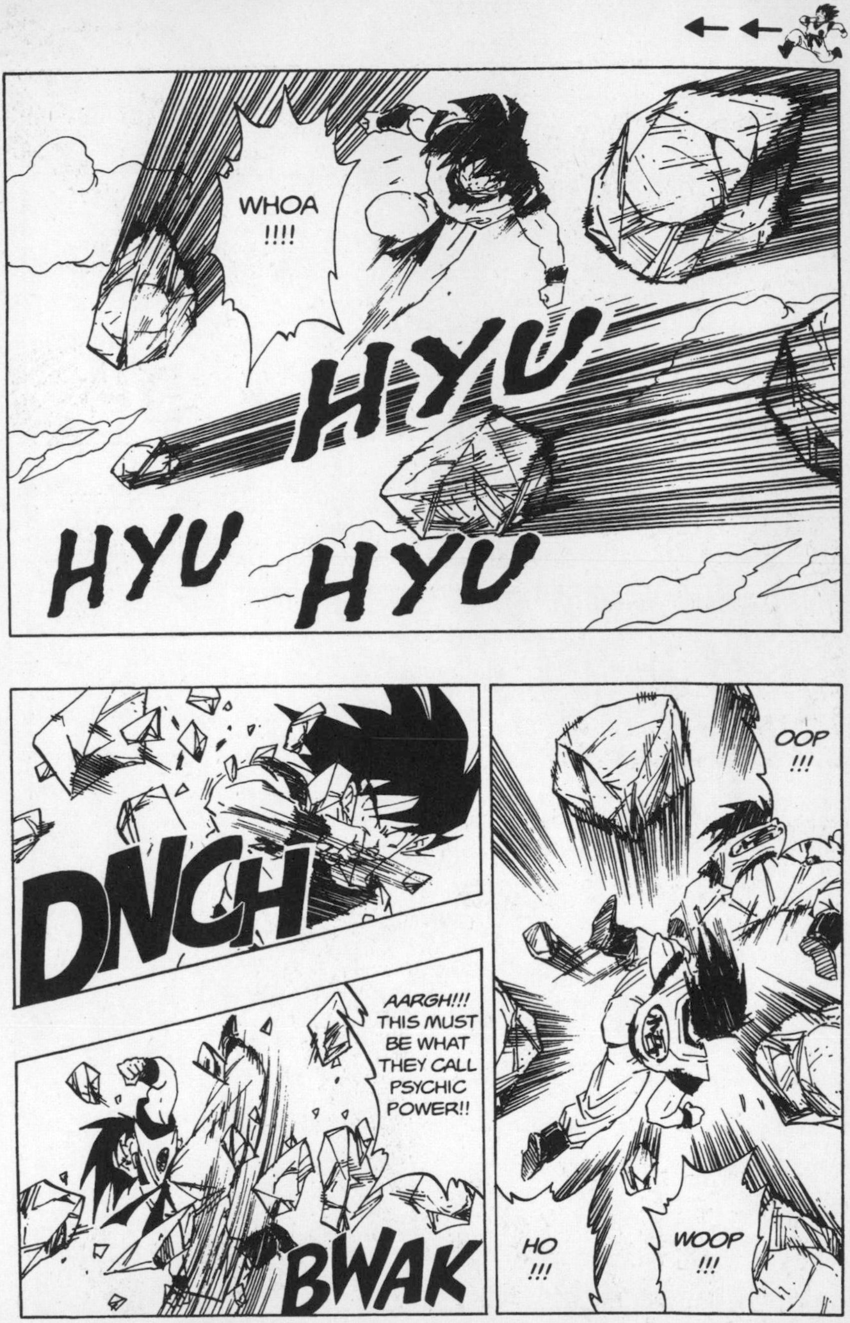
WHOA !!!!
HYU
HYU
HYU
OOP !!!
HO !!!
WOOP !!!
DNCH
AARGH!!! THIS MUST BE WHAT THEY CALL PSYCHIC POWER!!
BWAK

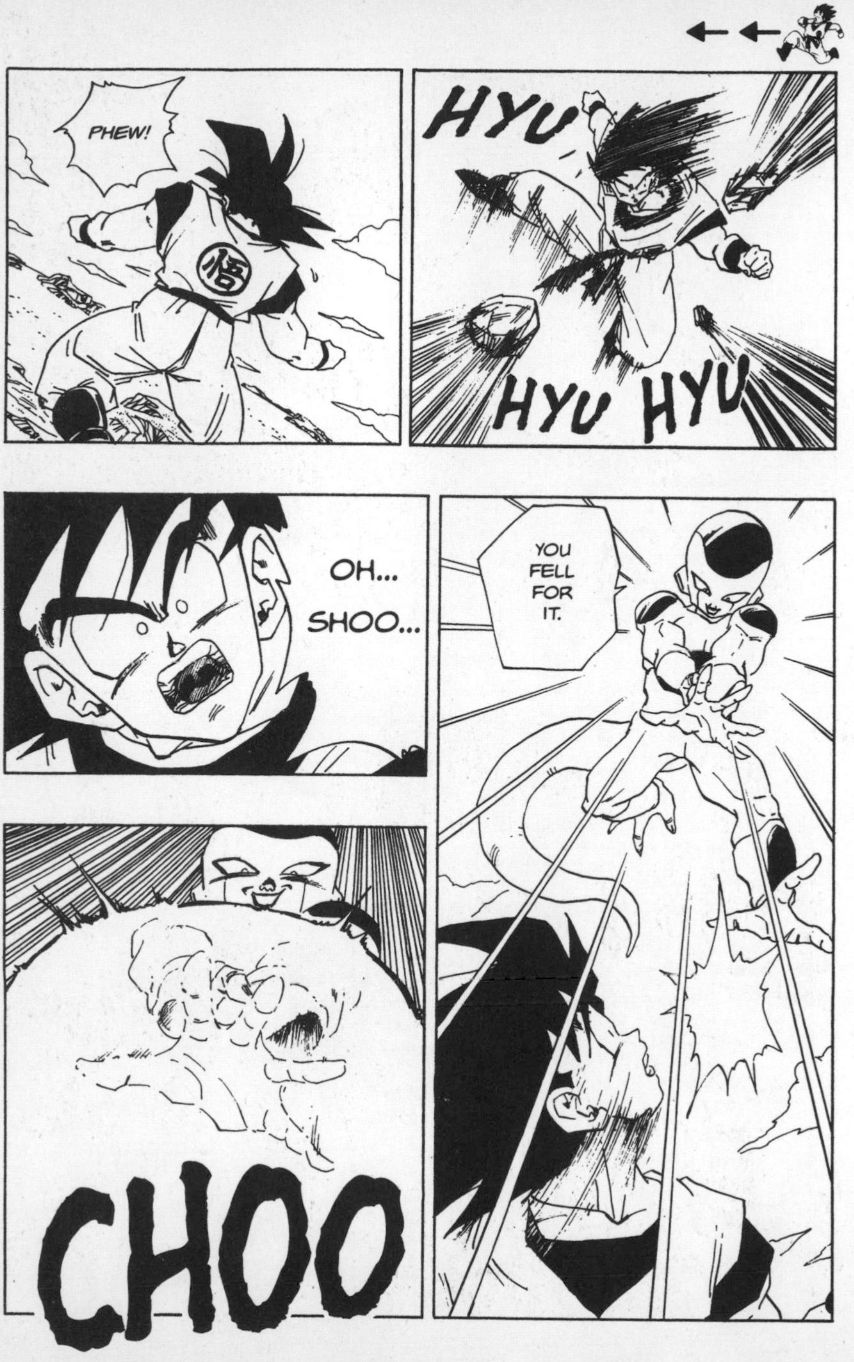
HYU
HYU HYU
PHEW!
YOU FELL FOR IT.
OH... SHOO...
CHOO

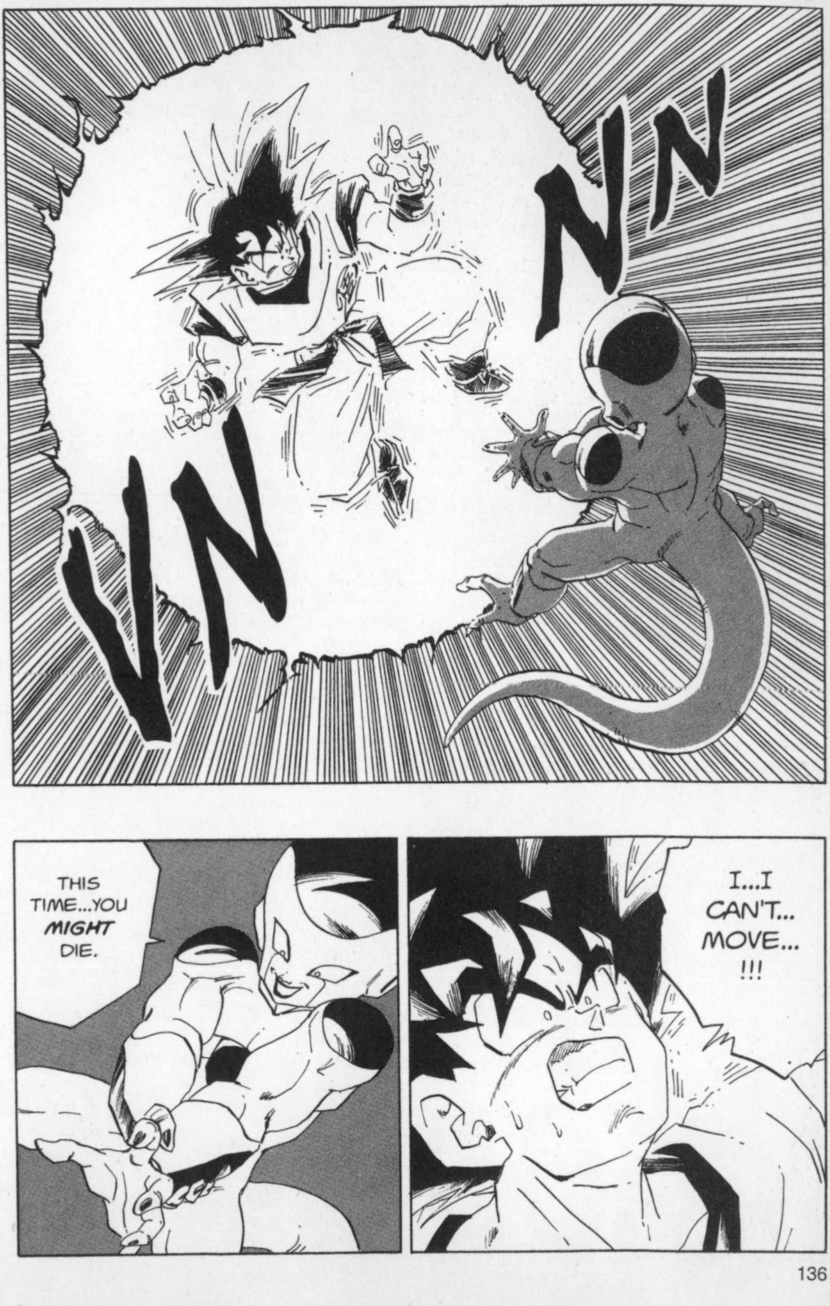
I...I CAN'T... MOVE... !!!
THIS TIME...YOU *MIGHT* DIE.

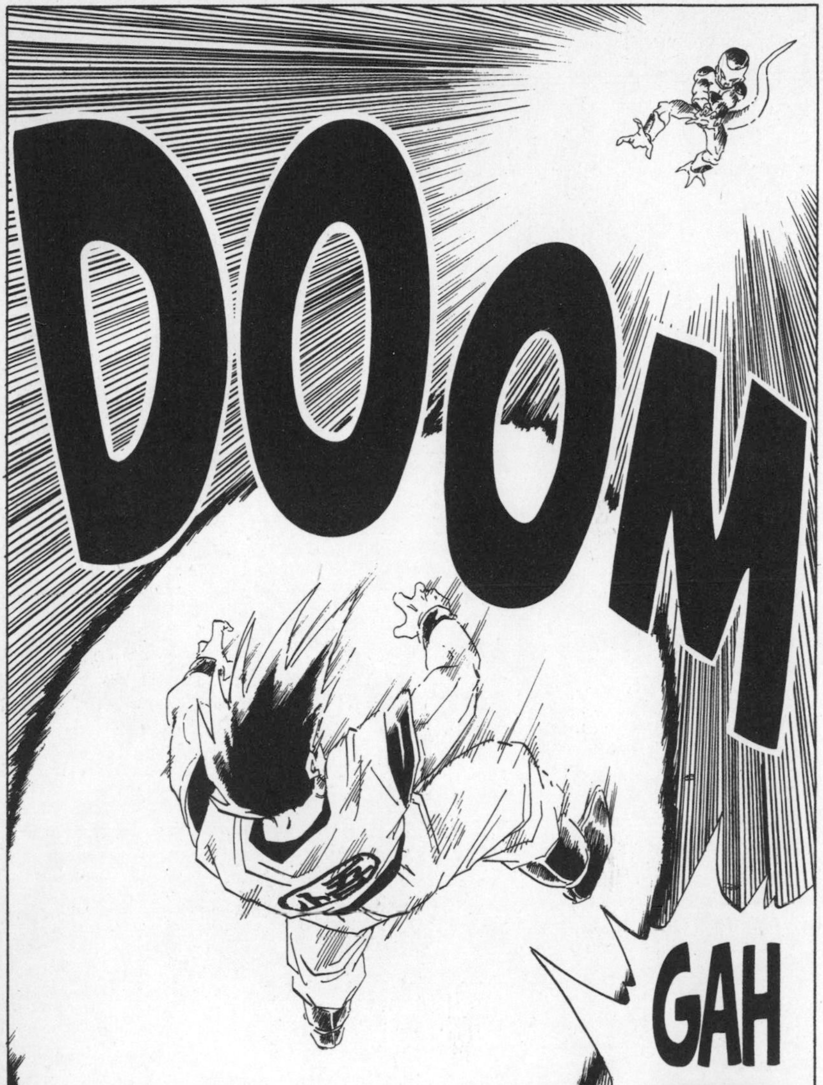
DOOM
GAH!!!!!

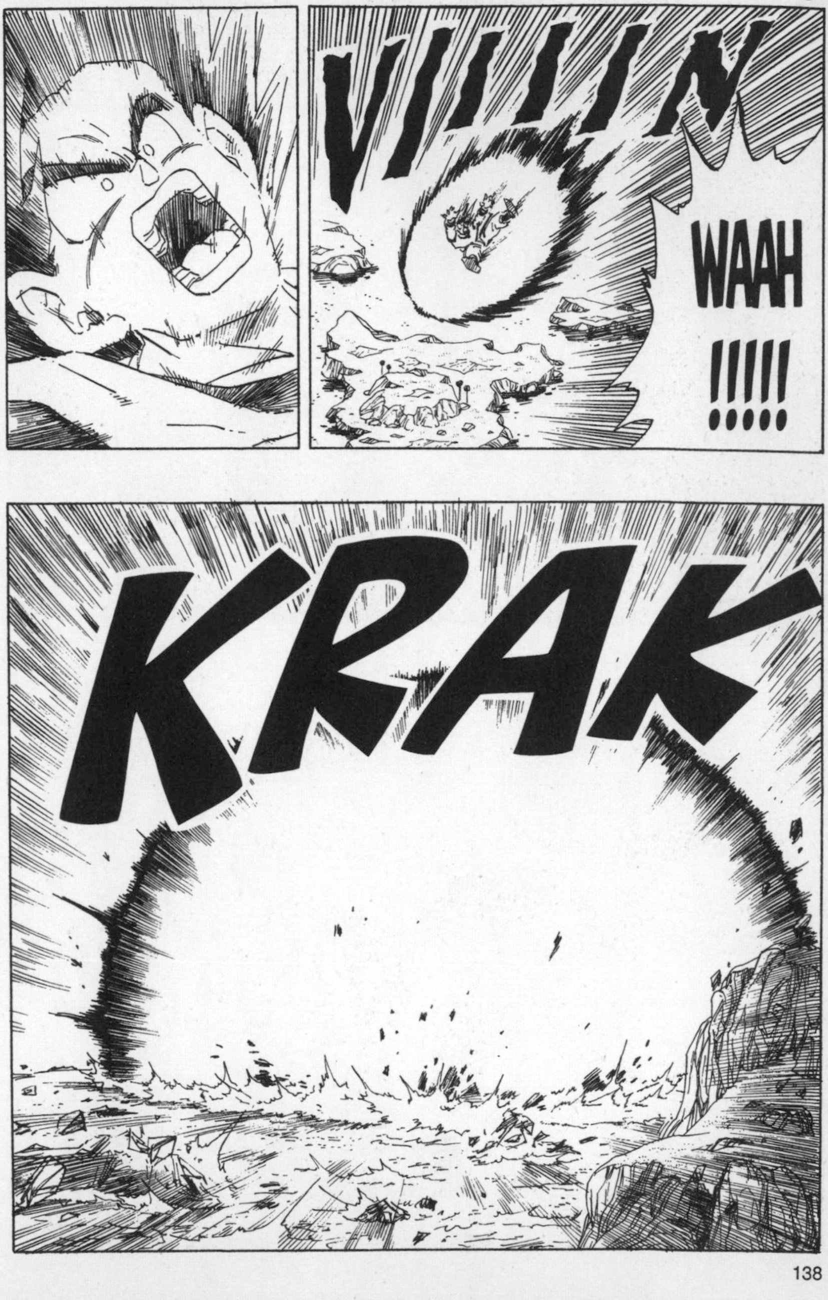
VIIIIN
WAAH!!!!!
KRAK

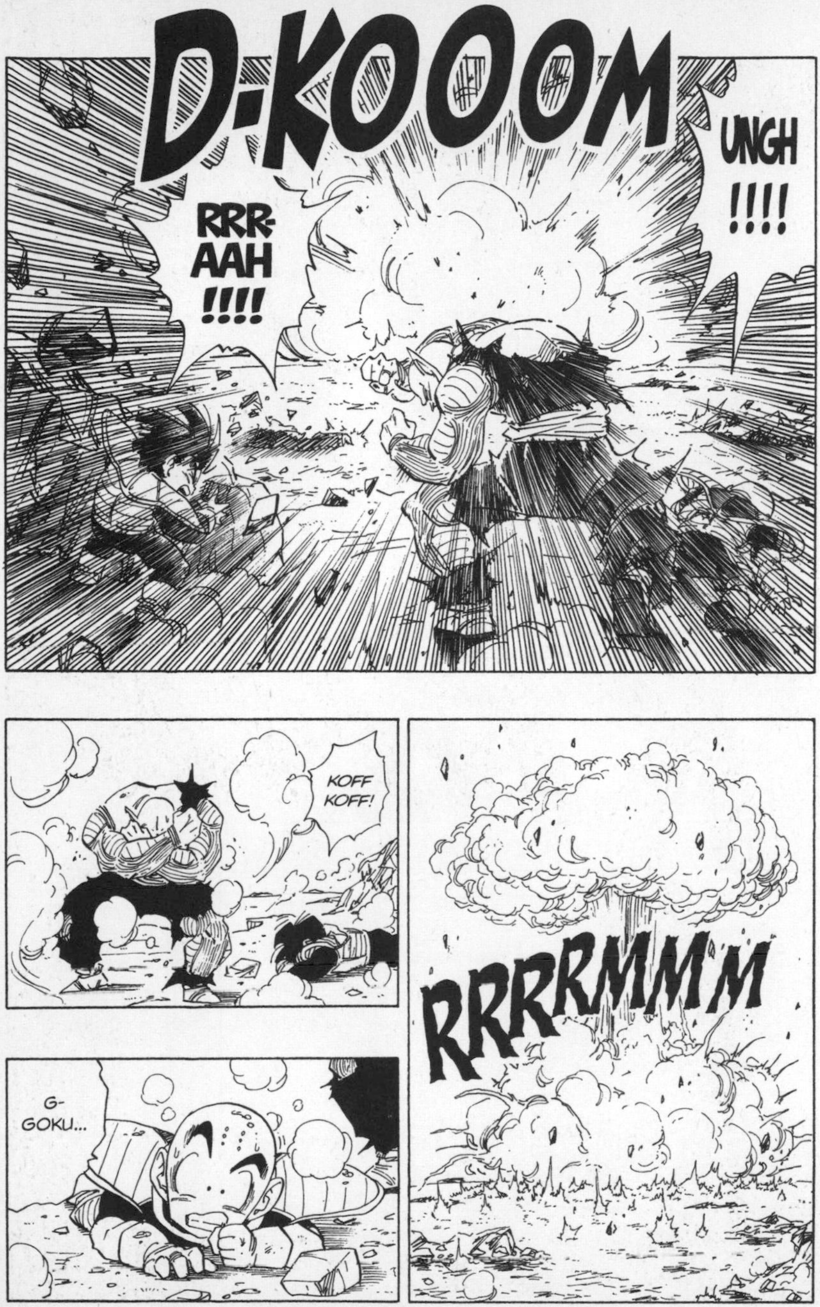
D-KOOOM
UNGH !!!!
RRR-AAH !!!!
RRRRMMMM
KOFF KOFF!
G-GOKU...

IF HE WANTED TO, HE COULD BLOW UP THIS ENTIRE PLANET.

FREEZA'S ONLY TOYING WITH HIM...

I...I CAN'T BELIEVE IT...

GOKU'S NOT GIVING HIS ALL EITHER...

BUT THERE'S NO POINT IN WORRYING...

WH- WHERE'S DAD...?

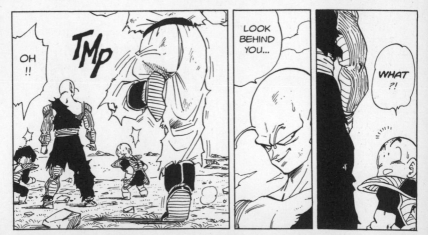

OH !!

TMP

LOOK BEHIND YOU...

WHAT ?!

140

142

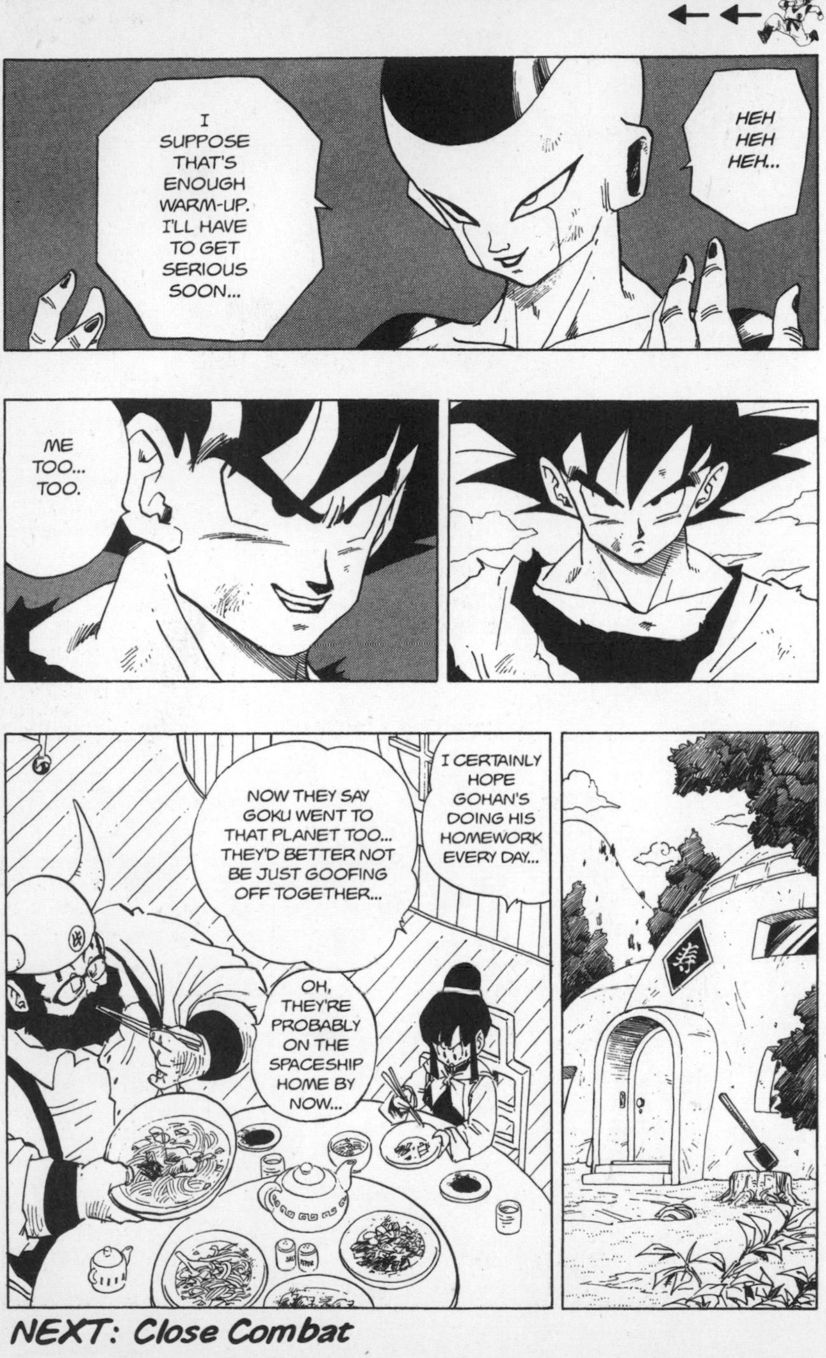

NEXT: Close Combat

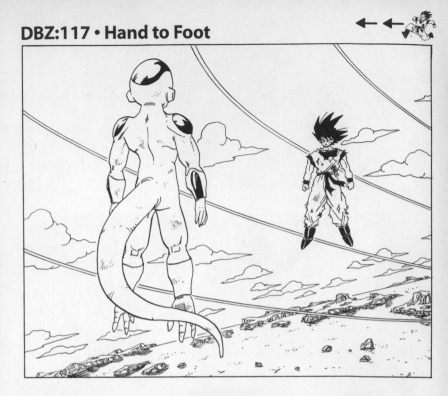

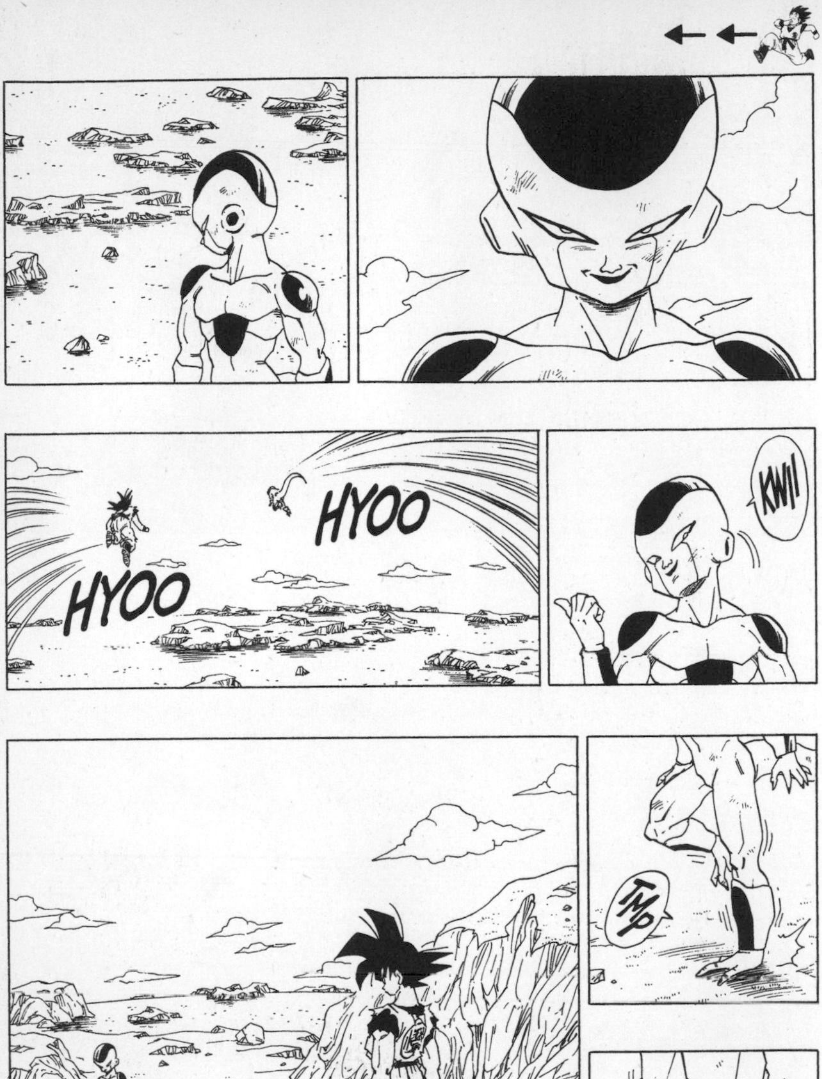
HYOO
HYOO
KWII
TMP
TMP

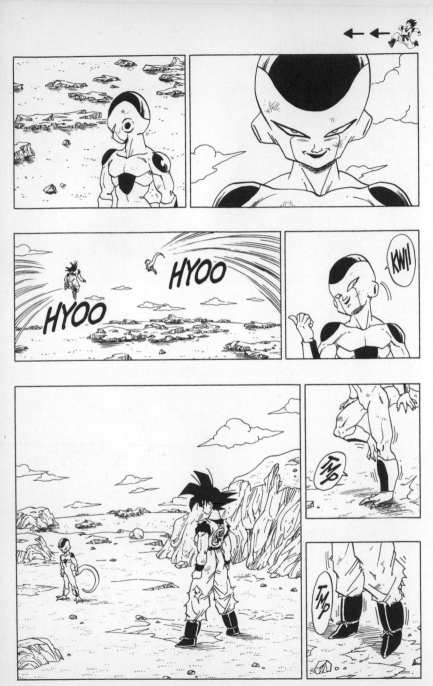

146

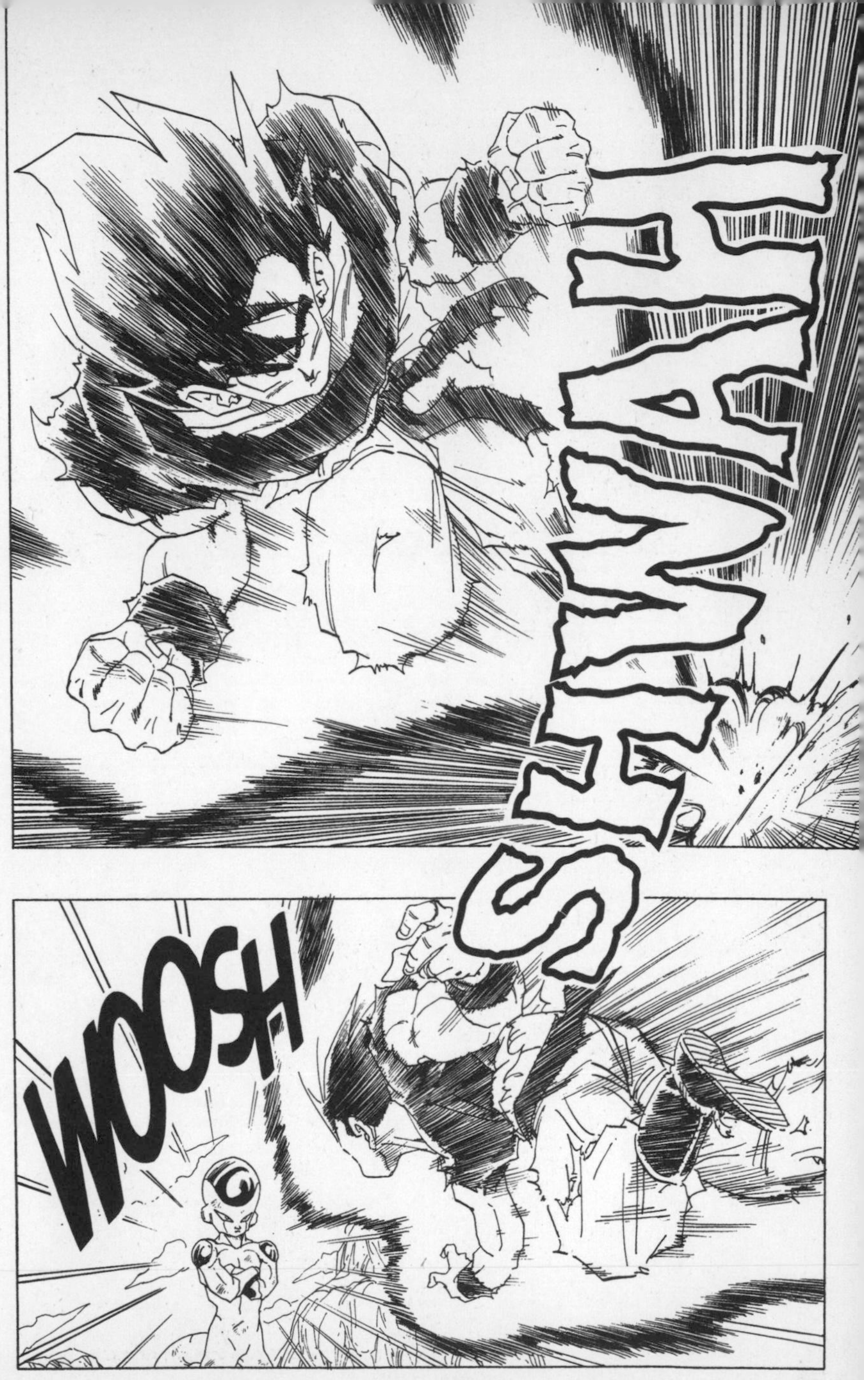
SHWAH
WOOSH

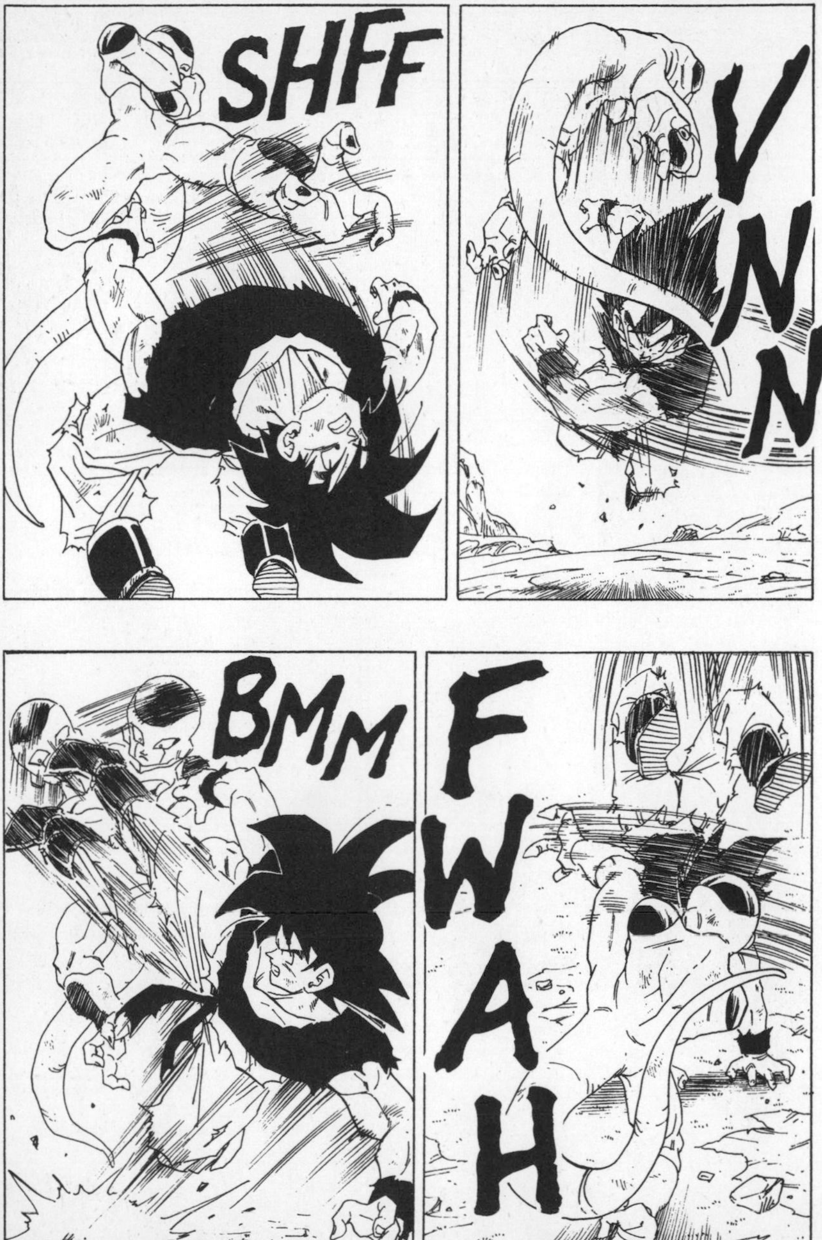
VNN
SHFF
FWAH
BMM

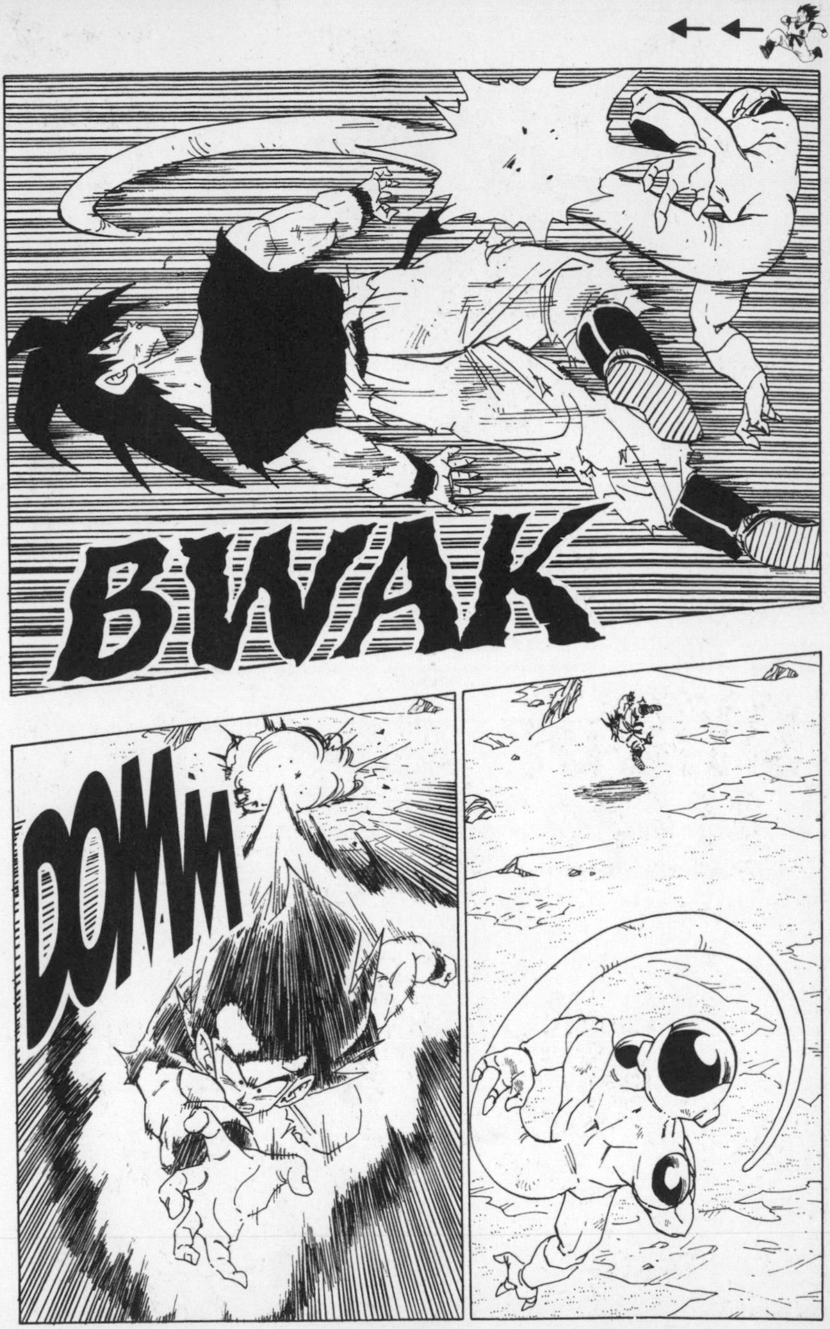
BWAK
DOMM

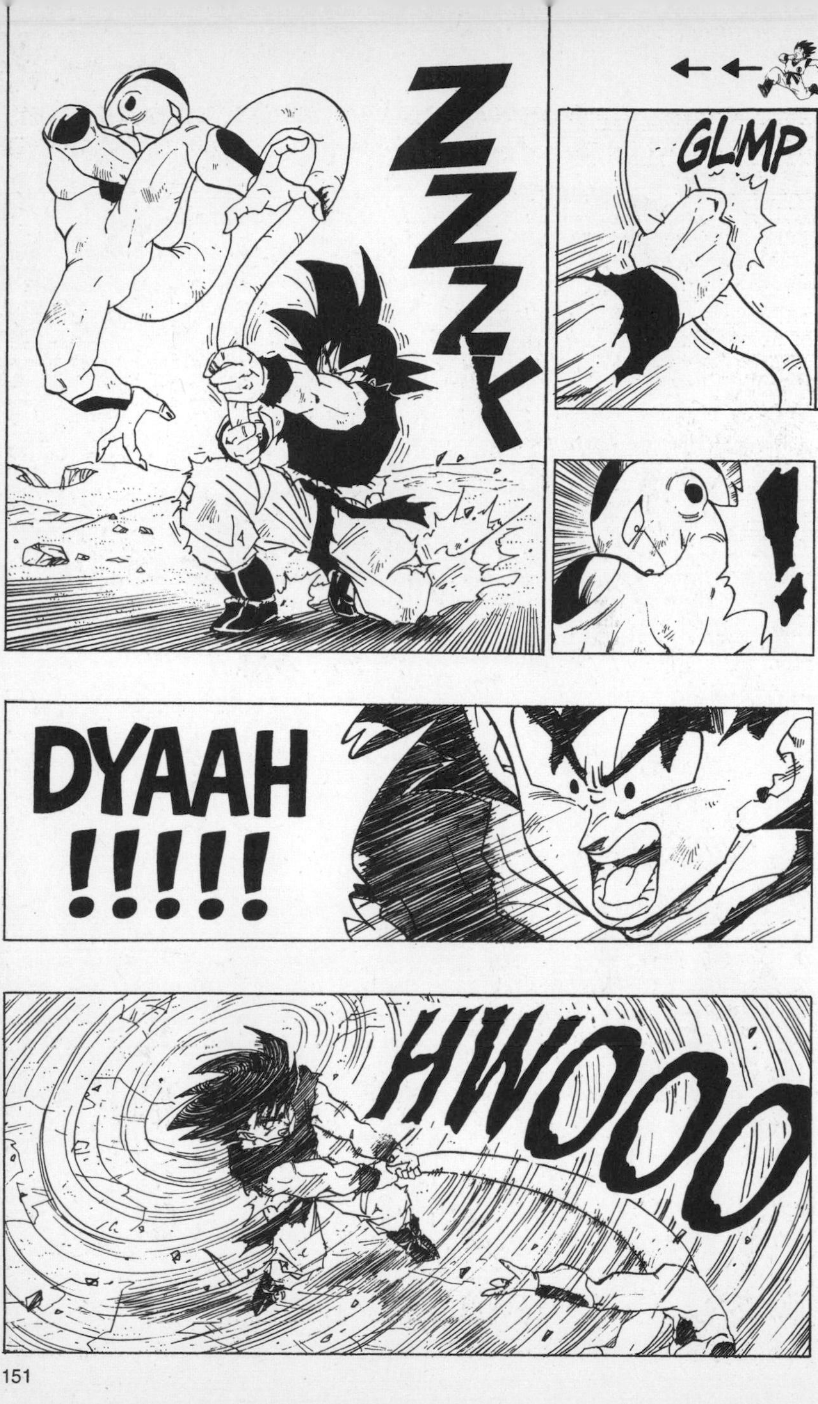
GLMP
!
ZZZK
DYAAH
!!!!!
HWOOO

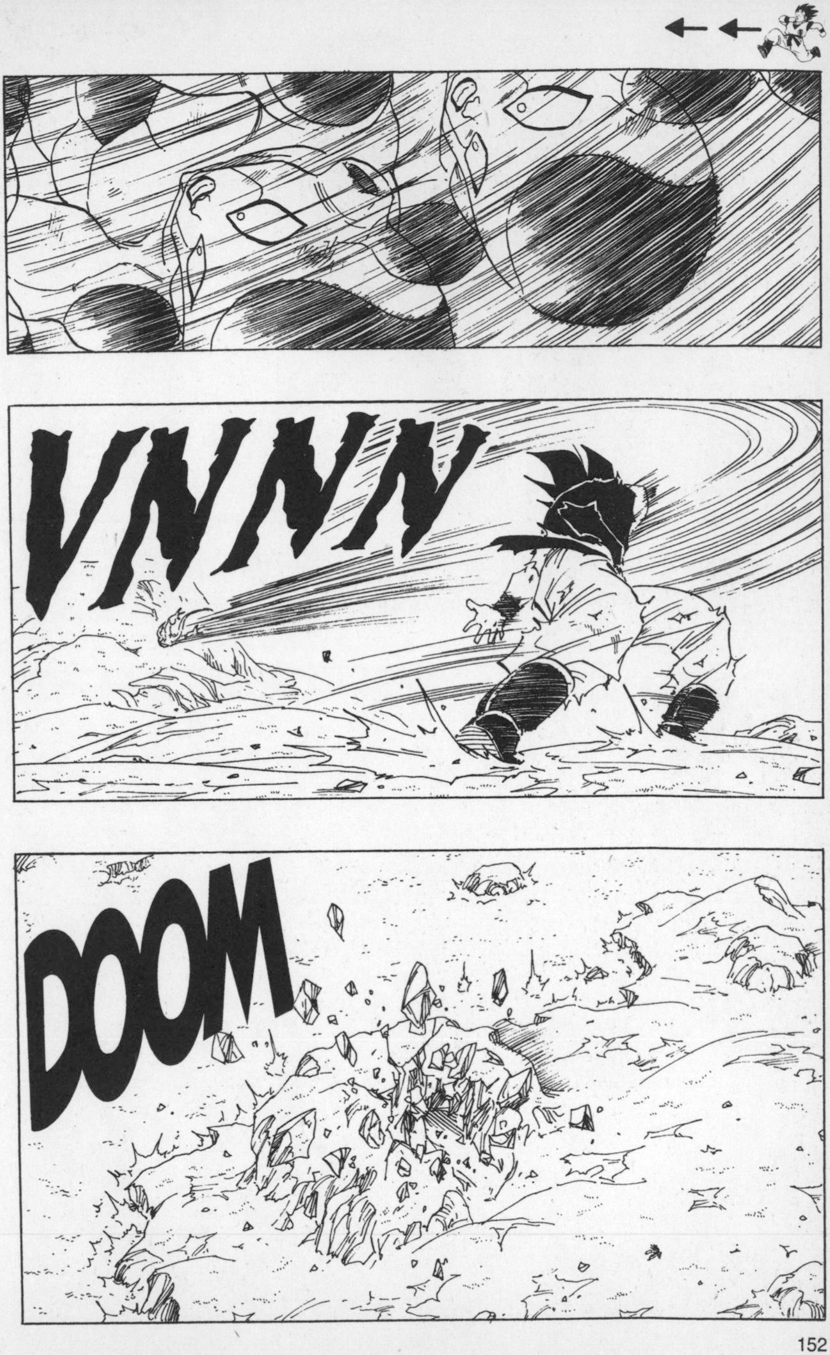
VNNN
DOOM

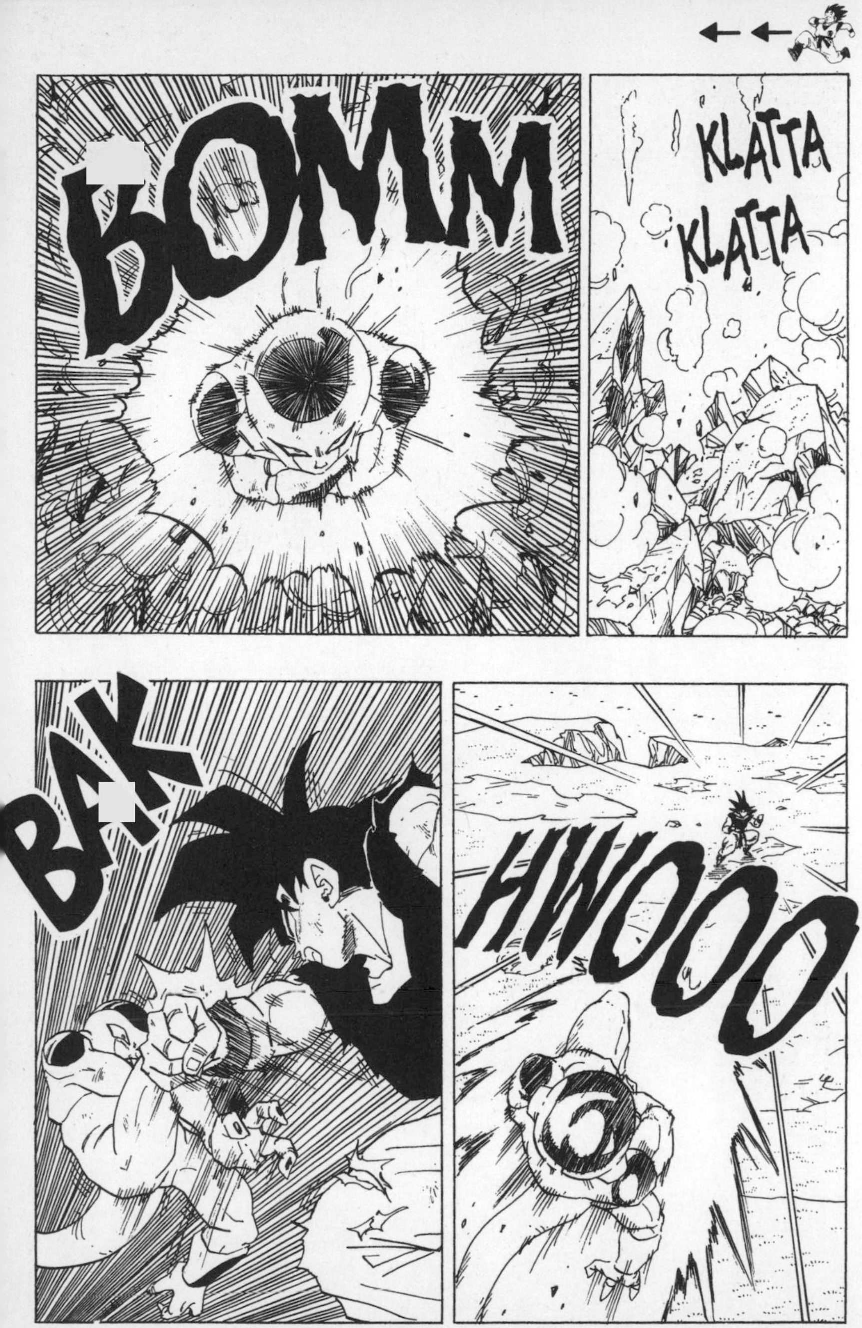
KLATTA
KLATTA
BOMM
HWOOO
BAK

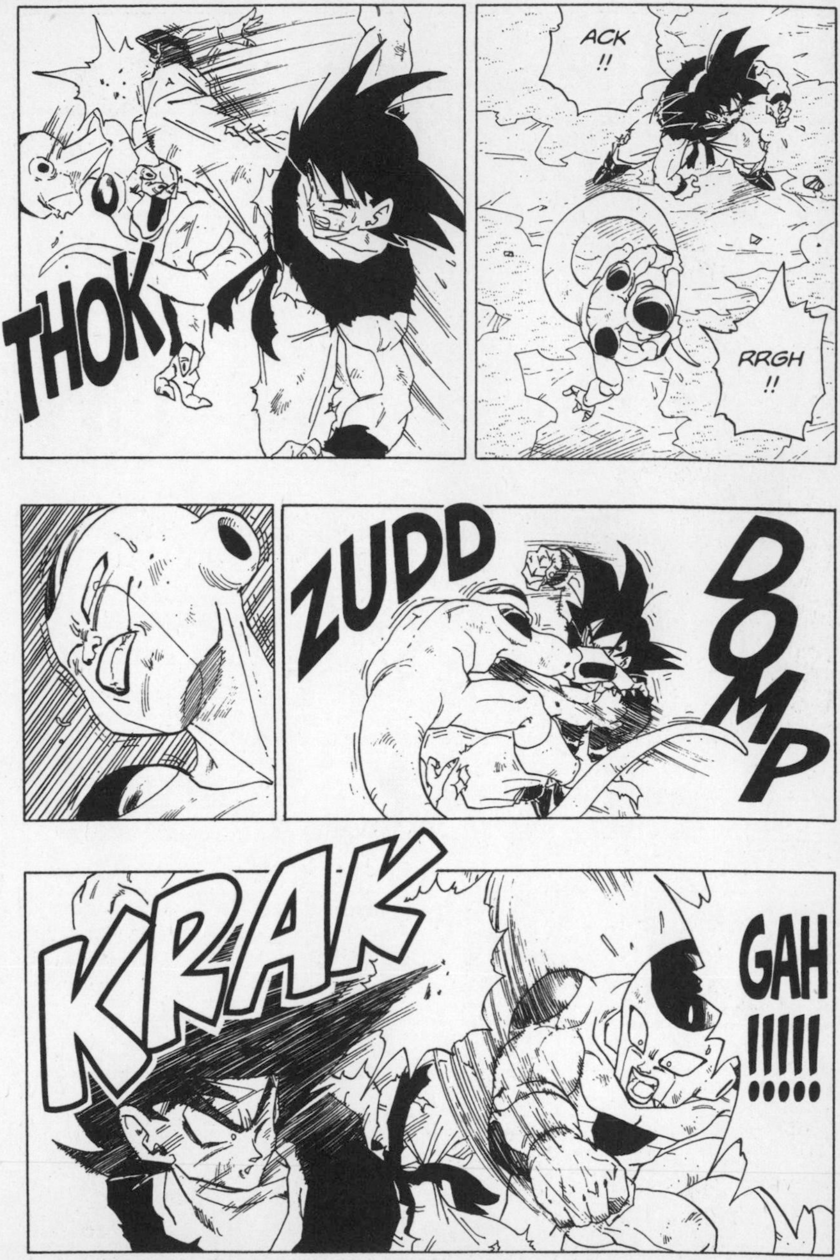
ACK !!
RRGH !!
THOK
DOMP
ZUDD
GAH !!!!!
KRAK

NEXT: *Freeza Gets Serious*

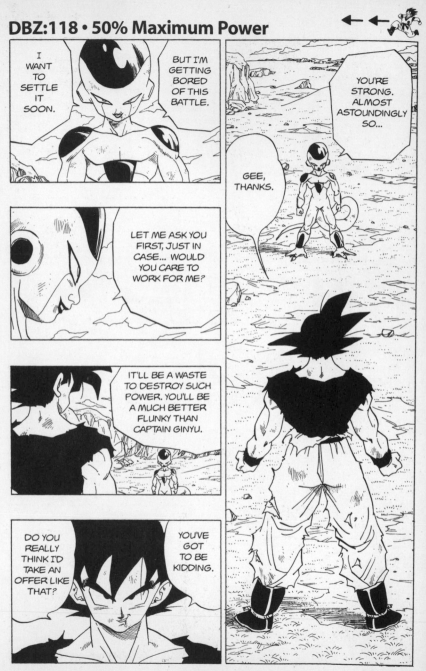

I WANT TO SETTLE IT SOON.

BUT I'M GETTING BORED OF THIS BATTLE.

YOU'RE STRONG. ALMOST ASTOUNDINGLY SO...

GEE, THANKS.

LET ME ASK YOU FIRST, JUST IN CASE... WOULD YOU CARE TO WORK FOR ME?

IT'LL BE A WASTE TO DESTROY SUCH POWER. YOU'LL BE A MUCH BETTER FLUNKY THAN CAPTAIN GINYU.

DO YOU REALLY THINK I'D TAKE AN OFFER LIKE THAT?

YOU'VE GOT TO BE KIDDING.

161

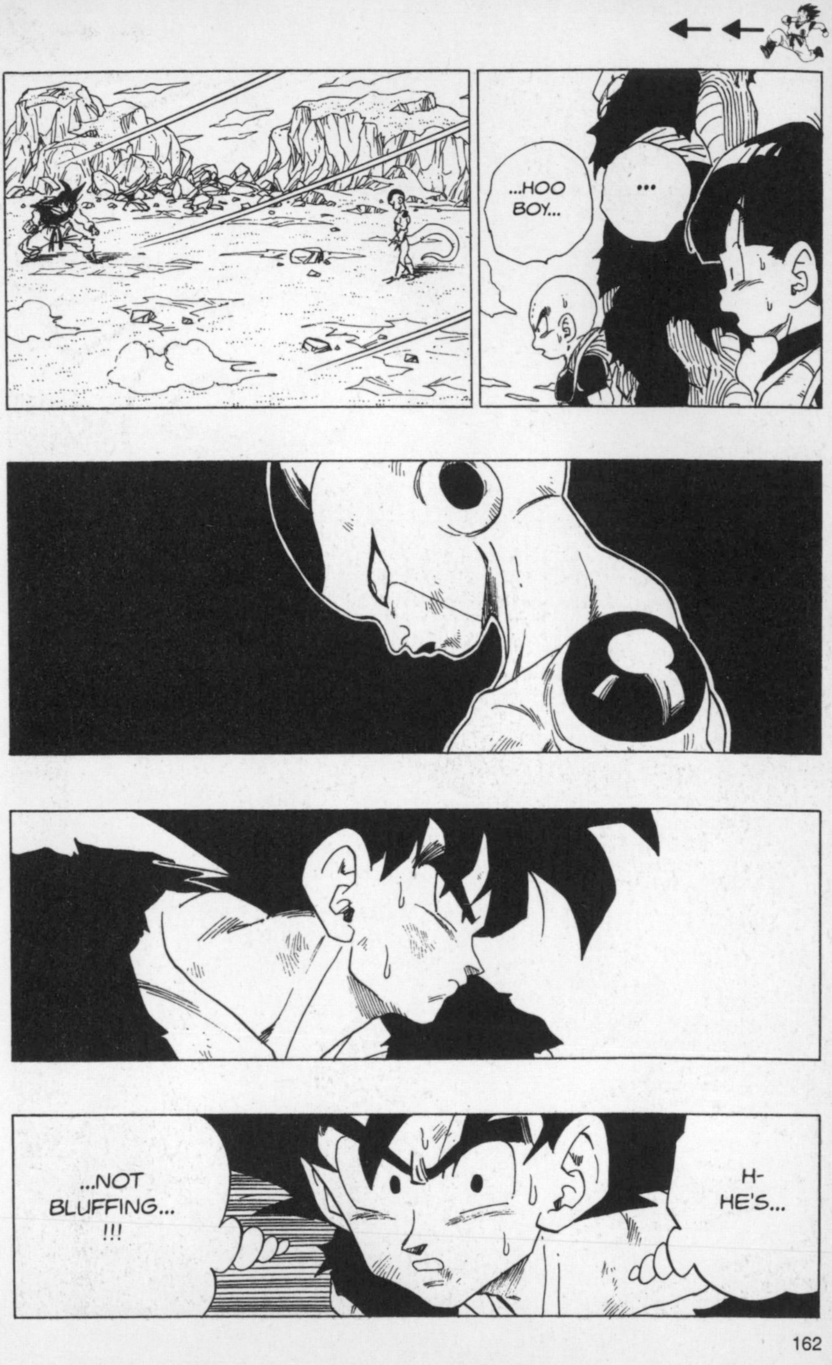
...
...HOO BOY...
H- HE'S...
...NOT BLUFFING... !!!

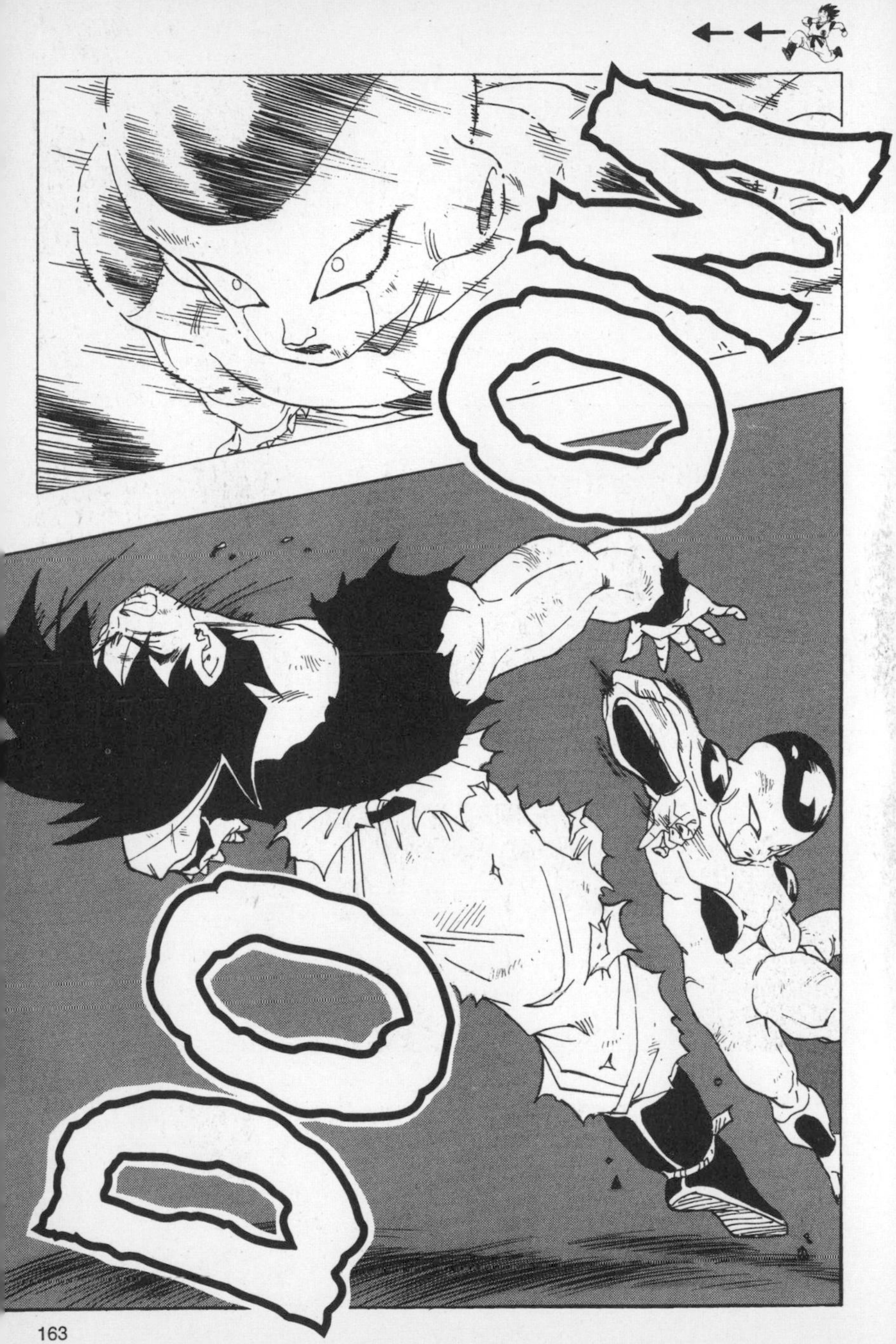
DOOM

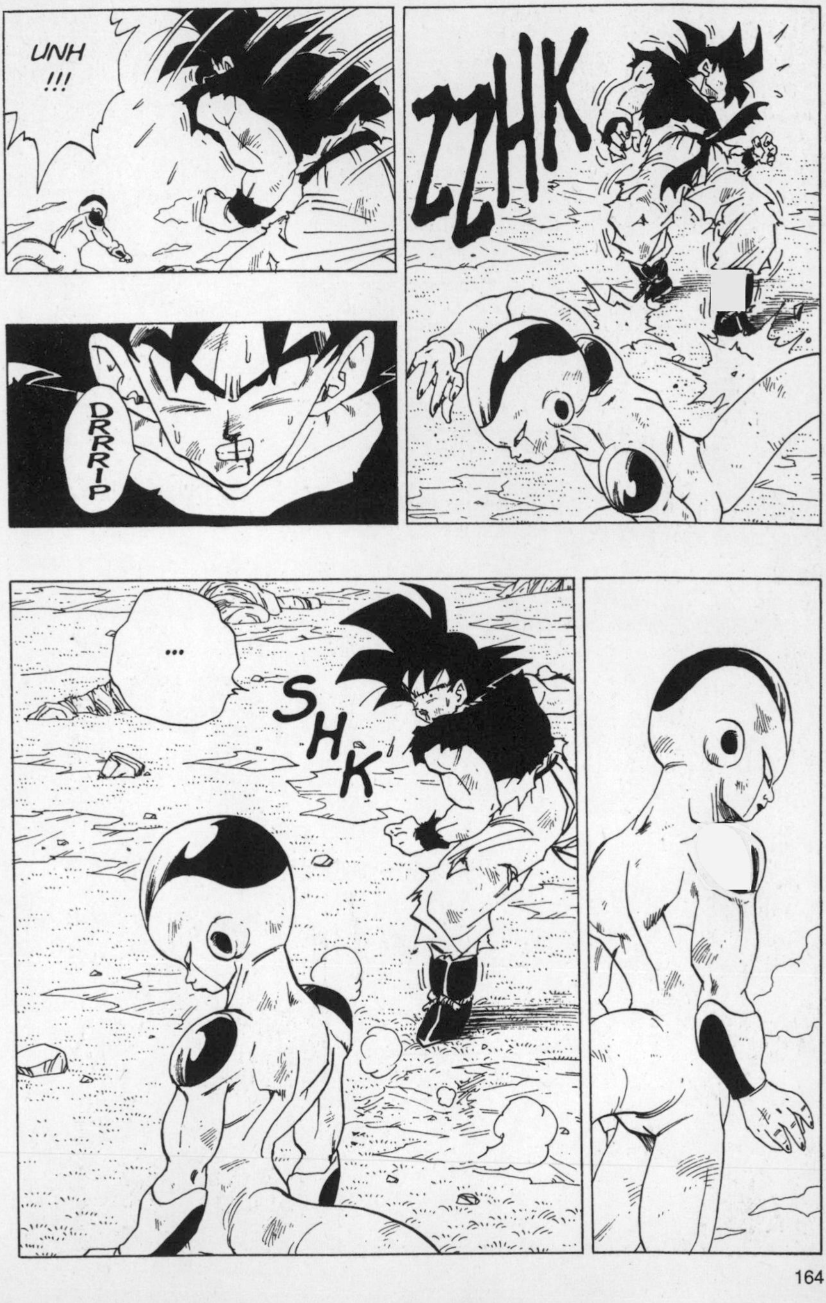
ZZHK
UNH !!!
DRRRIP
...
SHK

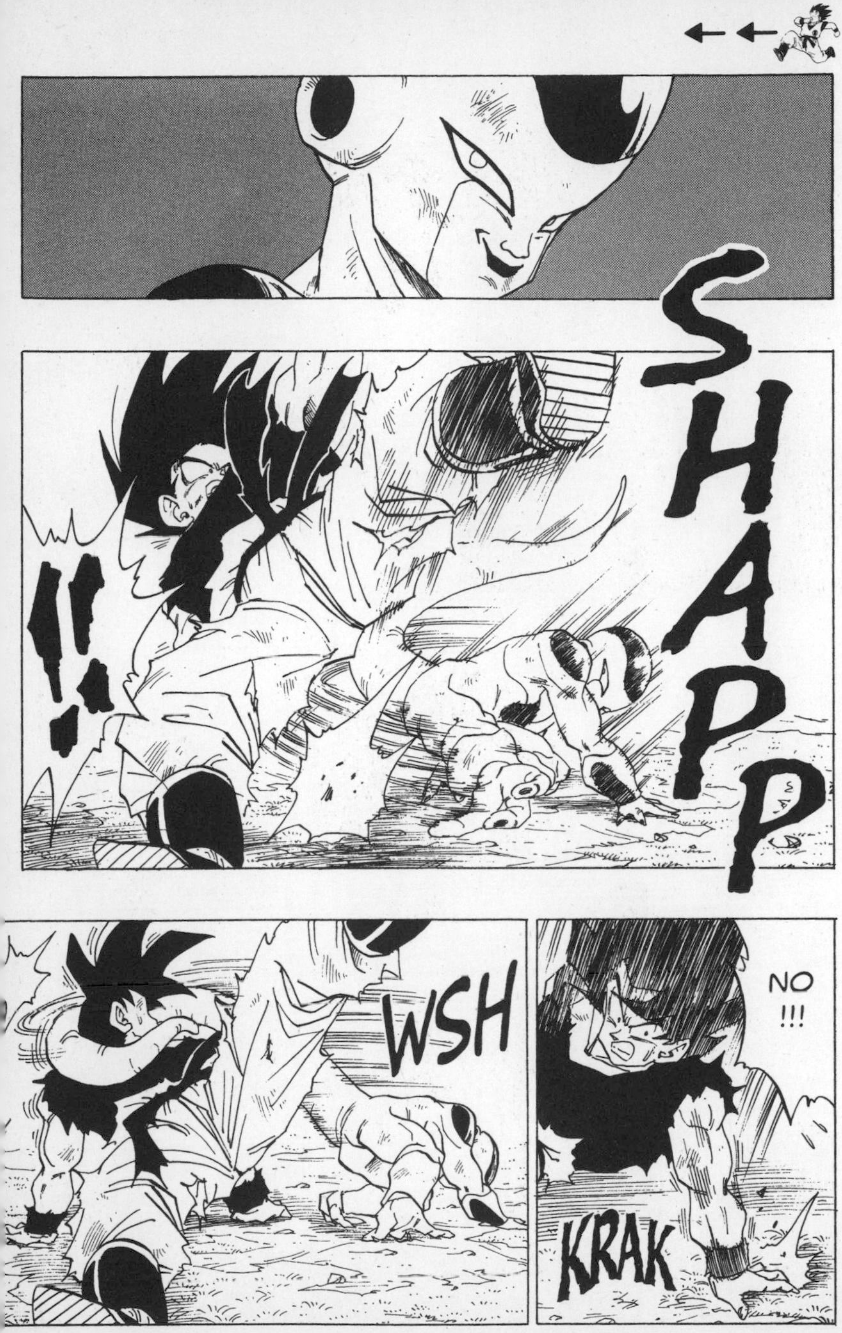
SHAPP
!!
NO !!!
KRAK
WSH

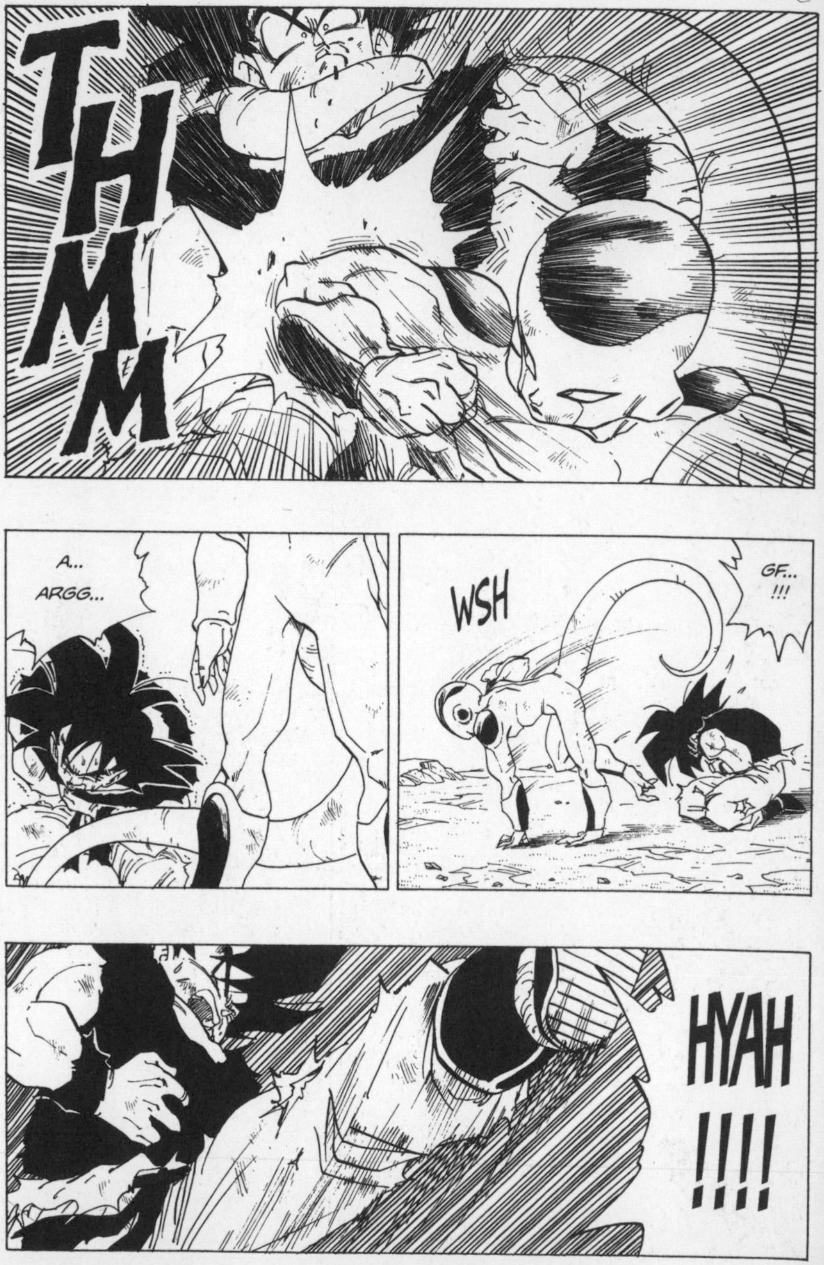
THMM
GF... !!!
WSH
A... ARGG...
HYAH !!!!

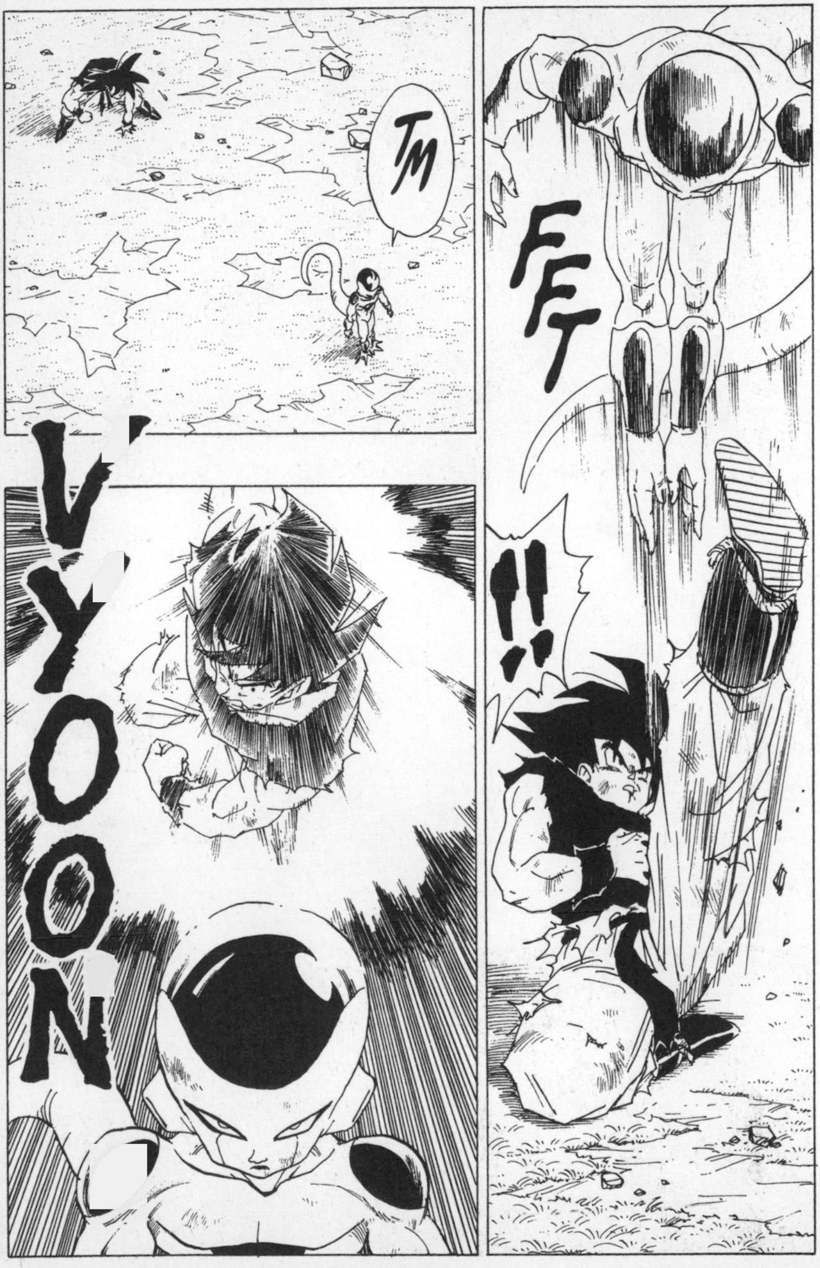
FFT
!!
TM
VYOON

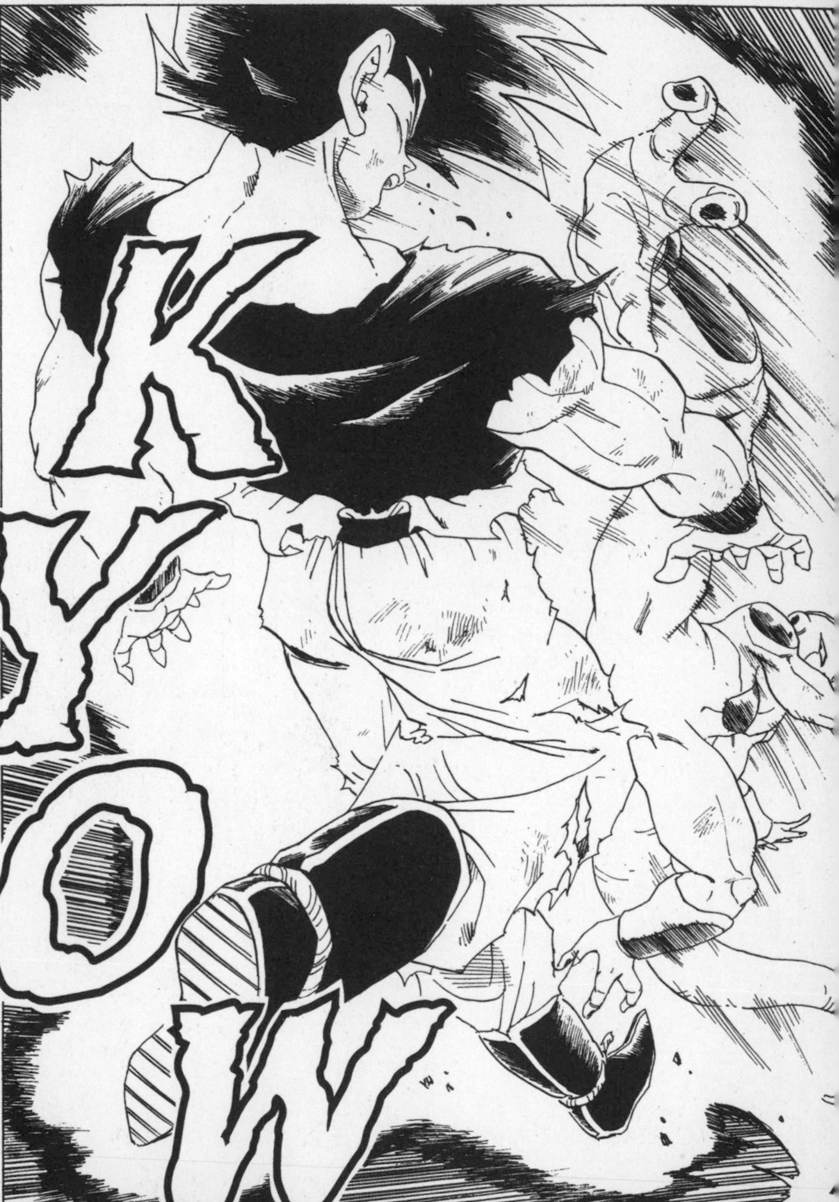
KYOW

THERE WAS TOO GREAT A DISCREPANCY BETWEEN THEIR RESPECTIVE RESERVES...

OH....

NO...

I...I CAN'T BELIEVE IT...

HE'S TOO POWERFUL...

THIS IS NO GOOD...

OH...

...

NO... WHAT HE'S WEARING NOW IS DURABLE... BUT NOT HEAVY...

MY LORD! ISN'T GOKU WEIGHED DOWN BY ONE OF THOSE TRAINING UNIFORMS...?!

AT HIS LEVEL OF TRAINING, HE SHOULD BE ABLE TO MULTIPLY HIS POWER UP TO A FACTOR OF *10*!

HAVE YOU FORGOTTEN ABOUT THE *KAIÔ-KEN*?

NOT TO WORRY. GOKU WILL WIN THIS BATTLE...

WHAT ?!

BUT HE'S ALREADY *USING* THE 10-FOLD KAIÔ-KEN ...

SORRY...

OH YEAH !!!

OH...

NEXT: *Kaiô-ken times 20!!!*

DBZ:119 • Kaiô-ken times 20!!!

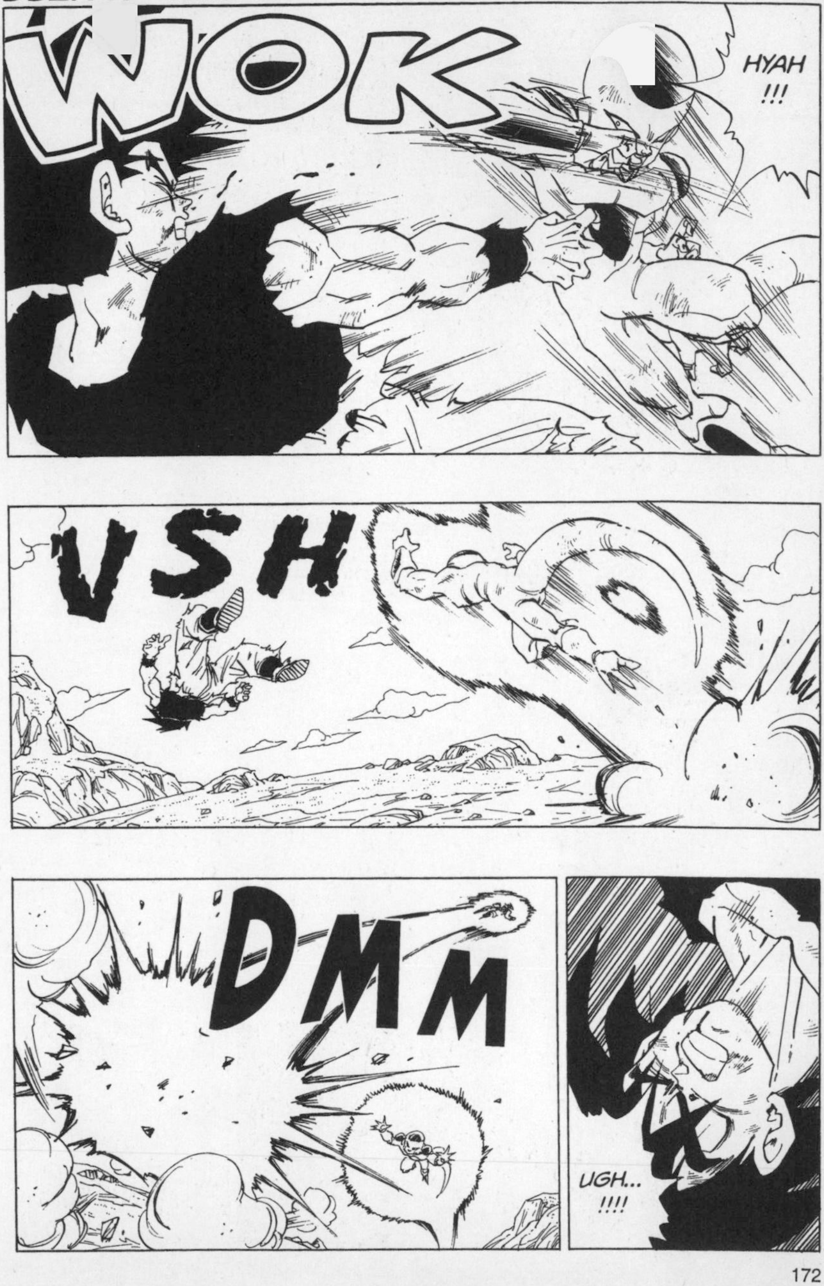
HYAH !!!
WOK
VSH
UGH... !!!!
DMM

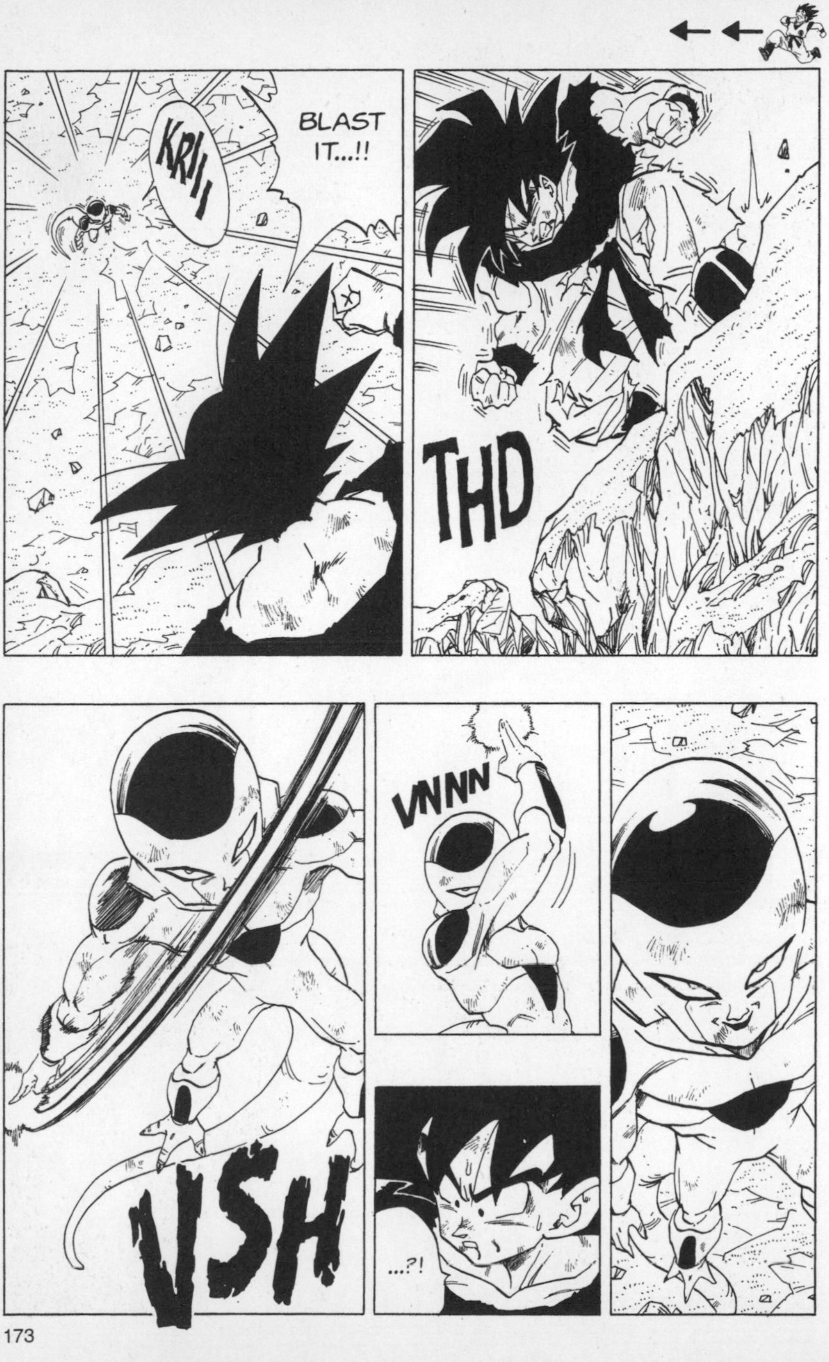
THD
BLAST IT...!!
KRIII
VNNN
...?!
VSH

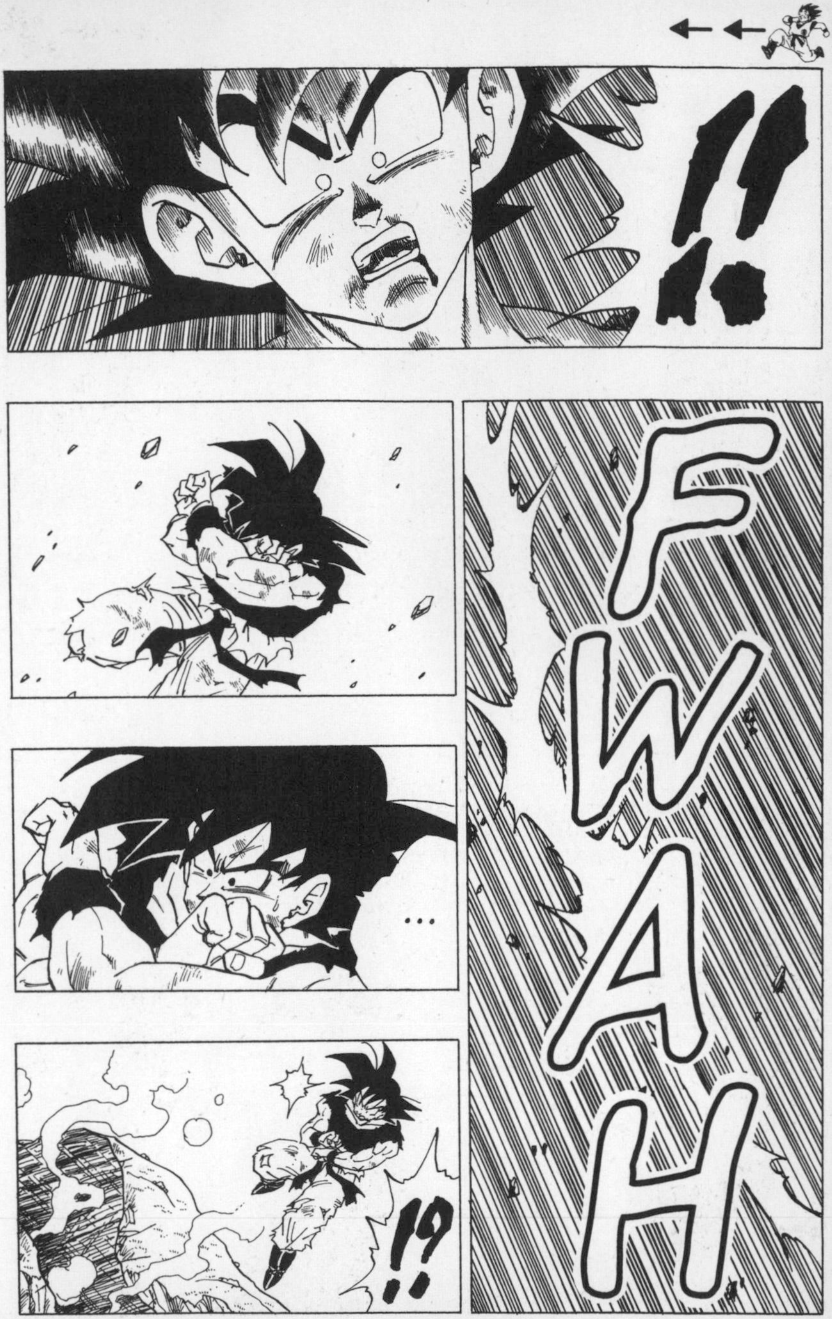
!!
FWAH
...
!?!!

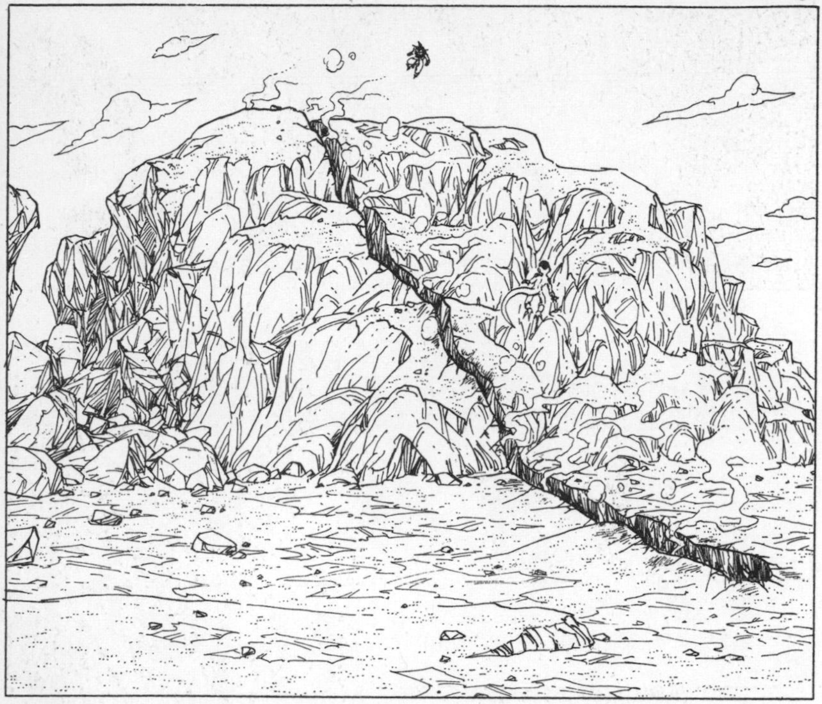

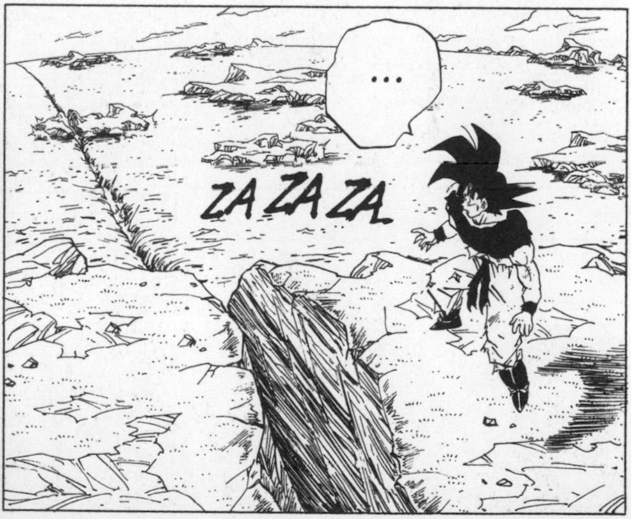
...
ZA ZA ZA

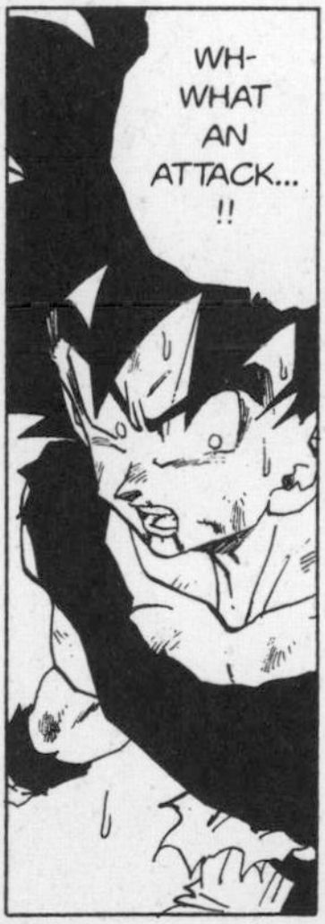
WH- WHAT AN ATTACK... !!

IT'S WHAT I DID TO PLANET VEGETA, YOU KNOW.

I TOLD YOU. I COULD DESTROY THIS ENTIRE PLANET WITH EASE.

I CAN'T WIN...

O-OH BOY...

H-H-HE SLICED UP THE PLANET...

WH-WHAT DID HE DO...?!

176

S-SAY WHAT... ?!

...!

...AND... FREEZA'S ONLY USING HALF OF HIS STRENGTH...

Y-YOU MEAN SON-GOKU IS *ALREADY* USING THE 10-FACTOR KAIÔ-KEN... AND HE'S STILL GETTING BEATEN UP...?!

...HE'S LOST...

THAT'S WHY I TOLD HIM...

NOT TO TANGLE WITH FREEZA... NO MATTER WHAT.

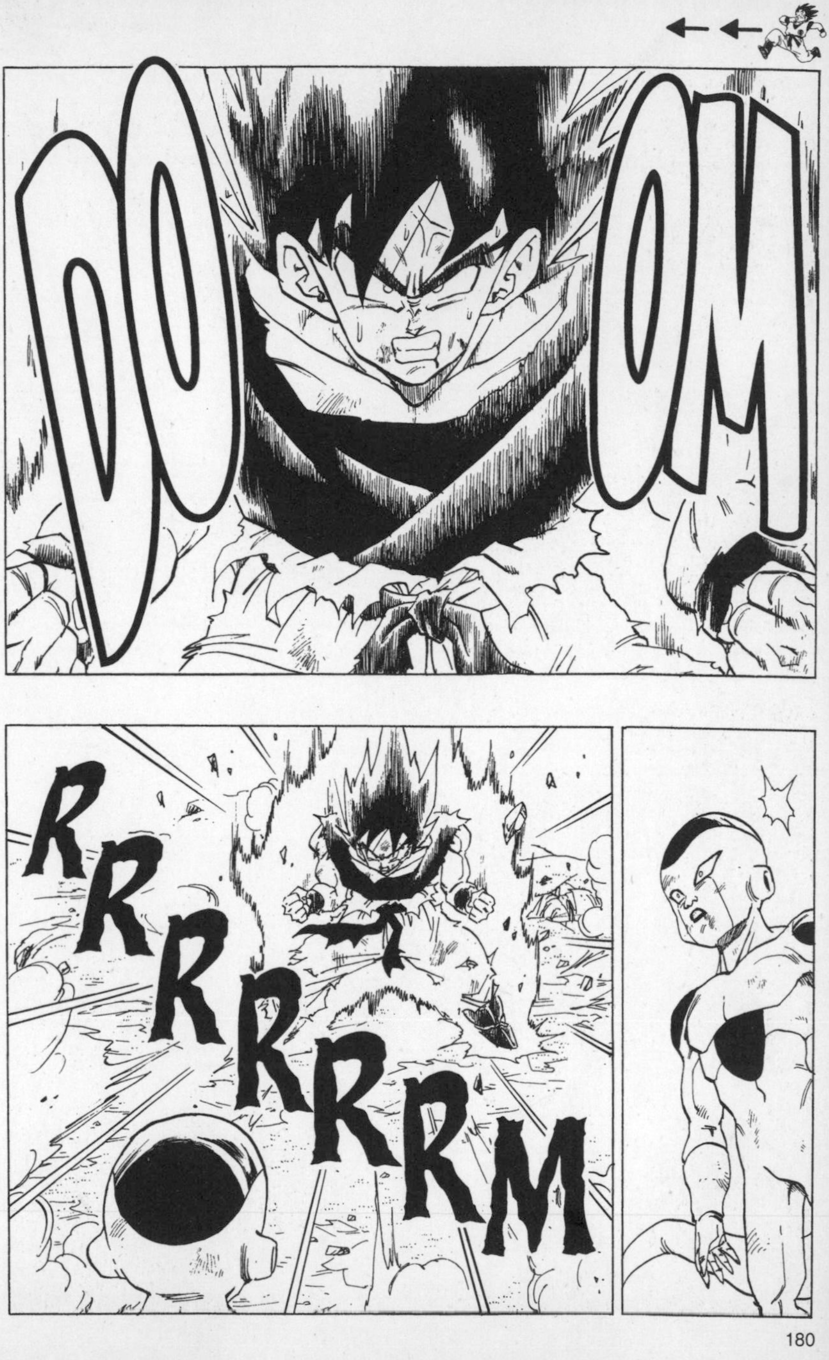
DOOOM
RRRRRRRM

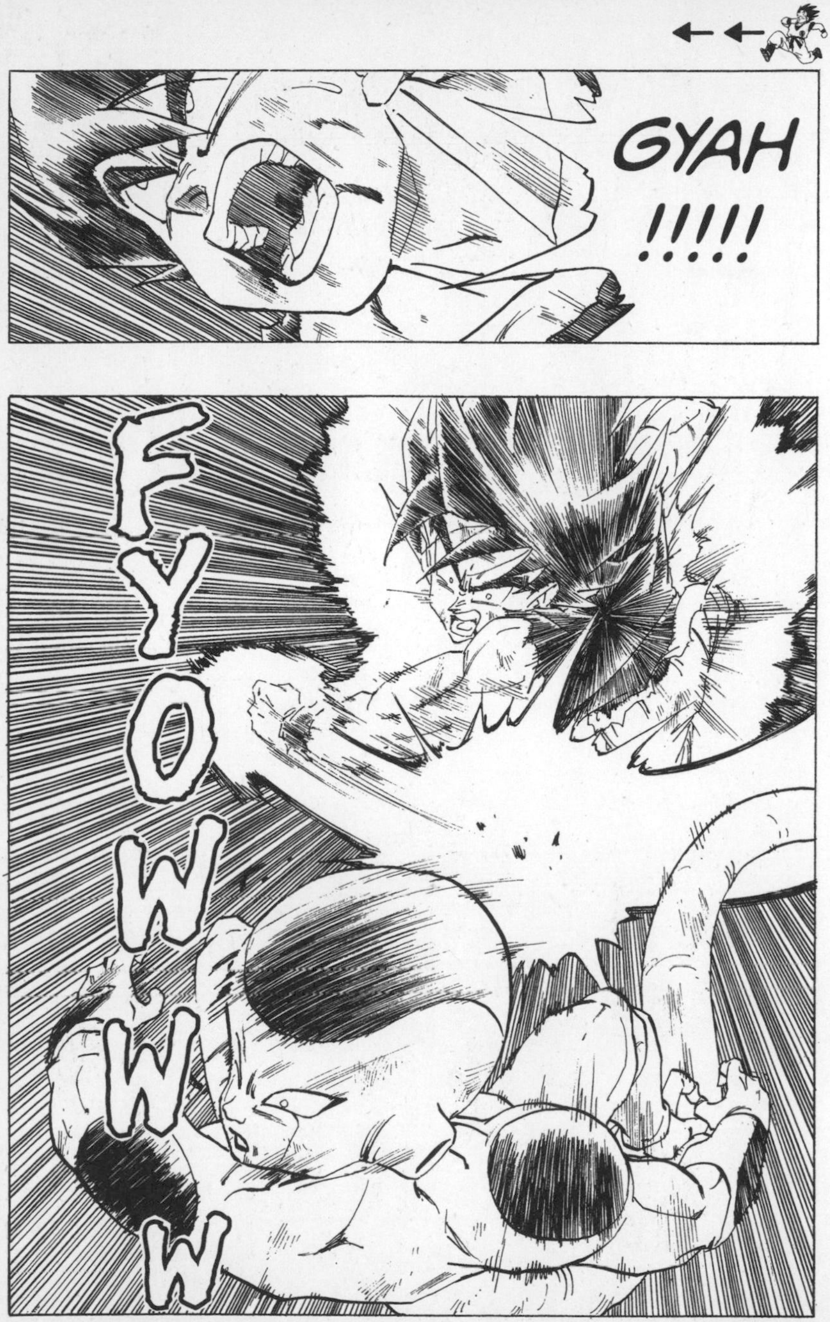
GYAH
!!!!!
FYOWWWW

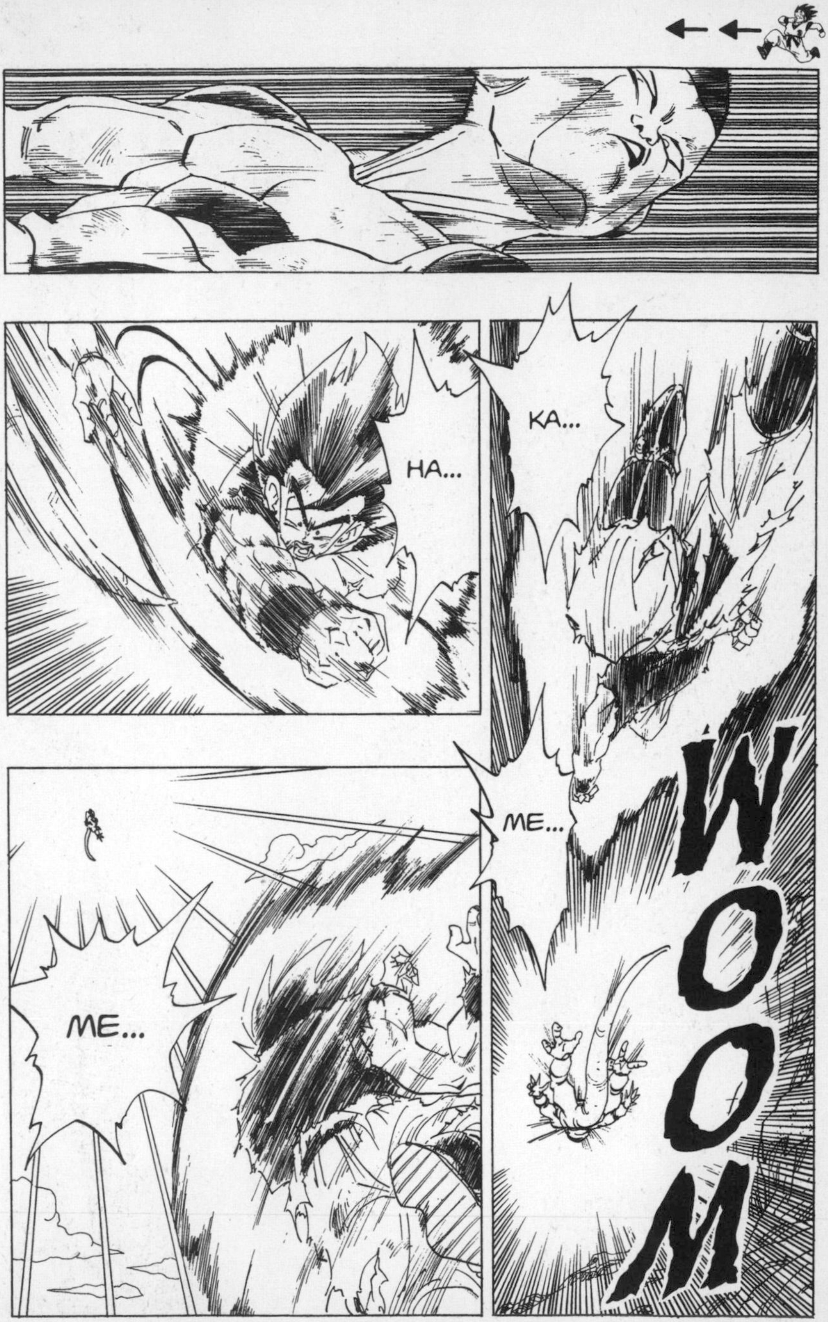
KA...
ME...
WOOM
HA...
ME...

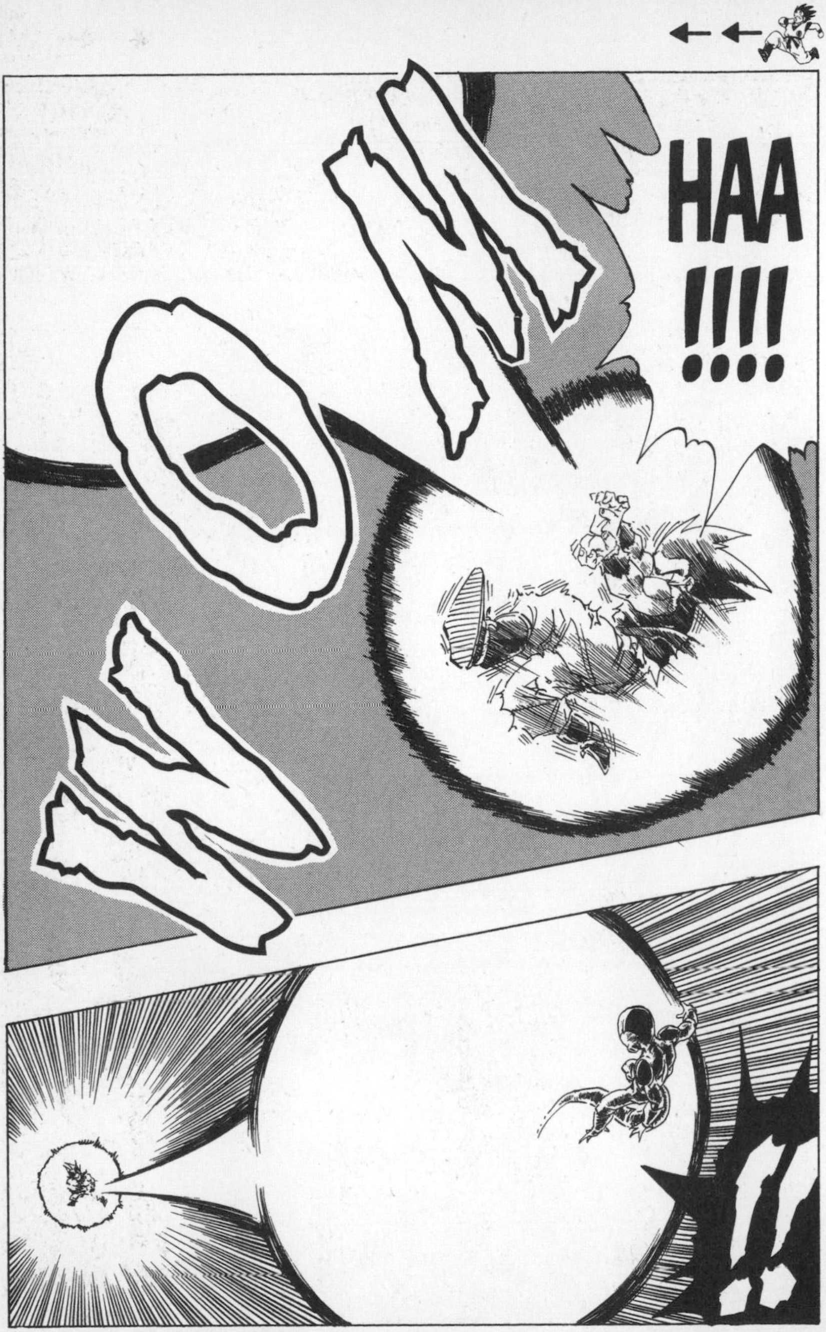
HAA!!!!
!!

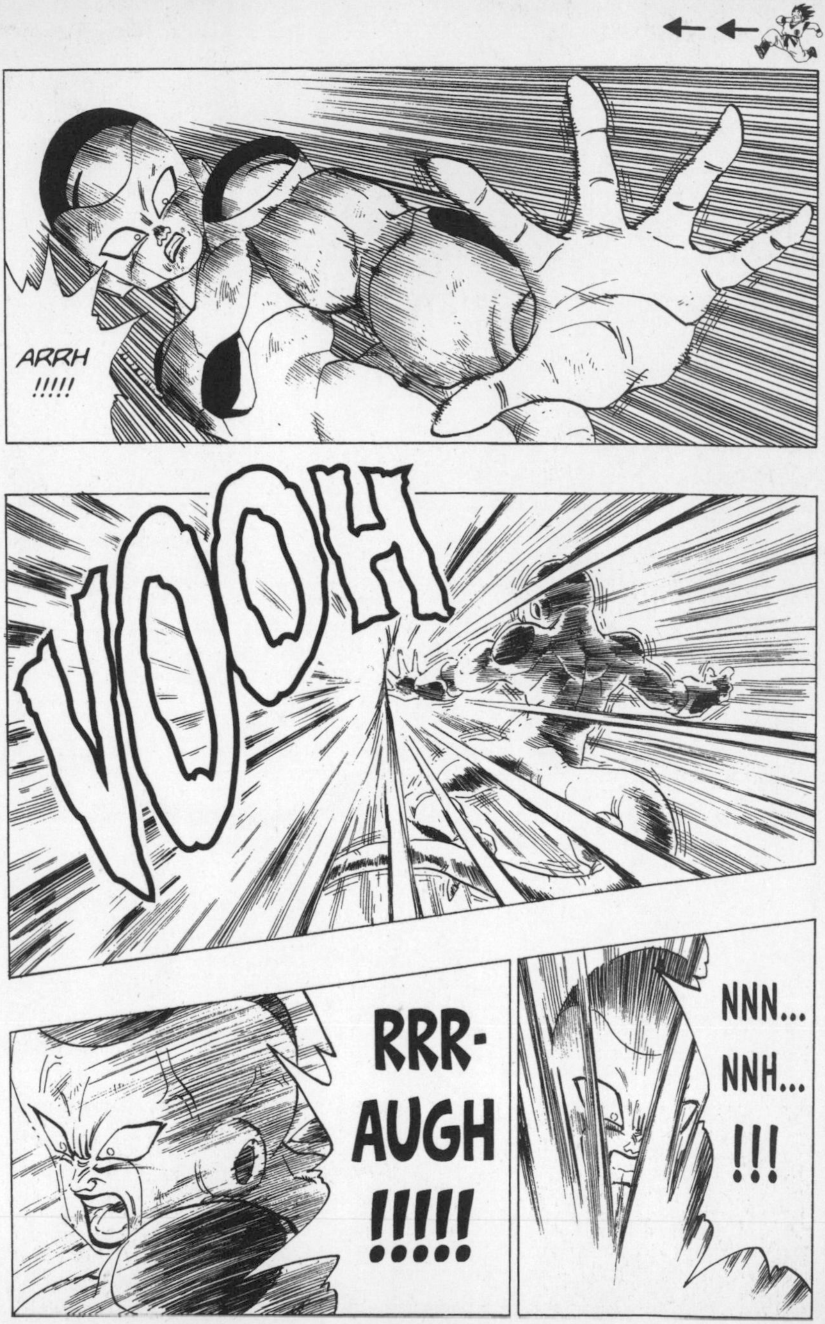
ARRH !!!!!
VOOOH
NNN... NNH... !!!
RRR-AUGH !!!!!

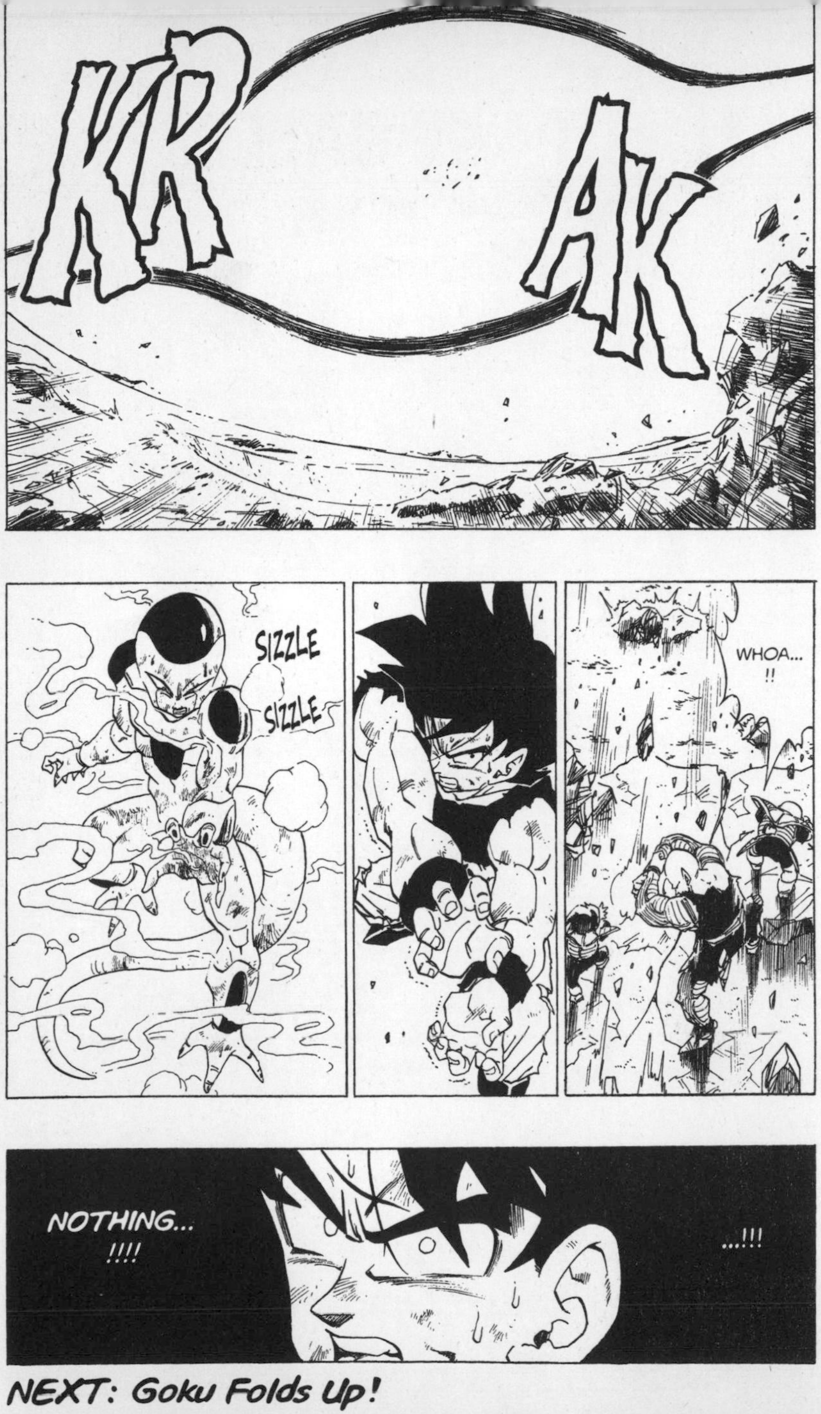
KR
AK
WHOA... !!
SIZZLE
SIZZLE
...!!!
NOTHING... !!!!

NEXT: Goku Folds Up!

TITLE PAGE GALLERY

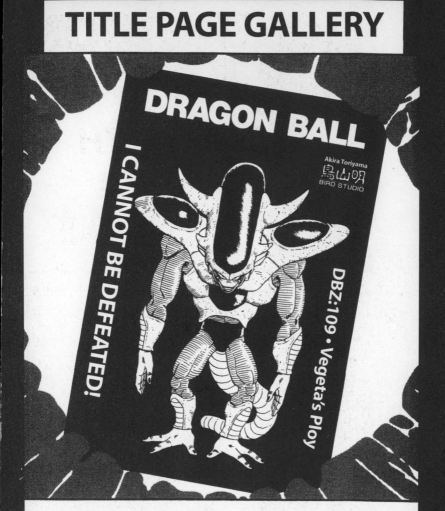

DRAGON BALL
Akira Toriyama
鳥山明
BIRD STUDIO
I CANNOT BE DEFEATED!
DBZ:109 • Vegeta's Ploy

These chapter title pages were used when these episodes of *Dragon Ball* were originally published in 1991 in Japan in *Weekly Shonen Jump* magazine.

DRAGON BALL

DEATH OF A SAIYAN!!!

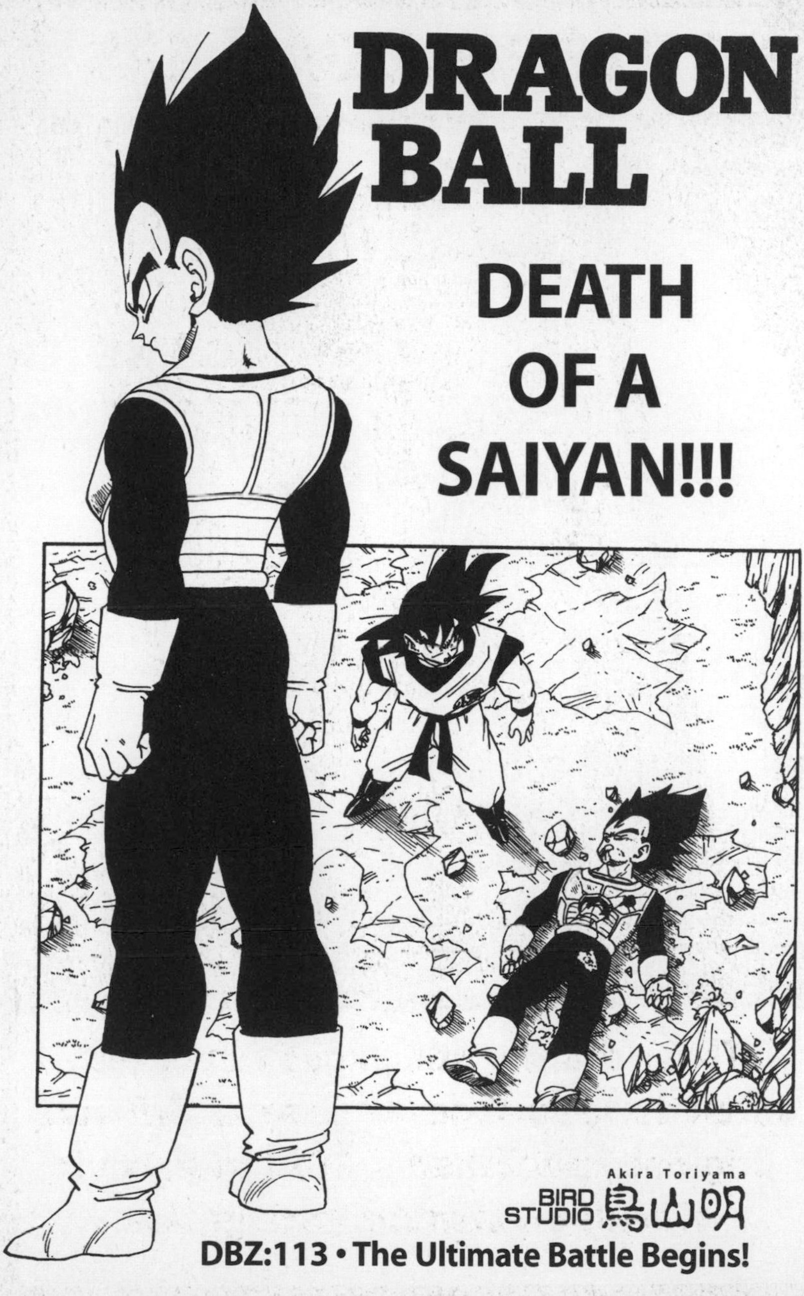

Akira Toriyama
BIRD STUDIO 鳥山明

DBZ:113 • The Ultimate Battle Begins!

DRAGON BALL

I'M GOING TO BEAT YOU UP!

I'M GOING TO KILL YOU...

DBZ:116 • Aerial Battle

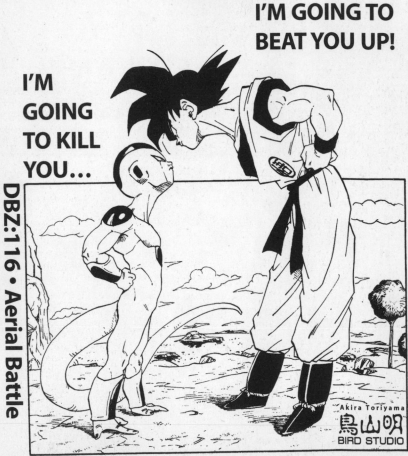

Akira Toriyama
鳥山明
BIRD STUDIO

SHONEN JUMP
GRAPHIC NOVELS
ALL NEW SHONEN JUMP GRAPHIC NOVELS!
Dragon Ball VOL. 16
Dragon Ball Z VOL. 17
Yu-Gi-Oh! VOL. 6
YuYu Hakusho VOL. 5
One Piece VOL. 5
Naruto VOL. 4
Shaman King VOL. 4
Rurouni Kenshin VOL. 8
Knights of the Zodiac VOL. 6
Hikaru No Go VOL. 2
The Prince Of Tennis VOL. 4
Bleach VOL. 3
Whistle! VOL. 2
Beet The Vandel Buster VOL. 1
All Books $7.99 and Under
VIZ
COMIC SHOP LOCATOR SERVICE
888-COMIC-BOOK
888-266-4226
ON SALE AT:
www.shonenjump.com
Also available at your local bookstore, comic store and Suncoast Motion Picture Company.
DRAGON BALL © 1984 by BIRD STUDIO / SHUEISHA Inc. ONE PIECE © 1997 by EIICHIRO ODA / SHUEISHA Inc.
NARUTO © 1999 by MASASHI KISHIMOTO / SHUEISHA Inc. SHAMAN KING © 1998 by HIROYUKI TAKEI / SHUEISHA Inc.
SAINT SEIYA © 1986 by MASAMI KURUMADA / SHUEISHA Inc. YU-GI-OH! © 1996 by KAZUKI TAKAHASHI / SHUEISHA Inc.
BOUKEN OH BEET: BEET THE VANDEL BUSTER. © 2002 by RIKU SANJO, KOJI INADA / SHUEISHA Inc.
BLEACH © 2001 by TITE KUBO / SHUEISHA Inc. WHISTLE! © 1998 by DAISUKE HIGUCHI / SHUEISHA Inc.
HIKARU-NO GO © 1998 by YUMI HOTTA, TAKESHI OBATA / SHUEISHA Inc.
THE PRINCE OF TENNIS © 1999 by TAKESHI KONOMI / SHUEISHA Inc.
RUROUNI KENSHIN © 1994 by NOBUHIRO WATSUKI / SHUEISHA Inc. YUYU HAKUSHO © 1991 YOSHIHIRO TOGASHI

SHONEN JUMP
THE WORLD'S MOST POPULAR MANGA

COMPLETE OUR SURVEY AND LET US KNOW WHAT YOU THINK!

☐ Please do NOT send me information about VIZ and SHONEN JUMP products, news and events, special offers, or other information.

☐ Please do NOT send me information from VIZ's trusted business partners.

Name: _____

Address: _____

City: _____ **State:** _____ **Zip:** _____

E-mail: _____

☐ Male ☐ Female **Date of Birth** (mm/dd/yyyy): ___ / ___ / _____ (Under 13? Parental consent required)

What race/ethnicity do you consider yourself? (please check one)

☐ Asian/Pacific Islander ☐ Black/African American ☐ Hispanic/Latino

☐ Native American/Alaskan Native ☐ White/Caucasian ☐ Other: _____

What SHONEN JUMP Graphic Novel did you purchase? (indicate title purchased)

_____

What other SHONEN JUMP Graphic Novels, if any, do you own? (indicate title(s) owned)

_____

_____

Reason for purchase: (check all that apply)

☐ Special offer ☐ Favorite title ☐ Gift

☐ Recommendation ☐ Read in SHONEN JUMP Magazine

☐ Read excerpt in the SHONEN JUMP Compilation Edition

☐ Other_____

Where did you make your purchase? (please check one)

☐ Comic store ☐ Bookstore ☐ Mass/Grocery Store

☐ Newsstand ☐ Video/Video Game Store ☐ Other: _____

☐ Online (site: _____)

Do you read SHONEN JUMP Magazine?

- [ ] Yes
- [ ] No **(if no, skip the next two questions)**

Do you subscribe?

- [ ] Yes
- [ ] No

If you do not subscribe, how often do you purchase SHONEN JUMP Magazine?

- [ ] 1-3 issues a year
- [ ] 4-6 issues a year
- [ ] more than 7 issues a year

What genre of manga would you like to read as a SHONEN JUMP Graphic Novel?
(please check two)

- [ ] Adventure
- [ ] Comic Strip
- [ ] Science Fiction
- [ ] Fighting
- [ ] Horror
- [ ] Romance
- [ ] Fantasy
- [ ] Sports

Which do you prefer? (please check one)

- [ ] Reading right-to-left
- [ ] Reading left-to-right

Which do you prefer? (please check one)

- [ ] Sound effects in English
- [ ] Sound effects in Japanese with English captions
- [ ] Sound effects in Japanese only with a glossary at the back

THANK YOU! Please send the completed form to:

VIZ Survey
42 Catharine St.
Poughkeepsie, NY 12601

All information provided will be used for internal purposes only. We promise not to sell or otherwise divulge your information.

鳥山　明

Our dog had puppies! She gave birth to three in all, but unfortunately one puppy died at birth, so now we have two puppies. When our cat gave birth, she didn't do so well on her own, and we had to assist with the labor and do things like cut the kittens' umbilical cords. We got ready several days in advance to help our dog with her labor, but she managed to do it all on her own. We really don't want to give the puppies away, so we are going to keep the both of them...
—*Akira Toriyama, 1991*

Artist/writer Akira Toriyama burst onto the manga scene in 1980 with the wildly popular **Dr. Slump**, a science fiction comedy about the adventures of a mad scientist and his android "daughter." In 1984 he created his hit series **Dragon Ball**, which ran until 1995 in Shueisha's bestselling magazine **Weekly Shonen Jump**, and was translated into foreign languages around the world. Since **Dragon Ball**, he has worked on a variety of short series, including **Cowa!**, **Kajika**, **Sand Land**, and **Neko Majin**, as well as a children's book, **Toccio the Angel**. He is also known for his design work on video games, particularly the **Dragon Warrior** RPG series. He lives with his family in Japan.

DRAGON BALL Z VOL. 10
The SHONEN JUMP Graphic Novel Edition

This graphic novel is number 26 in a series of 42.

STORY AND ART BY
AKIRA TORIYAMA

ENGLISH ADAPTATION BY
GERARD JONES

Translation/Lillian Olsen
Touch-Up Art & Lettering/Wayne Truman
Cover Design/Sean Lee & Dan Ziegler
Graphics & Design/Sean Lee
Senior Editor/Jason Thompson

Managing Editor/Elizabeth Kawasaki
Executive V.P./Editor in Chief/Hyoe Narita
Sr. Director, Licensing and Acquisitions/Rika Inouye
V.P. of Sales and Marketing/Liza Coppola
V.P. of Strategic Development/Yumi Hoashi
Publisher/Seiji Horibuchi

In the original Japanese edition, DRAGON BALL and DRAGON BALL Z
are known collectively as the 42-volume series DRAGON BALL. The
English DRAGON BALL Z was originally volumes 17-42 of the Japanese
DRAGON BALL.

Published by VIZ, LLC
P.O. Box 77010 • San Francisco, CA 94107

The SHONEN JUMP Graphic Novel Edition
10 9 8 7 6 5 4 3 2
First printing, May 2003
Second printing, October 2004

www.viz.com

THE WORLD'S
MOST POPULAR MANGA

SHONEN JUMP
GRAPHIC NOVEL

www.shonenjump.com